WE
HAVE
CAPTURE

TOM STAFFORD AND THE SPACE RACE

Thomas P. Stafford
with Michael Cassutt

WE

HAVE

CApture

Smithsonian Institution Press
Washington and London

This book is based in large part on research
and interviews conducted by James E. Alexander, Ph.D.

© 2002 by Thomas P. Stafford and St. Croix Productions, Inc.
All rights reserved

Copy editor: Craig A. Triplett
Designer: Brian Barth

Library of Congress Cataloging-in-Publication Data
Stafford, Thomas P.
  We have capture : Tom Stafford and the space race /
  Thomas P. Stafford with Michael Cassutt.
      p.   cm.
    Includes index.
    ISBN 1-58834-070-8 (alk. paper)
    1. Stafford, Thomas P.   2. Astronauts—United States—Biography.
    3. Astronautics—United States—History.   4. Space race.   I. Title.
  TL789.85.S73 A3 2002
  302.3'4'081022—dc21   2002021019

British Library Cataloguing-in-Publication Data available

Manufactured in the United States of America
09 08 07 06 05 04 03   5 4 3

For permission to reproduce illustrations appearing in this book, please correspond directly
with the owners of the works, as listed in the individual captions (uncredited photos belong
to Thomas P. Stafford). The Smithsonian Institution Press does not retain reproduction rights
for these illustrations individually, or maintain a file of addresses for photo sources.

To my family, to my co-workers, and to my colleagues in Russia

contents

acknowledgments

The authors wish to acknowledge the assistance of Maj. Gen. Aleksei Leonov for his insights into the Soviet and Russian side of the space race. Dr. Arnauld Nicogossian, Maj. Gen. Joe Henry Engle, and Anatole Forostenko also shared their valuable perspectives.

Photos and other materials were kindly provided by Chuck Biggs; Bill Moore at Oklahoma Educational Television; Kathy Strawn (Media Services) and Glen Swanson (History Office) at the NASA Johnson Space Center; and Gregg Linebaugh and Stewart Howard at the Oklahoma Air and Space Museum in Oklahoma City. Dennis McSweeney, Holly Stevens, and Mark Thiessen of the Stafford-Utkin Task Force performed support services above and beyond the call of duty, as did Patricia McCown and Karen Stover of FlexForce.

We offer a special thank you to our wives, Linda Stafford and Cindy Cassutt.

prologue
"We Have Capture!"

At 10:00 A.M. Houston time we were in sunlight when I saw the bright dot that was Soyuz 19. Seventeen minutes later, as we flew north of Australia, it was time for the terminal phase initiation maneuver. Closer and closer. By the time we approached the coast of Chile, Apollo was essentially station-keeping with Soyuz. I tweaked the reaction-control thrusters and continued to look outside, where I could now see Soyuz 19 clearly.

My crew mates, Vance Brand and Deke Slayton, and I were approaching the high point of a two-year journey, in which we had become the first American astronauts to work and train at the heart of the Soviet space program. A few short years ago, I had been a fighter pilot patrolling the Iron Curtain. My Soviet counterpart, Soyuz commander Aleksei Leonov, had done the same on his side. In working with the cosmonauts, in struggling to learn their language, in traveling in their world, I had stopped seeing them as faceless enemies, but now recognized them as complicated human beings trying to make the best of a terrible and complicated political system. And here we were, getting ready to link our two spacecraft 132 miles above the surface of the earth.

"I've got two messages for you," Dick Truly, the capcom in Houston, advised us. "Moscow is go for docking, Houston is go for docking. It's up to you guys—have fun." It was 10:46 A.M. CDT, the morning of July 17, 1975.

"Half a mile," I radioed in Russian to Aleksei.

"Roger, eight hundred meters," he said in English. He and his flight engineer, Valery Kubasov, had, as planned, closed the hatch between the orbit and descent modules, put on their pressure suits, and were in the couches. We had closed the hatch to our docking module, too. On my command, in Russian, Aleksei made a final sixty-degree roll to get Soyuz in the right orientation.

We edged closer and closer. At one point Aleksei said, "Tom, please don't forget about your engine." He was reminding me to inhibit the forward-firing thrusters. Already done. I called out the ranges in Russian. Five meters, three meters, one meter, contact. "Capture," I reported.

"We have capture," Aleksei repeated, in Russian. It was 11:10, and we had linked up over the Atlantic Ocean just east of the coast of Portugal.

WE

HAVE

CAPTURE

one
Gaining Altitude

It's a long way to Russia and earth orbit from Weatherford, Oklahoma, which is where I was born on September 17, 1930, the only child of Thomas Sabert Stafford, a dentist, and the former Mary Ellen Patten, a teacher. I was a small baby, weighing only four and a half pounds, and was fortunate to survive infancy. Weatherford, which lies seventy miles due west of Oklahoma City, had a population of twenty-four hundred supported by cotton, wheat farming, and cattle, and by the presence of the Southwestern State Teachers College, with its eight hundred students.

The first transcontinental airline route happened to run right across Weatherford, following U.S. Route 66, which was also the town's main street. Every afternoon a silver DC-3 would glide across the sky on its way to Amarillo, then Los Angeles, having flown from New York, Chicago, St. Louis, and Oklahoma City. Even as a small boy, I would stand there and watch, and think, I want to do that.

Weatherford was small enough that you knew everyone but not so big that you couldn't get around quickly and easily. We lived in a five-room, one-story house at 215 Washita Street, two blocks north of Main and two blocks south of the junior and senior high schools. We never needed an automobile.

We did have books, however. My mother, who gave up her teaching job to raise me, read to me from the time I was a baby, everything from Big Little Books, to the Bible, from fairy tales to funny pages in the newspapers. (I became a big fan of Buck Rogers.) It helped make me a lifelong reader.

There were drawbacks to life on the prairie, however. Summer nights were so hot that the family would take cots out back and sleep under the stars. (This was long before air-conditioned homes.) My father knew some of the constellations, and he would point them out to me. I would look at the Moon, which seemed so close, and wonder whether we would ever touch its surface. I thought that perhaps some day people might go there. But I never dreamed it would be me.

The middle 1930s was also the time of the dust bowl, when the hot wind would start blowing from the south, and the sky would turn red, then gray. Then we'd get hit by a black cloud so thick that the family would have to shove dampened towels against the doors and around the windows to keep out the flying dirt. I was too young to know about farmers losing their land and having to go on the road, but I knew times were tough; we never had much money because many people would postpone dental work for as long as possible, and when they finally had to have it, they would often pay in trade, not cash.

Nevertheless, my childhood was a happy one. I had the run of the town with buddies like Richard McPhetridge, who lived across the street. And though my parents (especially my mother) were tough when they needed to be, sometimes they let me push the envelope. When I was four years old, for example, we visited a farm near the town of May, which had a windmill that was eighty-five feet tall, one of the tallest in the world. I took one look at that thing and headed right for it, my little legs churning as fast as they could. I was up that ladder and all the way to the platform at the top—eight stories up—before my parents noticed I was gone. I had never been up that high before. I can still remember seeing for miles in every direction, all the fences, roads, farm houses, the low hills, and some of the few trees of western Oklahoma. Typically, there was a good stiff breeze blowing, making the vane at the top of the windmill creak as it swung back and forth. I had to keep ducking out of its way, but I didn't care: As far as I was concerned, I was on top of the world. Spotting me up there, my parents pleaded with me to be careful. My father was about to climb up and get me, but I yelled that I would come down myself. Which I did. I learned several things that day. First, that I liked the feeling of being way up high. Second, that rules could sometimes be broken. And third, that climbing down can be a lot harder than going up.

Right about the time of my adventure on the windmill, halfway around the world in the Siberian forests of the Soviet Union's Kemerovo region, a baby boy named Aleksei was born to an electrician named Arkhip Leonov and his wife, Yevdokia. Aleksei had six older sisters and one older brother, who became an aircraft mechanic and inspired young Aleksei to dream about a career in aviation. As he grew up, however, first in the village of Listvyanka then in the larger city of Kemerovo, his greatest interest would be drawing and painting. His subjects? Wounded soldiers, strafing aircraft, tank battles. Aleksei's country was being invaded.

As World War II loomed, we didn't think much about the Soviet Union in Weatherford; it was too far away, too mysterious. My father, a very conservative Methodist, would occasionally make critical remarks about Communism and other atheistic beliefs, and we heard about famine, fighting, and the horrors of show trials that allowed Stalin to execute the old Bolsheviks. But it was Hitler who had our attention, as his Nazi armies attacked Poland, then France, and eventually the rest of Europe. It was a tense time, with my parents listening to war news on the radio and me thrilling to Movietone newsreels showing brave English pilots flying their Spitfires against the Nazis in the Battle of Britain.

On Sunday, December 7, 1941, my mother and I were decorating our Christmas tree when my father walked into the room saying the Japanese had attacked Pearl Harbor. I was only eleven and had no idea what or where Pearl Harbor was, but I understood his next words: "We're at war."

World War II meant rationing in Weatherford. It also meant local boys who went into the service, and some who never came home. Southwestern College dedicated part of its facilities as a school for Army Air Corps aircraft mechanics, much like Alexei Leonov's brother in the Soviet Union. Forty miles east of us, El Reno hosted an Air Corps primary training base. The pilots in training would sometimes practice takeoffs and landings at Weatherford's airport, a fancy name for a grass field, and I would ride my bike out there and watch them. Occasionally there would be some excitement, like the time an Army Air Corps C-46 overshot the runway and got stuck in the sand. The good people of Weatherford put the crew up overnight while they waited for wreckers from Tinker Field in Oklahoma City to come to the rescue.

Inspired by Spitfires and DC-3s, I started building balsa wood and paper model airplanes. The airframes themselves were cheap but not the engines. When I asked my father for the cash to buy them, he said, "I could give you the money, but you'll appreciate these things more if you work for them." So I got a paper route delivering *The Daily Oklahoman* and the *Oklahoma City Times* to the western half of Weatherford.

When I needed twelve dollars to buy shoes for the junior high school football team, my father said the same thing, so I "snapped cotton" for weekends to raise the money. Working on my knees in those cotton fields with the red dirt blowing in my face made flying away from Weatherford seem even more attractive. I knew I had to leave the area to be a success. When I was fourteen, my mathematics teacher, Letha Spann arranged for her friend, a woman named Jessie Duncan, to take me for a plane ride in her yellow, two-seater Piper Cub. It wasn't a Spitfire, but it was a genuine airplane.

That ride made me eager to become a fighter pilot and help win the war. First, however, I had to finish school. I was a good student throughout junior high and the early part of high school, especially in math, thanks to Letha Spann, who had us winning prizes in mathematics every year at the Southwestern Interscholastic Meet. I also helped organize a football team for the junior high, which used the senior high team's old equipment. By the time I was a sophomore, I had grown to six feet, 185 pounds, and for the next three years I lettered on the senior high football team, playing left tackle. During my senior year I was elected captain.

Though I looked like an adult, I still had some growing up to do. From time to time I had gotten myself into trouble when I was a kid. I once tossed a firecracker into the police station, and another time I shot out streetlights with a BB gun. (The neighbors could always tell when I had been caught: I would be out front painting the fence as punishment, like Tom Sawyer.) But at Weatherford High I got into a new kind of trouble. My class (numbering 62) was the biggest that had ever gone through the school, and the teachers were simply overwhelmed. Two English teachers quit rather than deal with us. To help ease the teaching load, the superintendent of schools called in Dora Mae Mitchell, Ph.D., who had been teaching English in Wichita Falls, Texas. She showed up one day in 1946, a very prim woman in her late thirties, standing about five feet, seven inches tall. My buddies—Stony Lockstone and Lloyd Hedge—and I thought we could get rid of this new schoolmarm in no time.

To cause Miss Mitchell grief, we spread out around the classroom, and whenever she tried to speak we started coughing in turn. "Please turn to your textbooks—" *Cough.* "I said, please turn—" *Cough.* Miss Mitchell kept talking right through our coughing spells, but at the end of class she made the three of us stay behind. "We aren't going to have any more of that here," she said. "I don't want to see any of you back in school until your parents come with you." That made an impression on the three of us, believe me. I quit causing trouble in English.

Miss Mitchell did me an even greater favor, however: Seeing my interest in science and engineering, she got me reading the science section of her *Sunday New York Times,* which arrived in Weatherford by mail about a week after it was published. It was there that I first learned about wonder weapons such as the Nazi V-2 rocket and read about America's first experiments at White Sands missile range. The *Times* also reported that Capt. Chuck Yeager had broken the sound barrier in the Bell X-1 rocket plane. But space flight, as far as I was concerned, was still something out of the funny papers or comic books.

In the fall of 1947, my senior year, the new University of Oklahoma football coach, Bud Wilkinson, made a recruiting tour around the state and talked to the four largest players on the Weatherford High team, including me. He offered us the opportunity to try out for a spot on the Sooners. I also competed for and was awarded a full Navy ROTC scholarship to the university. Back during my sophomore year I had read a book called *Men of Annapolis,* which had triggered my interested in attending the Naval Academy and going on to a career in military aviation.

By this time I already had a bit of military experience. In early 1947 I had joined the 45th Division of the Oklahoma National Guard. At sixteen I had been too young to sign up without parental permission, and my mother had been reluctant at first. Eventually, however, she decided it would do me more good than harm and finally signed the document. I had not been sworn in for more than a couple of months before I was called to temporary duty. The small town of Leedey, Oklahoma, about sixty miles northwest of us, was hit by a tornado that went right down the main street, killing six residents and injuring many more. Our unit was put on guard duty there.

My commanding officer, 1st Lt. Joe Fred Lohrengle, assigned me to drive a jeep without knowing I'd never been behind the wheel of a car in my life. Because so many people did it, I figured driving couldn't be that hard, so I started up the jeep and took off—and slipped right into a ditch. Fortunately the only damage was to my ego.

I did better with my next Guard assignment, serving with the Fire Direction Center of C Battery, 158th Field Artillery Battalion, on maneuvers at Fort Sill that summer. This unit used information from forward observers to plot targets for 105-mm howitzers. It involved a good deal of math, and I turned out to be fast at the calculations using a worksheet and slide rule and even doing some of them in my head. C Battery won the award as outstanding artillery unit.

Getting to Annapolis was a challenge. Fortunately, two earlier graduates of Weatherford High—Charles Kyger and Billy Spradling—had become Annapolis midshipmen, and they guided me through the application process. I needed to be nominated by a member of Congress, and the representative for our district was Preston Peden. My mother discovered that Lloyd Lowery, our family lawyer, knew Peden, so I made that all-important contact.

Qualifying academically was a challenge of a different kind. For a small-town high school, Weatherford High was good, but I knew my classes wouldn't be enough to get me through the entrance exams, which were so tough that many candidates spent a year in college or even special prep schools before going to Annapolis. I had not studied mathematics beyond algebra II, and our curriculum did not offer a foreign language.

To overcome these difficulties I wrote away for a twenty-five-dollar guide to the exams. Once football season ended, I started studying at home during the evenings, often until well after midnight, and even weekends. Miss Spann and Miss Mitchell were great help to me. All my other activities came to a halt—sports, dating, even hanging out with my buddies.

In April 1948 I rode a bus forty miles northeast to Watonga, where the exam was to be given at a U.S. Post Office. It was a draining, six-hour ordeal. A few weeks later, during our senior-class picnic, the school principal told me I had a phone call from my mother. She had opened the letter from the U.S. Naval Academy: I had been accepted as a member of the class of 1952.

Just as my academic life got brighter, my home life became pretty bleak. Back in 1944 my father had been diagnosed with skin cancer, and it had been too far advanced for the available treatments; nevertheless he had driven to Oklahoma City every other week for radiation therapy. Like most people in those days, my dad didn't have any health insurance, so the bills ate up the family's money.

While I was preparing for and taking my Annapolis tests, it became clear that my father was dying. Eventually he just stayed home, getting weaker and weaker, slipping into and out of consciousness. I spent as much time with him as I could, holding his hand, wondering how this happened. Until this time, I had thought my father and mother would always be a part of my life.

My father died on June 22, 1948. We held his funeral on Saturday, June 26, at First Methodist Church where he had been an elder. A few days later, I said good-bye to my mother and boarded a train heading east to Annapolis. My mother had had to borrow $175 to pay for my ticket and the entrance fee at the Naval Academy. I was not airborne yet, but I was leaving Weatherford and my childhood behind.

two
Silver Wings

The United States Naval Academy, "where the Severn meets the Tide," in Annapolis, Maryland, was to be my home for the next four years. Or so I hoped. I was one of twelve hundred new midshipmen reporting that summer, and I knew that a quarter of us would drop out before graduation. I wanted to make sure I wasn't one of them.

I arrived on June 30, 1948, for plebe summer, and I shared a room with Eddie Hicks. For fall and winter term, I roomed with four other plebes, two of whom had already been to college: Stanley Storper had two years at City College of New York, and Tom McEwen was fresh off a year at Vanderbilt. Charlie Wright, from Mississippi, came directly from senior high school, as did I, and Charlie Theodoreau, from New Hampshire, was repeating his plebe year.

The weeks before classes started were the most fun, since no upperclassmen were around to terrorize us. We ran and swam, learned to row and sail the Navy way, and got a taste of real military life. This intense activity kept me from dwelling on my father's death.

In August the upperclassmen arrived, and from then on it was "meals on the square," thousands of push-ups, and arbitrary harassment. I knew that if I survived plebe year life would get easier, but I didn't have to like it. And nobody liked it.

Football didn't distract me from my studies at the academy because my Navy football career ended before the season started. During practice I tackled a runner, and both of us landed on my knees, which swelled to the size of grapefruit. At the academy hospital the doctor drained fluid from my knees with a large needle. "You're through with football," he said. What he said next, though, really bothered me: "You'll never be able to fly." I refused to believe that.

By the end of my first year, I was ranked in the upper twenty percent of my class.

During the summer of 1949, I went on the youngster cruise, an opportunity for midshipmen to practice their skills at sea aboard a Navy ship. I was assigned to the battleship *Missouri,* the very ship where General MacArthur had accepted the Japanese surrender just four years earlier. We sailed for Cherbourg, France, with academy and Navy ROTC midshipmen manning some of *Missouri*'s duty stations. I served as a "pointer," the sailor who sits in the turret of a five-inch gun and manually controls its up and down movements. This gun could lob a fifty-four-pound projectile a distance of nine miles.

Seated next to me in that turret was the "trainer," who manually controlled the movements left and right. My trainer was a midshipman from Georgia Tech named John Young. John and I bunked with a group of about thirty midshipmen two decks below the main deck. We got to be good buddies during that cruise, working in the gun turret and holystoning *Missouri*'s wooden decks. We would have laughed at the suggestion that someday we would become astronauts flying in space and circling the Moon together. That summer the newspapers showed the first picture of the earth taken from 250 miles up. The camera had been taken aloft by a V-2 rocket using a WAC Corporal missile for an upper stage.

Out from under the upperclassmen's tortures, I found that my second year at Annapolis was easier. I had a bit of free time and dated some of the local girls. I did well in my classes and finished as a "star man," meaning that I ranked in the upper ten percent of my class. I even got a star added to the collar of my uniform.

Instead of being assigned to ships that summer, the whole class headed for the naval air station at Pensacola, at the tip of the Florida panhandle on the Gulf of Mexico. At NAS Pensacola we took classes in aerodynamics, navigation, and engineering, and we saw survival training films showing how to bail out of an aircraft in flight or get out of one in the water.

We also got rides in the SNJ trainer, the Navy version of the ancient T-6 Texan; North American built fourteen thousand such aircraft before and during World War II. Far from a high-performance aircraft, the SNJ was a rugged beast designed to withstand punishment from clumsy students. Nevertheless, it could pull Gs and do aerobatics, and some of my classmates came back from flights with their barf bags full. Not me, though. I loved flying and aerobatics. The rides left me more determined than ever to become a pilot.

As I was tearing up the Florida sky in the backseat of an SNJ, my future Apollo-Soyuz partner Aleksei Leonov was living in the Baltic city of Kaliningrad, the former Koenigsburg of East Prussia, lost to the Soviets by Germany at the end of World War II. Like thousands of other Russians, Leonov's parents had moved to Kaliningrad from far off Siberia in 1945, in hopes of a better life. It was better for Aleksei, who became a member of the Communist Youth League and an avid bicyclist. He was able to shift his artistic subject from wounded soldiers to seascapes, and he became a big fan of an artist named Ivan Avaizovsky. Aleksei considered enrolling in a local art institute, though aviation was still a lure for him.

The outside world intruded on life at Annapolis beginning June 25, 1950, when the Communists in northern Korea invaded the south. Two days later, the United Nations voted to send troops to Korea to repel the invaders. For the next few weeks, Korea was all we talked about. Back home in Weatherford, my National Guard unit was called to active duty and shipped to Korea. I felt a twinge of envy knowing that my old buddies Steve Stroud, Gordon Pulliam, Stony Lockstone, David Tautfest, and Mac McPhetridge were going into action, but I couldn't just resign from the academy. Besides, we all figured this war would last long enough for the class of '52 to see action.

On this trip home, I started to get serious about a girl. Elva Shoemaker and her family lived on the same street we did. Elva and I were the same age, and our mothers used to take us strolling together when we were babies. I thought about dating Elva, but in high school I started to go out with her younger sister, Faye. By summer 1950 she had graduated from Weatherford High, and was the reigning Football Queen. Marriage, though, like graduation, was still a long way off.

I made star man again my third year at Annapolis, 1950–1951, ranking tenth out of nine hundred. As I had predicted, we had lost a quarter of the class that had arrived for plebe summer in June 1948.

The 1951 summer cruise was aboard *Burdo,* a destroyer escort accompanying battleship *Missouri* and other ships to Oslo, Norway. To help us choose what type of work we would do after graduation, the Navy rotated us through different billets to get experience. First I served as an engineering officer in *Burdo's* engine room, then as a fire control officer in the combat information center. Finally, I worked on the bridge as a ship handler. I liked all three, but none of them compared to flying.

The most impressive lesson about life at sea, however, has nothing to do with a billet. On the way to Norway, the *Missouri* task force ran into a North Atlantic hurricane. *Burdo,* which ran top-heavy, pitched twenty-four degrees fore and aft and rolled as much as forty degrees side to side. Of the sixty-five middies on board, at least sixty of them were violently seasick. I happened to be one of the lucky five. During the storm I spent my free time in the aft passageway looking back on the fantail, watching the action of the big waves. It was amazing to see how, when the ship pitched forward, the whole fantail would come out of the water, propellers churning in the air. Then, *splash,* down into the water again. It was a vivid lesson in the power of nature.

Senior year was a dream. I was now one of the dreaded first classmen, though I did very little hazing of the poor plebes. Not that I was above the occasional escapade. The night before the Navy-Maryland football game, several first classmen and I went over the hill, purchased some cans of gasoline, and drove to the University of Maryland campus. At the center of the Terps football field, we poured gasoline in the shape of an *N*—then torched it. The next day the television cameras showed the big *N* burned across that turf. I'm happy to say that the perpetrators were never caught.

I never lost sight of my main goal, however, which had now become to qualify for the Air Force. Why not Navy aviation? At the time, the Air Force flew the fastest jet in the world, the swept-wing F-86E Sabre jet, and I was eager to fly that baby against Soviet MiGs. If I couldn't get into the Air Force, the I hoped to become a Marine Corps aviator. Naval air was third.

In those days the Air Force did not have an academy, so twenty-five percent of the graduating classes at both Annapolis and West Point could chose service in the Air Force. I was open about my desire to exercise that option, but company officers and many other midshipmen did not share my enthusiasm, and it undoubtedly hurt my final standing at graduation. (That, and one unauthorized trip "over the wall.") Based on academic grades, I would have ranked about tenth out of 783 students. But attitude and conduct counted for twenty-five percent of the final standing, so I wound up fiftieth.

To complicate matters, midshipmen graduating in the class of '52 could no longer choose their service based on their academic ranking. The previous year a new superintendent, Vice Adm. Harry Hill, had joined the academy. A graduate of the class of '12, Admiral Hill was an old sea dog who had probably done his midshipman cruise aboard a sailing ship. Hill watched with fury as many of the top midshipmen officers of Annapolis '51 (including a future astronaut named James Irwin) volunteered for the Air Force. Hill made sure that wouldn't happen again. He simply divided us into thirds by class rank, then had us draw numbers out of a box. Those with the high numbers had the first pick.

I drew number 167. I had made it.

On June 3, my group was called into Memorial Hall, sworn in, and commissioned second lieutenants in the Air Force. We were commissioned on the same day that our colleagues from West Point graduated, so we all had the same date of rank. After the ceremony, we were then told to resume being midshipmen—for three more days. I sailed through the graduating ceremonies in a golden haze, enjoying the aircraft flybys and the formal parade, and tossing my white hat into the air.

The class of '52 did send a message to Admiral Harry Hill that day: We deposited our old shoes on the parade ground and carried jock straps on our bayonets during parade. As we passed in front of the reviewing stand, we even tossed our gloves over our shoulders—a backward salute to a backward superintendent.

There was one glitch. By Christmas 1951 Faye and I had gotten engaged.

We had also talked about getting married in the academy chapel, but never officially put our names on the list. (We both realized we were rushing things and postponed the wedding for a year.) Nevertheless, when my mother came east for my graduation, driving the first car she ever owned, she brought Faye with her. Faye eventually took the train back to Weatherford, but my mother and I took a more roundabout drive home, visiting relatives in Connecticut, New York, Indiana, and Illinois.

Joining the Air Force was the first step toward becoming a Cold Warrior; now I had to pass through several bases in the hot, humid South, beginning with Greenville, Mississippi. Situated on the big river about midway between Vicksburg and Memphis, Greenville Air Force Base was a leftover from World War II, re-opened in 1951 to train pilots for Korea. So were our planes, the ancient two-seat, prop-driven T-6 Texans. I reported to Greenville Air Force Base (AFB) for primary training on Labor Day, 1952, where I became a member of class 53-G. I was still hoping to get qualified as an Air Force fighter pilot in time to shoot it out with Soviet MiGs.

The initial training was a breeze. I soloed, and after six months I moved on to San Marcos AFB in Texas, for phase I basic training. At San Marcos we were supposed to transition to the T-28, an advanced prop trainer, but lately the plane had been slinging propellers, suffering engine failures, and having all sorts of problems you didn't want to inflict on new student pilots. So we wound up in T-6s again, but these were D models, older than the T-6Gs we'd flown at Greenville! Even their paint schemes were old, just a variety of colors. As if having to fly older planes wasn't bad enough, the weather in San Marcos that winter was terrible. It was rain, rain, rain. None of us accumulated enough flight hours, and we fell behind in the syllabus.

Finally the weather started to break, and early one Sunday morning I took off in a T-6 with my instructor, 1st Lt. Paul Grasso, for a lesson in instrument flying. I was in the backseat with a hood over my cockpit blocking my view of the outside world, using only my altimeter, airspeed indicator, and other instruments to tell where I was. Grasso was in the front seat with an unobstructed view.

The sky was heavy, filled with black clouds, and the air was bumpy. I was at six thousand feet, head buried under the hood, listening to a low-frequency beacon when—*bam!*—the instruments went haywire. My heading fell off, though I quickly corrected it. Airspeed indicator read zero and so did the rate of climb. But the altimeter was still holding steady at six thousand feet. I knew the plane was still flying the same airspeed. The engine was still growling with the same rhythm. Stick and rudder *felt* normal, but Grasso was yelling, "Get out from under the hood!" When I pushed back the hood, I saw immediately that the right wingtip had been smashed flat. The pitot tube, which measured the air speed, was bent back, useless. "What the hell's going on?" I said.

"We've just been hit by another airplane!" Grasso said. The plane had appeared out of the clouds, smacked us, then vanished back into the clouds. Grasso got on the radio to report the accident as we dodged in and out of clouds, searching for a parachute. We saw wreckage on the ground first—then, nearby, a parachute all strung out. No sign of the pilot.

Pilots often used the operating area next to ours for aerobatics. Unfortunately, the controllers at San Marcos weren't too rigorous about enforcing separations, and sure enough, we had been clipped by another T-6, flown by a solo pilot trainee named Otto Kraxburger, who was doing a loop. The top of our propeller sawed off part of his right wing. Had Kraxburger looped two feet lower, he would have decapitated us. The parachute we saw was his. It hadn't opened fully, and, tragically, Kraxburger was dead.

The accident never should have happened. Doing aerobatics was questionable given the cloudy weather and bumpy air, especially so close to planes flying on instruments. It taught me, however, to keep my head swiveling when flying, always, *always* watching for other aircraft.

On July 8, 1953, just as the Korean War was ending, nineteen-year-old Aleksei Leonov entered an air force school in the city of Kremenchug, on the Dnepr River in the Ukrainian Soviet Socialist Republic. Though he had taken entrance exams for the Riga Art Institute, the school did not provide student housing, and Aleksei's parents had no money to support him there, so he had decided to become a pilot.

The Soviet system for training pilots was different from ours. The U.S. Navy and Air Force wanted their trainees to have a college education before they put them in the cockpit. In the Military Air Forces of the USSR, however, you got the equivalent of a junior college education while you did your preliminary and basic flight training. So even though I was four years older than Aleksei and had a college degree, Alexei's and my flying careers were almost in sync.

The next phase of my training began in May 1953, at Connally Air Force Base near Waco, Texas. At Connally we would transition from T-6s to the jet-powered T-33, the trainer version of the F-80 Shooting Star, our first operational jet fighter. I had arranged to room with two other student pilots, Ralph Waddell and Larry Lucas, and in what was then the affluent part of Waco we found a second-story place in an old house owned by an elderly couple. We were moving in one afternoon in May—none of us had more than a suitcase and a car—when we heard a siren start to wail. When we turned on Larry's radio, we learned that a tornado had ploughed into downtown Waco. We reported to the base, where we were immediately ordered to forget flight training and help with rescue and cleanup. For three days, we dug through the rubble in Waco, pulling out the dead and injured. The death toll eventually reached 124. It was grueling, sad work, seeing so many lives ruined, and a grim reminder of the reality of my new career—making war.

By this time, the summer of 1953, it was clear that I wasn't likely to fly in combat any time soon. The Korean War had degenerated into a tense cease-fire and a stalemate, with our forces being drawn down and sent home. Nevertheless, I knew there would be other opportunities to shoot it out in the sky with Soviet MiGs. Under the instruction of 1st Lt. Barney Brooks from Tulsa, Oklahoma, I soloed and qualified on the T-33, my first jet aircraft. By the time basic was over, I had logged almost three hundred hours of flying time—more than pilots at a similar stage have these days.

On September 1, 1953, I pinned on my silver wings. And three days later, Faye Shoemaker and I were married at the Methodist Church in Weatherford. Stony Lockstone, Richard McPhetridge, and David Tautfest, my classmates from high school and the football team, served as best man and ushers.

three
Cold Warrior

Before I could take my place on the front lines of the war against the communists, I had to undergo advanced training on the F-86D Sabre at Tyndall Air Force Base in Panama City, Florida. Panama City was a town of ten thousand dominated by the air base and a giant paper mill. The Environmental Protection Agency did not exist in 1953, so the emissions from the mill were completely unregulated. When the wind was wrong, you could smell it for miles, even on approach to the runway at Tyndall. We referred to it as landing with "nasal flight rules," as opposed to landing with instruments.

Faye and I moved into a small, furnished two-room cottage in a motel on the East Bay. In spite of the challenging conditions, Faye adjusted to married life very nicely. It helped, I think, that the Air Force community at Tyndall resembled a small town like Weatherford. Most of the other renters were young lieutenants going through training, and their wives—Henry (Hank) and Hanny West, Donn and Harriett Eisele, and Jim and Joannie Morrison.

Hank was a West Pointer, but Donn was a fellow graduate of Annapolis. Though he had graduated in the class of 1952, we had not met there, but I had heard about one unfortunate midshipman who took the lack of his name on a duty roster as an invitation to skip formations. The omission was a mistake, of course, and when his absences were discovered, the midshipman caught all kinds of hell.

That was Donn Eisele.

The F-86D was the hottest thing in the sky in those days, a single-seat, all-weather interceptor with an afterburner capable of reaching speeds of almost seven hundred miles per hour at sea level, and just over six hundred miles per hour at its operating altitude of forty thousand feet. Designed to shoot down Soviet bombers, it carried radar in its nose that could detect a target thirty miles away.

But in 1953 its electronic fuel control system still had a few bugs, and it failed from time to time. If the engine froze and didn't windmill, your controls froze after a few minutes, too. In the T-33, by contrast, if your engine flamed out you still had manual elevator control, manual rudder control, and unboosted aileron. Flying a T-33 under those conditions was tough, but you could still do it.

Under those same conditions, the 86D fell like a brick. This flaw in the 86D caused thirteen serious accidents that season, among them one young Tyndall pilot named Fryer, West Point '52. Fryer's engine failed, and when the battery power ran out and the controls froze, he crashed and was killed. The string of accidents caused the Air Force to ground the whole fleet of 86Ds temporarily in December 1953. Because of these mechanical problems, we took much of our advanced training in the T-33, where we flew on instruments. We had yet to fire any weapons.

In early December, Faye took the train from Panama City back to Weatherford to be matron of honor at Elaine Tautfest's wedding to Stony Lockstone. Elaine had been Faye's maid of honor. I left for Weatherford shortly before Christmas, ready to become a Cold Warrior.

Very few warriors were colder than those who had survived a winter at Ellsworth Air Force Base, Rapid City, South Dakota, where I got my first operational flying job. Rapid City sits between the Badlands and the Black Hills not far from Mount Rushmore. It was cold that winter, ten below when we arrived in January 1954. To like such a place, you have to be young. You also have to have distractions, and we had an important one: Faye was pregnant.

I was assigned to the Air Defense Command's 54th Fighter-Interceptor Squadron. Our mission was to intercept and shoot down Soviet Tu-4 bombers flying across the North Pole and Canada to drop nuclear bombs on American cities and military bases. Ellsworth itself would be a prime target because, in addition to the 54th, it was home to the 28th Bomb Wing and a fleet of B-36 nuclear bombers.

Some of the pilots of the 54th were new; others were veterans who had flown fighters like the P-47 and P-51 in World War II, then served after the war with Gen. Joe Foss's original South Dakota Air Guard unit. These Dakotans, who had names like Swensen and Downey and Sacker, called us new arrivals "sprogs." All of the sprogs from Tyndall—including Stafford, West, and Eisele—moved with our pregnant wives into a new civilian housing development situated on a cold, windy hilltop. We were renters, of course. None of us could afford to buy a house.

In those days new officers still made formal calls on their commanders, leaving cards. When I had been promoted to first lieutenant in December, I had had new ones made. I'm not sure that the formalities meant much to Lt. Col. "Big Red" Benedict, the commander of the 54th. He had been an ace in World War II, flying with the famous Eagle Squadron and shooting it out with Nazis over Europe. Big Red liked to remind us that our new F-86s cost $750,000, more than *ten times* as much as a P-51. "I want you sprogs to take care of these planes! I want you to love them! And by God, if that plane goes down, you go down with it!" He delivered all this at the top of his voice because Red was a shouter. "Get out there and get as many hours as you can!"

Fortunately, building up hours was just what I wanted to do. Not only was I happy to stand alert every other day and fly on the days when I wasn't standing alert, I also volunteered for extra work when on temporary duty at the gunnery range in Yuma, Arizona. I would fly T-33s in a position called safety chase, helping signal rocket-firing aircraft that the planes towing their targets were far enough to one side that it was safe to fire away. I even flew as co-pilot on B-45 Tornadoes, four-engine, straight-wing North American bombers that towed the target.

One night when weather conditions had improved, Big Red called for a night scramble with instructions to generate maximum flying hours. I took off in my 86D and climbed above the top of the twenty-five-thousand-foot cloud cover. It was a beautiful night; you could see the stars, not to mention a lot of other airplanes zooming around.

We were all boring holes in the sky, building up hours, happy to be flying again. Since we had all scrambled together, naturally we all started to run out of fuel at the same time. (The 86D could only fly for a maximum of two hours.) Unfortunately, just as we started running low on fuel, the weather conditions deteriorated.

Along with its air traffic control tower, Ellsworth had a manned air defense radar site that often helped with vectored approaches, but both stations were overwhelmed with a whole squadron suddenly having to land in poor weather. I had instinctively throttled back to conserve fuel while orbiting in the night sky and managed to get down safely, on fumes, after an hour and fifty-five minutes in the air. But one pilot had to eject. I'm sorry to say I don't remember that poor pilot's name. He left us shortly after the night scramble, after being on the receiving end of a Big Red tirade and a transfer to someplace further north and even colder.

At no point did I ever question Big Red's wisdom in sending us all up under those conditions. I was too happy to fly, too certain that accidents happened to other people. But when I look back on it, I see the parallels to that day in San Marcos, when I was lucky to survive a mid-air. Once again, weather had kept us from flying, and our commanders and operating officers were so desperate to catch up on flying hours that they ignored common sense.

Since Faye, Harriett Eisele, and Hanny West were all pregnant that first winter and spring, they faced the same problem: where to get prenatal care. Though Ellsworth was expanding, its support facilities were primitive, and so were the medical options. Because the local Air Force obstetrician had a long waiting list, Faye and the other women had to drive all the way to Igloo, South Dakota, to visit a military physician at an Army munitions depot there. Finally, on July 2, 1954, our daughter, Dionne, was born, delivered by an Air Force psychiatrist in a barracks at Ellsworth that had been converted to a hospital. Sheets had been hung from the ceiling to create "rooms."

In the Soviet Union, the home of those Tu-4 bombers I was being trained to intercept, Aleksei Leonov was a cadet at the Kremenchug Air Force School in the Ukraine. Soviet air cadets, most of them eighteen or nineteen years old, weren't allowed near aircraft for a year or more. First they had to take college-level courses in mathematics, engineering, and aerodynamics, as well as literature, and most importantly, politics and military history. Aleksei wouldn't make his first flight until January 1955, in a two-seat Yak-18A prop trainer. His would take his first solo flight on May 10.

The facilities at the Kremenchug School were limited. It wasn't possible for cadets to fly at night, or on instruments, so Aleksei moved on to intermediate training at the Chuguyev Higher Air Force School, located near the city of Kharkov. At Chuguyev Aleksei learned to fly the prop-driven Yak-11 and later made the transition to jets, qualifying on the MiG-15. He would graduate in the spring of 1957.

My two-year tour in Rapid City would end soon. As my next assignment I had requested Germany because flying along the Iron Curtain was the closest thing to combat I could find. The orders came in right after Thanksgiving, in early December 1955. I was to join the 496th Interceptor Squadron at Landstuhl Air Force Base. To celebrate, I bought a new two-door Oldsmobile coupe, packed up Faye and one-year-old Dionne, and headed for New York. We planned to get together with Hank and Hanny West, who were also on their way overseas, to Wheelus Air Force Base at Tripoli, Libya.

The military shipped the new Olds and our small collection of furniture, one of the bonuses of an overseas assignment, and we boarded the military transport SS *Rose* at the Brooklyn Navy Yard, headed for Bremerhaven. From Bremerhaven, we took the train down to Landstuhl, near the city of Kaiserslautern in the Palatinate. The nearest major city was Frankfurt, sixty miles to the northeast. The border with East Germany, meaning Soviet soldiers, tanks, and fighters—and short-range nuclear missiles—was less than a hundred miles due east. Both sides of the Iron Curtain had numerous bases and thousands of tons of matériel, all of it ready to be flung at the other side on a moment's notice. It was obvious that the next world war would start right here. The joke was that in West Germany, distances between towns and bases were measured in kilotons.

Landstuhl was a former Luftwaffe air base located across the autobahn from 12th Air Force Headquarters at Ramstein. I barely had Faye and Dionne moved into Army housing at the edge of Kaiserslautern when I had to fly to Libya. The 496th, under Lt. Col. Carl Hawbeck, was on temporary duty at the Wheelus Air Force Base gunnery range, where all the USAF units in Europe went to fire rockets and cannon.

The rest of the squadron—planes and personnel—had recently come to Germany from Hamilton Air Force Base in California. They had moved as a group, but I was new. Thanks to two years at Ellsworth, though, I had more time in the 86D than any of them, and that helped me fit right in. I also turned out to be good at rocketry—good enough to be chosen for the 86th Fighter Wing's team in the European competition. Air Force units spent six weeks tracking and firing away at targets over the Mediterranean to see which unit could earn the highest score. The 86th wound up in the finals against a unit from England, and we came in a close second.

Faye and I loved living in Germany. The mark was trading at 4.2 to the dollar, which meant that Americans enjoyed a low cost of living. A haircut was twenty-five cents. A gallon of gasoline cost a quarter. A bottle of Coca-Cola or Löwenbräu would set you back a whole nickel. We saved money and used it to buy some decent furniture for the first time in our married lives. It was especially nice once we moved from the Army housing at Vogelweh to larger quarters across the autobahn at Ramstein Air Force Base.

Having three squadrons of 86Ds at Landstuhl made the base an inviting target for nearby Soviet forces, so plans were made to disperse us: One of the other squadrons in the wing, the 525th, was moved to Bitburg. My squadron, the 496th, was scheduled to deploy to Pfalzburg, France. But in October 1956, a revolution against Communist rule broke out in Hungary. Soviet tanks and planes moved in to crush resistance, and every American and NATO unit in Europe went on twenty-four-hour alert. Overnight, it seemed, the 496th was sent to Hahn Air Base, forty miles northwest of Ramstein. The 50th Tactical Fighter Wing had recently vacated Hahn on their way to France. Knowing they would be living in sticks and mud at a newly built base, they had stripped Hahn of everything useful and taken it with them. Even the telephones were gone. We had to truck up some portable power units just to keep the lights on.

To go with the lack of creature comforts, Hahn had terrible flying conditions. At this time, the worst flying weather in the United States, in terms of the number of days you had to use instrument flight rules, was Pittsburgh, Pennsylvania. Even so, Pittsburgh had fewer IFR days than the best American base in Germany. And Hahn had the most IFR days in Europe. For one thing, it was up in the mountains, so what was a five- or six-hundred-foot overcast ceiling at Landstuhl/Ramstein was only two to three hundred feet at Hahn. You would take off, hit the soup, and not see the ground again until you broke out on a final instrument approach. During one six-week period there I never made a single landing under visual flight rules. Most pilots don't like that kind of flying, but I did. And I logged enough hours on instruments to grow confident of my skills.

Confident or not, in late 1956 and early 1957 I was thinking about getting out of the Air Force. I loved flying, but I had watched all my Annapolis classmates who had stayed in the Navy get promoted to full lieutenant right on schedule, three years after graduation. Here I was, over four years out of the academy and still wearing that single silver bar. A lot of Academy grads chose to serve in the Air Force because it offered greater opportunity for promotion. But the Korean War had brought all kinds of Reserve and Air Guard pilots back to active duty, and some of them had stayed at senior ranks, clogging the system for young officers like me.

A buddy back in the 54th at Ellsworth, Capt. William "Norky" Norris, had talked to me once about joining the airlines, which would have been a great way to keep flying. My service commitment had only been two years coming out of Annapolis and two more years after flight training. So I was free to resign in 1957. One night I sat down and started drafting letters to American Airlines and TWA. But I changed my mind. The F-100, first of the Century series, had started flying in Europe. And I saw the F-101, F-102, and especially the hot new Lockheed F-104 coming. If I went to an airline, I'd be flying the equivalent of cargo planes and could say good-bye to high performance fighters. So I tore up those letters. And didn't make captain until early 1958. Norris didn't get out, either. He stayed in the Air Force and later became a three-star general.

During the winter and spring of 1957, Faye was pregnant again. The facilities and support at Hahn turned out to be better than we'd had at Ellsworth, and on August 27, 1957, we became parents of a second daughter. We wanted to give the baby a German name, in honor of her country of birth. It was our maid who suggested the German spelling of Karen—"Karin."

One day not long after Karin's birth, I got scrambled for another MiG intercept. It was late summer and, unusual for Germany, beautiful weather. I was element lead, with 1st. Lt. John Howard on my wing, as we headed northeast out of Hahn with afterburner full thrust. Flight control told us, "Make Angels Five-Zero." Go to fifty thousand feet? The F-86D was a relatively heavy airplane; the only way we might possibly approach that altitude was to drop our empty external fuel tanks. I requested permission, but it was denied. They didn't want these two aluminum tanks falling down on top of some German citizens.

Fine, but then I had to report, "We can't get up there." We had barely made it to forty-six thousand feet. As John and I would climb, our 86s would start to burble, on the edge of stalling. Then we'd drop back down to forty-three or forty-four thousand feet and start the process all over again. We were burning up fuel at a tremendous rate, and we still didn't know what we were supposed to be intercepting. But ground control ordered us to orbit.

Then I saw this strange sight coming at me—four contrails heading my direction inside the Eastern Zone. One of the contrails would suddenly shoot upward for a few moments then spiral back down, much as we were doing, but at a much higher altitude. Then another one would do the same thing—climb, stall, then spiral down. John and I were burbling around at forty-five or forty-six thousand feet while these Soviet fighters were getting up to fifty-two or fifty-three thousand.

I had no idea what was going on until I saw the sun glinting off a small spot up much higher than we were. It was a U-2 spy plane, headed west, outbound from the Eastern Zone, and these MiGs were trying to get up there and shoot it down—with no luck. Eventually they gave up and turned back. So did John and I.

By this time the U-2 had been flying out of Wiesbaden, then Giebelstat, for a year or so. I had no official knowledge of the program, of course; it was highly classified. But occasionally you'd run into a former Air Force pilot who was working for some top secret organization, and it didn't require a lot of imagination or inside knowledge to figure he was doing recon behind the Iron Curtain.

I had heard about the International Geophysical Year and America's plans to put a small artificial satellite called Vanguard into orbit, but I hadn't paid much attention; I was too busy flying airplanes. Suddenly there was word that the Soviets had tested an intercontinental ballistic missile, and then they put a satellite of their own into orbit. On the morning of October 4, 1957, we woke up to find Sputnik in space. This was a huge surprise. What was next? Nukes from orbit? A flight to the Moon? We spent a lot of time at the O-club wondering just how far behind America was, and what we would do to catch up.

My "extra" duty with the 496th was as assistant maintenance officer under Capt. George Hochstettler, a former P-38 pilot in World War II. One of my jobs involved flight testing the squadron aircraft once they returned to the flight line after maintenance, certifying them as safe for operations again. That kind of work, combined with my desire to keep flying the newest, fastest jets, led me to apply for the Air Force Test Pilot School as I looked at the end of my German tour of duty in 1958.

Hochstettler, who had given me good reviews on my Officer Efficiency Reports, wrote a recommendation for me. So did Colonel Hawbeck, and Maj. Jack Rockwell, the squadron ops officer. But even with all these great endorsements, my application seemed to go nowhere. Days and weeks went by with no response. I wondered if there was a problem somewhere along the line. Finally I just got on the telephone and called the personnel desk at Air Force European HQ at Wiesbaden and found out that the damn application hadn't been forwarded to the States yet; it was still sitting there. The personnel officer apologized; he was just swamped. I think I was polite, but I was firm in asking him to send it out *now*. He did, and in June 1958 I learned that I would be assigned to the USAF Experimental Test Pilot School, Edwards AFB, California, as a student in Class 58-C.

But first—the Mark VI.

The Royal Canadian Air Force had a squadron of fighters based across the border from us in France, on the Moselle River. I had gotten to know some of the pilots and had listened to them brag about the power of their Mark VI fighter. This was an F-86 that had been stripped down to 13,200 pounds, compared to the 21,000 pounds for the 86D I was used to flying, but it was powered by an engine with more thrust than the one we used. At two-thirds the weight, with more thrust, the Mark VI was *hot*. It had such a light wing loading that it could do a barrel roll at forty-eight thousand feet; the 86D could barely lumber up to that altitude at all, even without tip tanks.

I got the Canadians to let me fly a Mark VI, and wound up logging ten hours in it. On one of my last days in Germany, I took a Mark VI over to Hahn. Using my best Canadian accent, I requested permission to make a "compass check"—to make sure my compass was properly aligned by flying down the length of the runway. Permission granted—I zoomed down to fifty feet off the deck and roared up the runway at 520 knots, then stood the Mark VI on its tail and did a series of aileron rolls out of there.

It was my way of saying, "Auf wiedersehen!"

four

Higher and Faster

I arrived at Edwards Air Force Base on a Sunday morning in September 1958, piloting my new orange Volkswagen beetle down the Barstow-Bakersfield Road, which ran for seventy miles west out of Boron without so much as a bend. The same purple mountains rose in front me, just as they had in 1946 when I passed through on my way to a summer job at Tuolumne National Forest. The desert lake bed stretched for miles on my left.

I had followed the new I-40, which was still being built on top of old Route 66, all the way from Weatherford. I had parked Faye and the girls with Faye's parents, the Shoemakers, who lived in the small town of Thomas, Oklahoma. There was no housing for my family at Edwards yet. But as I turned south into the base and ascended the low hills that gave me a spectacular view of Rogers Dry Lake, I felt I had not only arrived at a destination—I felt I was starting a real adventure. Just seeing the famous lake bed from that viewpoint was exciting.

I had followed the exploits of famous test pilots, of course. You couldn't be an Air Force fighter jock without knowing about Chuck Yeager, Frank "Pete" Everest, or Iven Kincheloe, hearing about breaking the sound barrier, reaching Mach 2, or climbing to altitudes of one hundred thousand feet or more in those exotic X-planes. It was exciting work, and it was also dangerous: Kincheloe had been killed when his F-104 crashed just a few weeks before my arrival. That wouldn't stop me, though. I was eager to qualify for an X-plane. Failing that, an F-104 would do just fine.

USAF Experimental Test Pilot School Class 58-C consisted of sixteen students, including Harvey Prosser, who had been an academic instructor at West Point, and Jack Craigie, who had just completed a master's degree in aeronautical engineering at Princeton University. Some of my other classmates were equally intimidating at first—Joe Guthrie, Charlie Kuyk, Pete Knight, Russ Rogers. I would cross paths with many of them over the next twenty years in the space program, the Air Force, and the Pentagon.

Our curriculum consisted of two sixteen-week courses, one in performance, the other in stability and control. Harry Spillers and James King were the performance instructors, and Dick Jackobsen and Ralph Matson were the instructors in stability and control. The operations officer was Maj. Dick Lathrop, and the commandant of the school was Lt. Col. Herb Leonhardt.

I moved into the bachelor officer's quarters, prepared to devote every waking hour to excelling at the school. At the BOQ I found Ed Givens, Annapolis '52, who was completing his studies in stability and control and would become an instructor when he graduated. I had known Ed only slightly at Annapolis, but we were the only two members of the class at the school, and we became friends. We often had dinners and drinks together, and I took every chance I could to ask Ed for his advice on everything about the school.

We flew in the morning and attended classes after lunch. Our desks were each equipped with a Monroe calculator and a slide rule. Each morning's flight generated a pile of data from handwritten notes, recording cameras, oscilloscopes, and other instruments. We had to reduce this data to a terse report that we submitted to the instructors, and we had a test every Friday. I worked harder than I'd ever worked in my life. I really had to concentrate on the academics. I hadn't been exposed to much math since leaving Annapolis, but here at Edwards I was competing against people with graduate degrees.

I felt very confident and comfortable, though, with the stick-and-rudder · part; I had no problems adapting to precision flying, controlling airspeed to a very exact figure, whether the plane was bouncing around or not, and I learned to organize tasks for a flight test. I would rise before five A.M. most mornings, getting to the flight line and into the air when the desert was calm and clear. Mornings were the magic time, before the afternoon winds started, the product of cold air rushing down from the Sierra Nevadas and hot air rising from the lake bed. The sand would start to blow so hard you'd wind up with a dust storm and even pebbles and rocks flying off the roofs and around the buildings. Next morning, calm again.

Despite the struggles, I not only survived; I prospered. I learned to think about the average pilot and how best to make a difficult plane safe for him to fly. I also learned to be more objective: You fall in love with the planes you fly and tend to overlook their shortcomings. That's a trap a test pilot has to avoid.

In October my domestic situation improved when Faye and the girls finally arrived, and our household goods arrived from Germany. We moved into a stucco house with a flat roof, right near the Edwards base elementary school.

When Class 58-C graduated in May 1959, I placed first in the class, barely beating out Jack Craigie, and won the A. B. Honts Trophy for best combined flying and academic record. Our graduation speaker was a retired lieutenant general who had been the first American military pilot to fly a jet back in October 1942 and later served as Air Force deputy chief of staff for research and development. This gentleman, Lawrence "Bill" Craigie, happened to be Jack Craigie's father.

As Honts winner, I expected to have my choice of assignments, and I ranked them: First choice was, of course, fighter test operations. Second was to be an instructor at the test pilot school. Third was to go to Del Rio Air Force Base and qualify as a U-2 pilot. (The U-2 program was still classified, but I had seen the high-flying bird in Germany and lately out of the North Base at Edwards, too.) But Colonel Leonhardt convinced me that staying at the school as an instructor would be smartest because Edwards had a surplus of test pilots. "Anyone going to fighter ops right now is going to the end of the line," he said. "You won't be doing anything but flying chase and pace for the next two years." I could do that kind of flying at the school, he said, with a greater variety of aircraft. And being an instructor would also allow me to make an important contribution. His sales pitch worked, and I became an instructor in the performance section. Jack Craigie became an instructor in stability and control.

Actually, by the time Class 59-B came on board a few months later, I had even more duties. Phil Neale, one of my students in 59-A, had been assigned as a performance instructor. Unfortunately, he soon came down with a sore throat that turned to strep and then a heart murmur. He got medically disqualified from flying, so I had to pick up his load of flight test instruction. Harry Spillers had been transferred out by this time, and that left Jim King and me to do all the flight instruction for performance.

As a student I had also noticed that our handbooks on performance and flight testing were at least ten years out of date. I went to Leonhart and complained about this, and he said, well, yes, we ought to rewrite them. So within a few months I was not only teaching performance, I was also scheduling all the flights and other activities, helping to demonstrate stability flying and control technique, and rewriting the two performance textbooks in the evenings, with some small help from Jim King (who rewrote only one chapter but managed to get credit as coauthor).

I enjoyed the teaching and had some great students. Ted Twinting (59-A) would go on to become commander of the Flight Test Center. Class 59-C had Jim McDivitt and Ed White, who would become Gemini astronauts. I would work with two members of Class 60-C—Frank Borman and Mike Collins— in the space program. In fact, for one brief time, the three of us would form a single Apollo crew.

Occasionally we had visitors to the school, such as my counterpart at the U.S. Naval Test Pilot School at Patuxent River, Maryland, Lt. Charles "Pete" Conrad, Jr. I showed Pete around, took him up in one of the school's TF-102s, and in a few days we became lifelong friends. Pete told me that the staff at the naval test-pilot school included civilian academic instructors who took up the slack and provided continuity when the military instructors cycled in and out. I thought this was a great idea, so I raised it with Maj. Dick Lathrop, who had succeeded Leonhardt as the school commandant at Edwards in June 1959. "Aw, we should be able to handle this ourselves," he said. But he let me go ahead, and I recruited Bill Schweikhard from the flight-test center engineering directorate to join the test-pilot school as a permanent, civilian academic instructor.

It wasn't all school work, of course. Half of the job was in the cockpit. We didn't have the world's hottest planes at the school. Those birds, the F-104s and F-100s, were down at the far end of the flight line, in test ops. At our end we had T-28s and T-33s as well as single-seat F-86Fs. These were the first of the series for most of the aircraft, still equipped with the original test instruments. We also had old B-57 bombers that were instrumented for stability and control. Later we got a pair of TF-102s. Even though these planes were old, they were fun to fly, especially since we were in the air almost five days a week, teaching maneuvers like stall and spin recovery.

While I was working through my first year as an instructor at the test-pilot school, Lt. Aleksei Leonov was making a career change, too. He had graduated from Chuguyev in 1957, and was now qualified as a MiG-15 pilot; he was also, incidentally, a full member of the Communist Party, a requirement for any officer with ambition in those days. His first assignment was with the 69th Air Army, which happened to be based back in Kremenchug, where he had undergone basic flight training. At Kremenchug Aleksei flew the MiG-15, and he met Svetlana Dotsenko, a beautiful young student. They married on October 13, 1959, her 19th birthday. At that time, Aleksei was under orders to transfer to Soviet forces in East Germany, a plum job for a young Soviet fighter pilot. It was, in essence, going into combat. Leonov would be piloting the same type of MiGs that tried to intercept high-flying American U-2 spy planes and keep at bay the other recon craft prowling the periphery of Soviet-controlled airspace.

Before leaving Kremenchug, however, in September 1959, Aleksei received another set of orders—to report before a traveling board of Soviet Air Force flight surgeons headed by a Lt. Col. Yevgeny Karpov. They were visiting bases in European Russia searching for candidates for a "special program," which was eventually revealed to be manned space flight. Leonov was interested and qualified, and he wrote out an application. It was approved and sent to Moscow with, it turned out, 340 others.

Aleksei and Svetlana had barely relocated to the Air Army in Altenberg, west of Dresden, when he had to rush back to Moscow to spend a week at the Central Aviation Hospital, where he was subjected to a lengthy series of examinations. At the end of the tests he was told he had passed and went back to Germany to continue flying while he waited.

In February he was called into his commander's office and told he had been chosen for this "special" new assignment. He reported to Khodynka Field—the central airport in downtown Moscow—and on Monday, March 14, 1960, he became one of the first twenty pilots to enter the Soviet cosmonaut program.

The seven Mercury astronauts had been selected, with great fanfare and public acclaim, in April 1959, when I was in my last months at the test-pilot school. I had followed the news of the Mercury program, whose goal was to put a man inside the nosecone of an Atlas rocket and fire him into earth orbit, but I didn't think it could possibly involve me. For one thing, the Mercury program was limited: It was supposed to accomplish a manned orbit of the earth by 1961 or 1962. My height (at six feet I was over the limit for Mercury astronauts) and the fact that I had not graduated from the test-pilot school meant I wasn't even eligible for consideration. The closest I got to the Mercury program was seeing Deke Slayton and Gordo Cooper celebrating their astronaut selection at the bar in the Edwards Officer's Club.

At about that time, the Air Force was reorienting itself toward space flight. In October 1961 the Experimental Test Pilot School was renamed the Aerospace Research Pilot School, following suggestions from Ed Givens, Bill Schweikhard and Frank Borman that the Air Force create a postgraduate course emphasizing space.

The group of twenty cosmonauts was too large to train for the first manned flight into space. So on May 30, 1960, after a few weeks of classroom work, lots of physical conditioning, and parachute training (cosmonauts would return to earth by ejecting from their spacecraft!), six of the twenty were selected for advanced training.

Aleksei wasn't one of them. Even after two of the "vanguard six" dropped out within the next eight weeks, Aleksei was held back. It had nothing to do with flying or academic ability: He was just too big. The designers of the spherical manned spacecraft knew that a cosmonaut had to eject at the end of his space flight and land by personal parachute. They were worried that the bigger cosmonauts would face greater risks when fired through the hatch. So Aleksei and the others continued their training, spending hours or days in various test chambers as various unmanned test flights took place without their active participation.

In September, the cosmonaut team moved into its new home near Chkalov Air Base, about forty kilometers northeast of Moscow near a town called Ze-lyony ("Green Town"). Eventually Zelyony would be renamed Zvyozdny Gorodok—"Star City."

Even though the Aerospace Research Pilot School had a variety of airplanes, they were usually the oldest survivors of the production line. We needed something more modern, and eventually the Air Force Systems Command provided us with five Northrop T-38 jet trainers. They were still some of the first T-38s ever built, but they were newer than anything else we were flying. Since I had lobbied to get them, I became the test-pilot school's project pilot.

On my third flight in the 38, I took Bill Schweikhard up to get him familiar with the bird. We took off nicely from runway 04, went out and demonstrated the 38's performance and some stability and control. Coming in for a landing, I had planned to do several touch and gos. I pitched out, pulled the throttles back, slowed, dropped the gear, lowered the flaps, and turned base leg. We were about a third of the way around base leg, turning 180 degrees from downwind back to final approach, when we heard a sudden explosion from somewhere inside the aircraft. And then the whole plane went over in a ninety-degree bank.

I had been in a forty-five-degree bank, turning to line up with the runway. When I heard that noise, I remembered that day down in San Marcos, and I first thought we'd been hit by another plane. But as we flipped over to where we were almost upside down, I was too busy to worry about another plane. I immediately put full left aileron to the aircraft. It came back up . . . then started to roll over again past ninety-degree bank angle.

One of my tasks as an instructor at the school was to teach pilots how to do rudder rolls, where you slow down the airplane, pull the nose up, then stomp full left rudder. As you yaw to the left, the angle of sideslip will just turn you over in a slow roll. Students initially found a rudder roll unnerving because most pilots have never experienced large angles of yaw and don't realize what a large aerodynamic surface the vertical stabilizer is: Modern jets don't have torque, the force imparted to old prop planes by the turning propeller. So the only time a jet pilot normally pushes the rudder pedals is when taxiing or during a crosswind landing.

When the T-38 yawed, I hit the afterburners to get some speed. We shot across the runway at a ninety-degree angle, a few hundred feet off the ground, with me holding full left rudder, full left aileron, afterburners firing. As I picked up speed, I could decrease the rudder and aileron force long enough to see that the flap gauge on the left side of the cockpit was just rotating around. I picked up the landing gear, which allowed me to ease off the rudder some more and hold the plane steady with just a modest bit of left stick force and a little left rudder.

Behind me, Bill Schweikhard was frantically clawing between his legs for the ejection seat D-ring, as you would in an F-104. Lucky for him, to eject from a T-38 you had to raise the seat armrest and squeeze the triggers. Since we were nearly upside down at low altitude, he'd have fired himself right into the ground and been killed.

Now I could shut off the afterburners, and see outside the window that the left flap was down, but the right flap was just floating in the breeze—"reflexed up." As I got more speed, I slowly brought the left flap up. With both flaps in the same position, I felt I could make a safe "no flaps," high-speed landing. I got squared away at three hundred knots, came back in, lowered the landing gear, slowed down, then touched down and rolled in, no problems. I looked out at the right flap, and it was already coming down on its own, as the airspeed decreased.

We taxied back to the test pilot school and popped the canopy. As we got out, I said to Schweikhard, "I think I hit another airplane." But the crew chief, who was looking over our T-38 the moment we stopped, told me, "There's a big hole in the bottom of your airplane." Sure enough, there was a jagged hole about six inches in diameter on the center line.

The T-38 had flaps that were electrically powered. The procedure on approach was to put the flap switch full down and *leave* it down. Not down, then back *up* to the neutral position. Every airplane that has flaps has a control mechanism linking the left and the right flaps, so you don't have asymmetric movements. This linkage goes through a gearbox known as the H-drive. The flap controls have limiters to shut down once they've reached the proper position. When I had put my flaps down, the left flap stopped right where it should have, and the motor shut off. But the right flap's limiter didn't work, so the motor kept pulling until finally it just pulled the mechanism in two. The flap exploded up and the H-drive mechanism itself blew right out the bottom of the fuselage. Had I crashed into the ground, the investigators might have said, "Well, the dumb bastard got too slow and low on final approach."

Nelly Nelson, a test pilot working the T-38 in test ops, took one of their instrumented T-38s out for a flight with one flap pinned up. When he tried to reproduce the conditions I was in, flying the recommended speed, putting the flaps down according to the manual, he lost control of the plane, too. So they upped the recommended speed for base leg and the start of final approach, and changed the flap limit switch designs and procedures. And I received an award for saving the airplane.

The Vanguard Six cosmonauts—Bykovsky, Gagarin, Nelyubov, Nikolayev, Popovich, and Titov—were ordered to take final examinations on the Vostok spacecraft between January 17 and 19, 1961. Those tests, along with personal evaluations and recommendations reviewed by Gen. Nikolai Kamanin, showed that the best candidates for the first Soviet citizen in space were Yury Gagarin, German Titov, and Grigory Nelyubov.

On March 9, 1961, an advanced version of the Vostok spacecraft was launched from Baikonur carrying a dog named Chernushka and a mannequin. Everything worked well. On March 23, however, tragedy struck the cosmonaut team. At the Institute of Aviation and Space Medicine in Moscow, Valentin Bondarenko, the youngest of the twenty candidates, was in the tenth day of a planned fifteen-day simulated flight in a chamber filled with pure oxygen when a fire broke out. By the time doctors and technicians could open the door and rescue Bondarenko, he had been so severely burned that he died within hours.

The other cosmonauts were told of Bondarenko's death, but launch schedules and the pressure of the space race left no room for mourning. Aleksei and the Vanguard Six were already in Baikonur: They would see the launch site and booster for the first time. And on March 24, another Vostok successfully orbited the earth carrying a dog named Zvyozdochka.

At Edwards, we knew very little of this. Television and newspapers reported on the Soviet successes, but none of us outside the intel community knew about the failures, especially the Bondarenko accident. Sure enough, on April 12, 1961, we heard that the Soviets had put a Maj. Yury Gagarin into orbit. I thought we were good. My worry was that the Soviets were better.

When Al Shepard made his Mercury flight on May 5, 1961, Faye and I were at Hamilton Air Force Base, north of San Francisco, visiting George and Betty Hochstettler. Now a major, George had been my boss in maintenance back in Germany and had recommended my selection for test-pilot school. We sat there in front of the television, through all the delays and holds, until the Redstone lifted off. I thought it was great, but it still didn't involve me.

Three weeks later, however, President Kennedy made a speech to Congress in which he committed the United States to landing a man on the Moon and returning him safely to earth, a feat we were to accomplish by the end of the decade. I knew, of course, that Kennedy needed something to take people's minds off Gagarin's flight and the Bay of Pigs fiasco. The new president had also had a rough time with Khrushchev at a recent summit. So here was a new initiative—a national goal. Go to the Moon? *That* was exciting. Apollo wouldn't be just a small, one-person craft going around the earth for a few hours. This would be a major program. I was really charged up about the idea, and for the first time I got interested in joining the space program. But NASA wasn't hiring new astronauts.

By now I had been at Edwards for three years, one as a student and two as an instructor. In 1962 I was due for a permanent change of station, probably returning to college for a master's degree in a technical field. One day I was complaining to Capt. Frank Cavanaugh, one of my students, that the Air Force had great technical people but relatively few good managers. "Why don't you go to Harvard Business School?" Cavanaugh said. He was from Boston and knew that Harvard accepted graduate students from the Air Force. Not only would a master's in business administration but useful to my military career, Cavanaugh said, it would be helpful when I eventually retired.

I got enthusiastic about this new idea and telephoned the Air Force Institute of Technology Resource Assignment Office, where I wound up talking to an old friend and classmate from my battalion at Annapolis, Capt. Mike Sorrentino. He confirmed that the Air Force did indeed assign two or three students a year to Harvard Business School, so I put my request through channels, and after passing a grad school test I was accepted.

In April 1962, however, I learned that NASA was going to select a new group of astronauts for the Gemini and Apollo programs. As a graduate of the test-pilot school, I now met all the requirements for experience, flying time, and age. The most important change, for me, was that they had raised the height limit from five feet, eleven inches, to six feet even. I sent that application in, too. I passed the Air Force's internal screening board, and with a dozen other pilots from Edwards and other locations, I was invited to Washington, D.C., in late May for a "briefing." This turned out to be an Air Force "charm school," complete with advice on how we should dress, speak, and hold ourselves in dealing with NASA. What I remember most about that briefing is that many of us kept slipping off to another room to watch a television showing Scott Carpenter making the second Mercury orbital flight. It was May 24, 1962.

Following our examination for charm, all the NASA final astronaut candidates were ordered to Brooks Air Force Base in San Antonio for a series of medical examinations. I arrived on July 9. The doctors had run amok with the Mercury candidates, subjecting them to all kinds of irrelevant and unnecessary poking and prodding, merely because they could, so the Mercury astronauts themselves had encouraged NASA to shorten and simplify the medical testing. We had the expected blood tests and EKG stuff but no centrifuge testing, for example. (We were all pulling Gs on a regular basis in high performance aircraft.) You didn't need to be some kind of physical superman to fly in space.

Nevertheless, we still wound up serving as unwitting test subjects for various studies. One required you to look into an ocular device long enough to see a sudden flash of light. Some captain was doing a special test to see how a pilot's eyes would adapt to the flash of a nuclear explosion! It wasn't enough to damage your eye—at least, I don't think it was—but you couldn't see for several minutes after the test. It had nothing to do with space flight.

I passed the medicals at Brooks, and was one of the candidates invited to Houston for personal interviews in August.

Even though I was confident I had a good chance at being selected by NASA, I had to operate on the assumption that I was headed for graduate school at Harvard. My tour at Edwards officially ended in July, a few weeks after my Brooks physicals. By August 1, 1962, Faye and the girls and I had shipped our belongings to Massachusetts then climbed into our new yellow Chevrolet to start a leisurely trip eastward. Classes at Harvard were scheduled to begin on September 10. Our plan was to stop in Oklahoma to see family for a couple of weeks.

While there, I took a detour to Houston for a week of further tests and NASA interviews. It was hot and humid, typical August weather for Houston, and I was assigned a room in the Ellington Air Force Base BOQ with a civilian test pilot named Jack Swigert. There were thirty-two of us by this time, including friends from Edwards like Frank Borman, Mike Collins, Greg Neubeck, Ed White, as well as some familiar Navy faces, such as Pete Conrad and John Young, and Jim Lovell, a classmate from Annapolis.

We had a series of new physicals, and new psychiatric tests by a Navy shrink named Robert Voas, who had been involved with astronauts since the Mercury selection. The main event was an hour-long technical interview at Ellington with Walt Williams, Deke Slayton, Al Shepard, and Warren North, where we covered my flying experience, with special emphasis on my incident in the test-pilot school's T-38.

After our "social night," where all the candidates mingled with people like Robert Gilruth, head of the new Manned Spacecraft Center, and several of the Mercury astronauts, I drove back to Oklahoma, picked up my family, and headed east once again. We stopped at Wright-Patterson Air Force Base in Dayton, Ohio, and spent two nights with one of my former students, Harley Johnson, and his wife, Dory. Harley had been in my company at Annapolis, a class behind me. We also saw Ed and Patricia White, and talked about our chances for astronaut selection.

Arriving in Boston late at night, Faye, the girls, and I checked into the temporary BOQ at Hanscom Air Force Base. The next day we moved into the duplex I had rented in Watertown. Our goods showed up shortly thereafter, but I think I surprised the mover by telling him not to unpack everything. "Just the stuff we need to live on for the moment," I said. "We may be leaving." I told our landlord the same thing, as well as Dean Baker, head of the Graduate School of Business. Everybody understood my situation.

Nevertheless, I enrolled at Harvard Business School with Dr. Richard Chapin as my faculty adviser. I had attended three days of classes—seven case histories—and was at home late on the afternoon of September 14 when one of my new neighbors came to the door.

"There's a phone call for you," he said. (We hadn't had time to get a phone installed, so I had given NASA the neighbor's number.)

It was Deke Slayton. "Are you still interested in the astronaut group?"

"Yes, sir!"

"Well, you're selected. Get down here on the sixteenth."

I went back to our duplex, and my face said it all. I was going to be an astronaut.

I'd been a Harvard man for three days.

five

Houston

"Pardon me, is this the Southern Texas Retail Grocers Association?"
Two startled, but familiar faces turned around toward me, then broke into
laughter. Pete Conrad, my Navy counterpart from Pax River, and John
Young, my old shipmate from the USS *Missouri,* were sitting at a table in the
lobby of the Rice Hotel having a beer and killing time.

I had met up with Pete and John and the other astronaut candidates during the "social night" in Houston several weeks back and at other stages in
the selection process but had no idea that they had finally been selected. None
of us had been told anything beyond instructions to fly to Houston Hobby
Airport, where NASA security officers were to pick us up and drive us downtown to the Rice Hotel. At the hotel we were registered under the name
"Max Peck," who turned out to be the manager. All of this cloak and dag-
ger routine was to throw off reporters who were supposedly on the lookout
for the new astronauts.

I had unpacked and gone down to the lobby, where I spotted Pete and
John and sneaked up on them. They told me that Jim Lovell had also been
selected, and so had Ed White. I went to dinner with Pete and a few of the
others, but it wasn't until the next morning, when NASA cars arrived to take
us all to Ellington, that I saw the whole team. The Navy test pilots were Pete
Conrad, John Young, and Jim Lovell. Conrad and Lovell had actually been

finalists for the Mercury program but had been dropped at the last stage for some minor medical reason. I had met Pete Conrad, of course. Jim Lovell had graduated from the same class at the naval test pilot school as both Pete and Wally Schirra, and he had been the student who placed first. From the Air Force, in addition to Ed White and me, Frank Borman and Jim McDivitt had been selected. As their former instructor, I knew they were outstanding choices. Both had gone through the first Aerospace Research Pilot course, the "space school" at Edwards, too. Elliot See was one of two civilians selected; I had only seen him from a distance during the social night and didn't know him at all. Then there was Neil Armstrong, who had been flying for NASA at Edwards. I knew Neil, but only slightly.

I had gone into the selection process confident in my skills and credentials. But none of us knew what yardsticks would be used to reduce our group of thirty to, say, less than a dozen. One of those criteria might be actual test flying or even combat experience. I had neither, but my academic standing at the naval academy and at the test pilot school, as well as my adventure in the T-38 (which showed what I could do in an emergency), were undoubtedly factors in my selection.

At Ellington Air Force Base, the morning of September 16, we were met by Deke Slayton and Al Shepard, as well as by Robert Gilruth (director of the Manned Spacecraft Center), Walt Williams (head of flight operations), and Shorty Powers (the public affairs officer). They ran us through the job description, our schedule for the next few months, and our responsibilities. Pictures were taken. We were told there would be a public announcement tomorrow, with a press conference at the University of Houston. At that time there were eleven manned Gemini flights on the schedule, at least four Block 1 Apollos (to be launched on the Saturn 1), and no one knew how many Block 2 Apollos, including the first lunar landing. A lot. "There'll be plenty of missions for all of you," Gilruth said. Great news.

Then Deke Slayton started talking about the new pressures we would have to face. He mentioned "flaps" they had had over the Mercury astronauts and their business dealings. People, especially contractors, could be offering us gratuities and freebies. "With regard to gratuities," Deke said, "if there is any question, just follow the old test pilot's creed: Anything you can eat, drink, or screw within twenty-four hours is perfectly acceptable."

We all smiled nervously. Bob Gilruth blushed, and Walt Williams choked, held up his hand, and said, "Within reason, within reason." I wasn't thinking about the goodies that day. I was thinking about the opportunity I'd been handed. Looking around at the nine of us, I thought, *one of us is going to be first on the Moon!*

September 17, 1962, the day of the press conference, happened to be my thirty-second birthday. One of the reporters noted it and offered his congratulations. I can honestly say I never had a birthday before or since quite like that one. Then I flew back to Boston. Among other tasks, I had to tell our landlord that the Staffords were going to have to break their lease. He was very gracious about it, and we gave him an extra month's rent—which hurt; we didn't have too much saved.

We reported to Houston on October 1, 1962. Not knowing where we were going to be living, Faye and I had dropped the girls off with their grandparents in Thomas, Oklahoma, before driving down to Houston. We moved into an apartment on the Gulf Freeway near Ellington Air Force Base. Neil and Jan Armstrong were there, and so were John and Barbara Young. We weren't entirely on our own: NASA had a transition office that was very helpful in getting people settled—not just new astronauts, but also the dozens of NASA engineers moving from Virginia, as well as Canadian engineers from the Avro Arrow program, who had been recruited by NASA after that Mach 2 fighter was cancelled.

It was a good thing we had help, though, because we nine new astronauts barely showed up when we were sent on the road, making what we called our "grand tour" of NASA and contractor facilities—the places we would be living and working for the next seven years.

First stop was the Cape, where Wally Schirra was ready to be launched on the third manned Mercury orbital flight. I had never seen a rocket launching before, and it was exciting to see that Atlas light up and move out. I wasn't the only one who was excited. Pete Conrad was standing right next to me, with fingers crossed on both hands. Wally's flight lasted six orbits, nine hours, and ended with a splashdown in the Pacific near the carrier USS *Kearsarge*.

We finally began to spend some time with the Mercury astronauts, who were very friendly, even Gus Grissom, who had the reputation of being tough to take. He didn't offer much in the way of conversation, but he was pleasant. Some people were intimidated by Al Shepard, who could turn icy at the snap of a finger, but I got along well with him. Scott Carpenter had a smile on his face and seemed to like everybody. John Glenn was absent a lot of the time. I barely got to know him at all. Wally was flying the mission, with Gordo Cooper as his backup, so we didn't see much of those two at this stage.

From the Cape we went up to Huntsville, Alabama, to the Marshall Space-flight Center. Wernher von Braun, the center's chief, had just fought the big battle over how we were going to get to the Moon. He had ultimately agreed that the lunar-orbit rendezvous method was more likely to work, in less time, than his preferred mode—earth-orbit rendezvous between two spacecraft. Von Braun was very articulate, knowledgeable, and impressive.

From Huntsville we flew to Baltimore, where the Martin Company had a special manufacturing line for the final assembly of its Titan 2s for the Gemini program. From Baltimore, it was off to St. Louis, home of McDonnell Aircraft. Our Geminis were going to be built at the plant there. Our hosts were James McDonnell—"Mr. Mac" himself, the founder—and David Lewis, president of the company.

Following a stop in Denver, to see the plant where Martin assembled the ICBM version of the Titan 2, we arrived in northern California, visited NASA Ames Research Center, then headed down to Los Angeles, where we saw two major facilities: North American Aviation's plant in Downey, where the Apollo would be built, and the Douglas facility in Huntington Beach, where the S-4B upper stage would take shape for the Saturn 1B and Saturn 5.

The trip was grueling. We were all flying commercial, four of us on one flight, five on another. Most of the time I found myself assigned to flights with the Navy guys—Pete, John, and Jim. Pete was by far the funniest and most outgoing member of the whole group, with Jim close behind.

And everywhere we landed we faced a full schedule of cocktail parties and dinners. People were excited to meet us, of course, because we were not only new astronauts, but we were also supposed to be the men who were going to go to the Moon. So they laid out lots of food and plenty of booze. The drinking never got out of hand. It was just a new challenge to be a celebrity, signing autographs, meeting the chief executives of major corporations, and everything else.

Since the Manned Spacecraft Center was taking shape south of Ellington, we all began looking for homes closer to the new location. Faye and I picked out a lot in El Lago. We hired a contractor named Jim Blackstone, who had been a lineman on the football team at the University of Houston. Jim made a lot of money building houses for the NASA folks in those days. The price was $27,500, which seemed like a huge amount. When construction was complete in February 1963, Dionne and Karin were able to join Faye and me. Dionne entered second grade at Webster Elementary School.

The Bormans built a house four lots down from us, using a floor plan that was almost the same as ours. The Youngs built right across the street from the Bormans. The Whites and Armstrongs built next to each other at the end of the block and around the corner. Elliot See built on the water in Timber Cove, which was separated from El Lago by an estuary of Clear Lake. (He'd been a civilian test pilot and had made more money than the rest of us.) Pete Conrad and Jim Lovell were also in Timber Cove, where Glenn, Grissom, Carpenter, and Schirra already lived.

We spent Christmas 1962 back home in Oklahoma. I was there when I got a phone call from Jim Brickel, a fellow classmate and "star man" from Annapolis who had gone into the Air Force. "Congratulations, Major Stafford," Jim said. He told me that both our names had appeared on the list of new majors a year "below the zone," ahead of schedule. Not bad for a young officer who once thought he was being left behind his Annapolis classmates.

Our first astronaut offices were in the Farnsworth-Chambers Building in downtown Houston. Every Monday morning all astronauts would get together at 8 A.M. for the pilots' meeting chaired by Deke. There we would get our schedule for the week. In the fall of 1962, we spent much of our time back in school. We had courses in astronomy, rocket propulsion, computer science, meteorology, geology, space guidance and navigation, orbital mechanics, the Gemini spacecraft, and aerospace physiology. In spite of my typical pilot's disdain for flight surgeons, especially those at Brooks who had subjected us to unnecessary tests, I enjoyed the medical classes. I often thought if my father had lived, I might have gone into medicine rather than military aviation.

Once we had been onboard for a few months, in January 1963, Deke gave us technical assignments—areas of the Gemini program development we were to monitor and take part in, reporting developments to the whole group. We didn't have a choice in the matter; Deke just said, "Here they are." Frank Borman was assigned to the Saturn boosters. Jim McDivitt got guidance and control. John Young, environmental controls and pressure suits. Pete Conrad would handle cockpit layout. Neil Armstrong was responsible for trainers and simulators. Jim Lovell had recovery and re-entry matters. Elliot See was assigned to electrical systems and mission planning. Ed White would work on flight control. My area was to be range safety, instrumentation, and communications. Gus Grissom was appointed our branch chief.

We had been keeping up our flying proficiency by doing aerobatics out over the Gulf in the NASA fleet of T-33s and F-102s or flying to places like Flagstaff, Arizona, for geology class. The new assignments drastically increased our need for a fleet of aircraft because we would now be scattered all over the United States. The T-33s and F-102s were pretty old and slow, and NASA eventually realized it would be a good idea to have newer, faster birds. The debate in the astronaut office was, the Air Force's T-38 or the Navy's F-4 Phantom?

The Navy faction, led by my good buddy, Pete Conrad, wanted the F-4. It was a hotter plane and would do Mach 2, for example. But the F-4 was also a large, complicated machine requiring a lot of maintenance between flights. And it burned a lot of fuel. Having been the project pilot introducing the T-38 to ARPS, I knew the T-38 was far less complex and significantly less expensive to maintain. The T-38 had its drawbacks, notably shorter range and problems with icing. But I knew of a technical fix for the icing, and when someone broke out the cost-per-hour for operations, there wasn't much of a contest: The T-38 beat out the F-4.

Soviet cosmonauts had made further flights after Gagarin. German Titov had spent twenty-four hours in orbit from August 6 to 7, 1961, greeting various Communist and socialist workers via television. (He was sick, too, though this wasn't disclosed for years.) Then there was a year-long delay, which none of us could understand. During this time, Aleksei Leonov and most of the cosmonauts in that first group were busy with schooling. General Kamanin knew that he wasn't going to need more than three or four cosmonauts in active training at any one time and wanted to groom these young, talented officers for management—so he enrolled them at the Zhukovsky Air Force Engineering Academy in Moscow, a very prestigious military university that usually took five years to complete. Aleksei had started at Zhukovsky on September 1, 1961. He did almost no flying during this time. And he and the other cosmonauts did none of the kind of development or engineering work we were doing on Gemini and Apollo.

When the Soviets got back into the manned space business, however, it was worth watching. On August 11, 1962, Andrian Nikolayev was launched on Vostok 3. A day later, Pavel Popovich went up on Vostok 4. The Soviet press made a big deal out of this, and the "salvo" launching was undeniably impressive. We couldn't have put two Mercury-Atlases into space one after the other like that.

Western observers leapt to the conclusion that the Soviets had accomplished a rendezvous between two vehicles or had proven that it would be their next step. It wasn't remotely true, of course: Vostok couldn't maneuver. But we didn't know that for years. Here, though, was another set of triumphs. The longest American manned flight, by Wally Schirra, had lasted about nine hours. Two Russians had done that several times over.

There was still one more flight to come in the Mercury series, an eighteen-orbit, thirty-four-hour marathon by Gordo Cooper. Our group had no responsibilities on Gordo's flight; we flew to the Cape for the launch and that was all. Gordo was flying, and Al was his backup. Wally was the primary capcom at the Cape, with Gus, Scott, and John scattered around the world at different tracking stations and ships.

Deke was now in charge of astronaut activities; he had been the one to select Gordo for the flight over the objections of Walt Williams, who had wanted Al Shepard. "Either fly him now or send him back to the Air Force," is what Deke told Walt. Nobody in NASA management wanted to ship an astronaut back to his service, so Gordo got the assignment.

Even before Gordo flew, in the late spring of 1963, another astronaut battle took place right over our heads. It concerned a possible a three-day long Mercury-Atlas flight called MA-10. The Mercury astronauts, especially

Al Shepard, were pushing for it as an answer to Nikolayev and Popovich. There was enough Mercury hardware available. Jim Webb, Brainerd Holmes, and the other NASA managers didn't want to fly MA-10. It was going to suck millions of dollars out of the budget that was already strained to cover rising Gemini costs. That should have been the end of it.

But the Mercury astronauts raised the issue in person with President John F. Kennedy. Kennedy was smart enough to stay out of the whole situation. He simply said the astronauts would have to get Jim Webb's approval. But Webb's approval wasn't forthcoming, period. And Webb was furious about the way the astronauts—especially Shepard—went around him to the president. From this point on, he took every opportunity he could to let us know he was boss.

Aleksei Leonov's group of Soviet cosmonauts was feeling less special at this time, too. General Kamanin, who headed manned space issues for the Soviet Air Force, and Col. Yevgeny Karpov, the flight surgeon who was the actual head of the training center, realized that even though Titov had suffered some kind of motion sickness during his flight, a cosmonaut didn't need to be a physical superman to fly in space.

So, figuring they would need more cosmonauts in the next few years, they went looking for new candidates. But this time they raised the age limit to thirty-five, eased some of the physical tests, and even dropped the flying requirement. This time, however, they wanted college or academy graduates, just as NASA did. All through 1962 they ran a new selection program that in January 1963 turned up fifteen new military cosmonauts, among them Vladimir Shatalov and Anatoly Filipchenko, who would become my colleagues on the Apollo-Soyuz.

Even more startling, Kamanin came up with the idea of flying a *woman* cosmonaut and within a few months had recruited five candidates from various Soviet sport parachuting teams. By November 1962, four of them were judged ready to fly on Vostok. The plan was to fly one female and one male cosmonaut on different spacecraft at the same time. The two leading male candidates were Valery Bykovsky and Boris Volynov, with Yevgeny Khrunov and Aleksei Leonov as support. On June 14, 1963, it was Bykovsky who got launched on Vostok 5, but his booster underperformed and left him in a lower orbit than planned, and his eight-day mission got shortened to five days. On June 16, Vostok 5 went into space with a woman cosmonaut, Valentina Tereshkova. She was on television waving and smiling all through her three days. (Like Titov, she was also sick from time to time.)

This raised all sorts of questions in the United States about our own lack of women astronauts. Before our group of nine had showed up, several women pilots, including one named Geraldine Cobb, had arranged to go through the same medical tests at the Lovelace Clinic that the Mercury astronauts did. They had all done fine. Of course, passing the medical tests was only one facet of the job. NASA still wanted astronauts to be pilots with extensive experience on military jets, and in those days there was no way for a woman to get qualified.

With the end of Mercury, attention turned to Gemini and Apollo. Both programs were growing like mad—in the case of Gemini, growing out of control. Originally budgeted at around $530 million, it was now expected to price out at twice that—or more. Every element of Gemini cost more than the original estimate: the basic spacecraft, the Titan 2 launch vehicle, the Atlas-Agena target vehicle, the ejection seats, the fuel cells. Money was spent on the idea of flying Gemini to a touchdown on return to earth using an inflatable wing a plan that never really had a prayer of working, but it ate up a couple of years and a few million bucks. (The North American test pilot for the Rogallo wing happened to be Jack Swigert, my former roommate from the astronaut interview week.)

Some of Gemini's growing pains got blamed on poor management. James Chamberlin, the father of Gemini, was considered to be a brilliant engineer but not necessarily a program manager. *Bam!* He was replaced by Chuck Mathews in February 1963. Higher up at NASA, Brainerd Holmes, the RCA manager who had been brought in to run manned space flight in 1961, left too. His replacement was also from industry—George Mueller, a physicist by training who had been a program manager for space and missiles at Space Technologies Lab.

Seeing the size of Apollo, Mueller got the Air Force to give him Maj. Gen. Samuel Phillips as the Apollo program manager. The two men had worked on the Minuteman missile. (When Sam was a colonel and the Minuteman program manager, he was the one who briefed President Kennedy on the plans to store the missiles in silos. Colonels aren't allowed to brief presidents these days. It's always the chairman of the Joint Chiefs of Staff.) Mueller also put Joseph Shea, a systems specialist from the missile world who had been a deputy at NASA headquarters, in charge of the Apollo program office in Houston.

Those changes were far above our heads, of course. We were moving offices, from the Farnsworth-Chambers Building to some of the newly rehabbed offices at Ellington Air Force Base, flying all over the country, and doing on-the-job training that sometimes threw us together in different pairs. For example, Neil Armstrong and I were assigned to help define the control systems for the planned lunar excursion module. We would take turns flying a simulator, trying to get the right gains in the system. The simulator was located at a North American Aviation facility in Columbus, Ohio, not far from Neil's hometown of Wapakoneta. So we flew up there a couple of times, staying a week each time, and spent some nights at the Armstrong home rather than in a hotel. All sixteen astronauts, including Deke, Al, and even John Glenn, traveled to Panama for jungle survival training in the spring of 1963. We did desert training, too.

Before we'd been astronauts a year, we saw that Deke was hiring reinforcements. In June 1963 word went out to the military services and the civilian flying world that NASA would be selecting an additional ten to fifteen astronauts this year. The requirements were similar to those for our group, with one minor exception—they couldn't be older than 34, rather than 35—and a major one: They didn't have to be test pilots.

Our group had no formal role in the selection, but all of us got phone calls and letters from various buddies who wanted help. I recommended three names to Deke Slayton and Al Shepard: Jack Swigert; Greg Neubeck, my former student and colleague at the test pilot school; and Donn Eisele, my old friend from Tyndall and Edwards, now a test pilot at Kirtland Air Force Base in Albuquerque. Swigert and Neubeck wouldn't make it, though Jack would ultimately come to NASA with the 1966 group, and Greg would become an astronaut with the Air Force's Manned Orbiting Laboratory. But Donn was one of the fourteen selected in mid-October 1963, along with Charlie Bassett, Mike Collins, and Ted Freeman, other students of mine. These four were test pilots, and so were Dave Scott (Air Force), Al Bean and Dick Gordon (Navy), and C. C. Williams (Marine Corps). The other six in the new group were Edwin "Buzz" Aldrin, an Air Force fighter pilot who had shot down a pair of MiGs over Korea and who had a Ph.D. in astronautics from MIT, with a dissertation in rendezvous. He had been working with the Air Force element at the Manned Spacecraft Center when he was selected. Bill Anders was another Air Force fighter pilot with an advanced degree, a master's in nuclear engineering. There were two young Navy pilots, Gene Cernan and Roger Chaffee. And two civilians with military flying backgrounds—Walt Cunningham from the RAND Corporation (ex-Marine) and Russell Schweickart from MIT (Air Force). They were all supposed to report in early January 1964. By then I hoped to be on a Gemini crew.

On Friday, November 22, 1963, I was having lunch with Gordo Cooper in the officer's club at Ellington Air Force Base when we heard the news that President Kennedy had been killed in Dallas. We were shocked, of course. JFK had seemed so young and vigorous, and now he'd been gunned down. What would it mean for the country? For the space program? We didn't know. I also remember Gordo's comment from that day: "Because of this, Dallas is never gonna become a great city." Hell, I thought, people have been assassinated in New York and Washington, and *those* are great cities. But over the years I, like many people, have associated Dallas with JFK's death, so maybe Gordo was right.

In late January 1964, the first Gemini-Titan launcher was stacked on Pad 19 at the Cape, with the Gemini 1 spacecraft about to join it. We were looking at the first manned flight in October or November of that year. The question for all of us was, who's going to fly? Our assumption was that the Mercury astronauts would be in command of the first few missions but that we were going to be in those right seats.

One afternoon not long after, in February, Deke Slayton called a special meeting in a briefing room at Ellington, where he announced, "The first Gemini is going to be flown by Shepard and Stafford. Backup crew is Grissom and Borman." That was it: We had no hint prior to the announcement. I was going to be the first of my group to fly. I accepted the congratulations from the other guys, and shook hands with my new commander. When I told Faye the news that night, she was elated. I cautioned her that she couldn't discuss the assignment until NASA had made an official announcement.

Over the next month, Al and I made a couple of trips to St. Louis and the Cape, and it seemed we would work fine together. One Friday night late in March the Rice Hotel in downtown Houston hosted a function with all the astronauts and their wives as guests. During the evening, Al pulled me aside and said, "Has Deke said anything to you?" I didn't know what he was talking about, so he told me he had been suffering from bad dizzy spells off and on over the past year or so, sometimes so bad he couldn't get out of bed, or he would have to crawl to the bathroom. Unknown to us, Al had actually been grounded the previous August because of these dizzy spells, which were diagnosed as Ménière's Syndrome. He'd gotten his ticket back, but with the official assignment to Gemini 3 he'd had to have another medical, and the news was bad. "I'm off the flight."

Maybe it was selfish, but in the best pilot tradition, my question was, "What about me?" He didn't know. All through the weekend I wondered what would happen. Were Shepard and I a team? With him gone, was I gone, too? Or would Grissom, the backup commander, move up? I figured I could work with Gus. I could work with anybody.

On Monday I was at the new MSC facility, where we were moving into our new offices, when I happened to run into Duane Ross, one of the flight surgeons. Duane said, "Hey, I heard you're not going to be on the prime crew. You and Wally are the backups." I don't know which was worse, the news itself or the fact that I was hearing it from one of the doctors.

I went straight up to Gus Grissom's office and told him I needed to have a chat. Seeing the look on my face, he closed the door. I related the "rumor" about the new Gemini prime and backup crews.

"Who told you that?" he snapped.

I wasn't eager to get Duane Ross in trouble, so I said, "It's just word that's going around."

I could tell this whole subject was making Gus uncomfortable. "You know, the commander gets to pick his crew." Now I was uncomfortable. "Look, talk to Wally," he said.

So I went looking for Wally. He closed his door and said, "Here's what we've got. You and I are the backup crew for Gemini 3, then we're going to turn around and fly Gemini 6, the first rendezvous. That's the way it's scheduled. Gus and John Young are going to fly Gemini 3, then turn around and be our backups."

"What about Borman?" I wasn't real happy about what I saw as a delayed assignment, but at least I was still in the picture. I was concerned about Frank, since he and I were good friends, and he seemed to have dropped completely out of sight.

"He's being held for later." So that's how it was done.

Gemini 1 got off the pad on April 8, 1964. Our crews were officially announced the following Monday, April 13, and we leaped into training.

SIX

The First Gemini

Beginning in April 1964, Gus Grissom, John Young, Wally Schirra, and I became virtual citizens of St. Louis, Missouri—"Mellow Old St. Louis," as Mr. Mac called it—flying in on Sunday night or Monday morning in our T-33s and T-38s, spending days at the McDonnell Plant at Lambert Field then going back to Houston on Thursday or Friday. We were there so much we eventually rented apartments at the Chase-Park Plaza Hotel. Wally and I shared a three-room suite on one floor, with Gus and John in another suite one floor down.

One problem quickly became apparent for me: Gus Grissom had been the first astronaut representative to the Gemini program, and naturally the cockpit reflected his views . . . and size. Gus was about five foot, six inches, 160 pounds; I was six feet, 175, and I was jammed in, especially when I had to wear a pressure suit and helmet. The top of my helmet nearly kept the hatch from closing. It was also painful. Once the spacecraft mockup was tilted to vertical, so that we were on our backs, I found that I developed an ache in my neck and back. (The same thing happened to Jim McDivitt.) I really complained for a few months. Finally, we made a plywood mockup of the ejection seat and took measurements in both horizontal and vertical positions.

We learned that McDivitt and I *grew* when we were rotated from the vertical to the horizontal position—an inch and three-quarters for me, two and a quarter for Jim. Eventually the McDonnell engineers removed some of the insulation from the inside of the hatch to create a slight bump that gave us room for our helmets. The bump was first installed on Gemini 6, so they called it the Stafford Bump.

Back in Houston, in July 1964, another Gemini prime and backup crew came on line. To my surprise, all four new members were from my group: Jim McDivitt and Ed White would fly Gemini 4, with Frank Borman and Jim Lovell as backups. So not only had I lost my status as the first to fly, I wasn't going to be first to command, either. Nevertheless, I was happy for Jim.

One of the questions this assignment raised was what about Gordo Cooper? He had flown a good mission on the last Mercury flight. Walt Williams hadn't liked him much, but now Walt was off at headquarters, out of the direct line of authority over crews. Deke, who by this time had become head of flight crew operations at MSC, had put Gordo in charge of the Apollo branch of the astronaut office, under Al Shepard. This was where about half of the 1963 astronauts were now assigned.

I didn't have much time to worry about these personnel moves. I was too busy with Gus, John, and Wally at St. Louis and the Cape. We had originally hoped to have the unmanned Gemini 2 off the pad in August 1964, and Gus and John flying in December. Gemini 2 would be the first "production" vehicle off the assembly line, a spacecraft completely equipped for a launch, suborbital coast, then re-entry and splashdown. Instead of astronauts, it would carry a pair of "crew simulator packages," cameras, tape recorders, thermometers, and other instruments to record the sights and sounds of a Gemini launch.

The launch vehicle for Gemini 2 was delivered to the Cape on July 10, and erected on Pad 19 four days later. Checkout got underway. Unfortunately, a month later, on August 17, a storm blew through the area and lightning struck the launcher. Down it came for a whole new set of checks, which was fine, because Gemini 2 was running behind. Two weeks later, however, Hurricane Cleo arrived, forcing the Martin launch team to de-stack the upper stage. They had just put it back in place when Hurricane Dora showed up. Down came the whole launcher a second time, while we waited out that storm. Then Hurricane Ethel threatened.

It wasn't until September 21, 1964, that the launch vehicle was ready to begin its final checkout. The spacecraft finally arrived from McDonnell in St. Louis and fell behind its schedule almost immediately. The earliest we could expect Gemini 2 to fly now was mid-November.

On October 12, 1964, while we were hiding Gemini 2 from the hurricane, the Soviets got back in the manned space business with a new vehicle called Voskhod. It only spent a day in space (and apparently did no maneuvering), but it carried a crew of three: A pilot named Vladimir Komarov, a scientist named Konstantin Feoktistov, and a doctor, Boris Yegorov. Voskhod, we learned years later, was a modified Vostok, its ejection seat removed and replaced by three simpler seats; life support and other equipment reduced to a minimum. All so the Kremlin could claim it had flown three cosmonauts while the United States was still struggling to launch a pair.

The flight of the Voskhod didn't do much for Khrushchev. While it was in orbit, he was kicked out of his job as Soviet premier and replaced by a *troika* of leaders—Brezhnev, Kosygin, and Podgorny. In fact, one of Khrushchev's last acts was to talk to the Voskhod crew by telephone. Once the cosmonauts returned to Earth, they were officially greeted by the new Soviet leaders.

Sunday, October 31, was Halloween—a day off. I was home with Faye early that afternoon when I got a phone call saying that Ted Freeman had been killed in a plane crash. He had taken a T-38 out of Ellington for some proficiency flying and had run into a flock of geese while coming back in for a landing. A goose shattered the aircraft's canopy and pieces of Plexiglas flew into the engine ducts, causing both engines to flame out. Ted tried to eject, but he was too low.

Ted had been one of my students at Edwards and had been a good choice for the astronaut program. He was one of the quieter men in his group, very intense, but a superb pilot. Since he and his wife, Faith, had moved to Houston in January, we had not seen much of them socially, and I didn't see Ted at work beyond the Monday meetings or the occasional geology class. Our schedules were rarely in sync and I was frequently out of town.

When I got the news I hurried over to see Faith, and found a very sad, angry scene. The tragedy of Ted's death was bad enough, but Faith had learned of the accident from an over-eager young reporter from the *Houston*

Chronicle, who had managed to get to her door before Deke Slayton did. None of us was happy about that. I heard years later that Deke Slayton had wanted to team Ted and me on a Gemini crew, and I'm sorry it never happened.

The Gemini 2 spacecraft was mated to its Titan launcher on November 6, 1964. From that point on, preparations went fairly smoothly toward a December 9 launch date.

Gus, John, Wally, and I were in the blockhouse with Bastian "Buz" Hello, one of the chief Martin Gemini managers, when, at 11:41 A.M., the Titan on Pad 19 lit up—and, just like that, shut down.

Buz, who had been watching events through a periscope, turned back toward us, his face showing shock and surprise. "It's still sitting there!"

It sure was. The expensive and complicated malfunction detection system we had put on the Titan 2 had done its job, saving the launcher and spacecraft for another day. I was just happy the thing hadn't blown up. A disaster like that, plus the investigation, would have delayed the whole program by months.

Finally, on January 19, 1965, Gemini 2 roared off the pad, separated on schedule and by design, and splashed down in the Atlantic eighteen minutes later, 2,150 miles downrange, clearing the way for Gus and John to fly Gemini 3.

We were at the Cape, a week away from the scheduled launch of Gemini 3, when we heard that the Russians had put a new manned spacecraft into orbit. Called Voskhod 2, it carried a crew of two, Col. Pavel Belyayev and Lt. Col. Aleksei Leonov. Most amazing about the flight was that an hour and a half after launch, Leonov opened the hatch and floated outside for ten minutes, making the world's first space walk, what NASA would call an "extravehicular activity" or EVA. It was a huge triumph for the Soviets, complete with black-and-white television footage beamed to earth shortly after Leonov got safely back inside.

What we didn't know was how close the cosmonaut had come to death on that EVA. The three-man Voskhod had been further modified to carry two space-suited cosmonauts and an inflatable airlock that would extend from the side. Packed for launch, the airlock was only 0.7 meters tall. Inflated and expanded in orbit, it reached 2.5 meters, still a tight fit for a cosmonaut in a bulky pressure suit and life-support backpack. Wearing his Berkut pressure suit, Aleksei got out of the airlock in good shape. But as soon as he finished his tasks, shoved an external movie camera into the airlock, and tried to slide in feetfirst, he discovered a serious problem. In the vacuum of space, the suit had ballooned so completely that his feet had come out of the boots, and his hands had come out of the gloves.

To regain a bit more control, he was able to lower the suit pressure to the emergency setting, .27 atmospheres, and crawl into the airlock headfirst; then, slowly and painfully, using all his strength, he turned himself around so he could close the outer hatch. Once the hatch was closed, he repressurized the airlock, and, violating the flight rules, opened his faceplate, gulping air and trying to recover his strength. Only then did he open the hatch and get back into the Voskhod cabin. He was red-faced, and his pulse rate had reached 143. And he was lucky to be alive.

Nine years later, Aleksei and I would have dinner at the Arugby Restaurant in downtown Moscow, just the two of us. Over Georgian food and drinks, he told me this story. He was still a member of the Communist Party in those days, technically an atheist, but what he said was, "Thank God I made it." It was the first anyone outside of the Soviet space team knew of his problems on the spacewalk.

Belyayev and Leonov also faced other challenges. On the seventeenth orbit, they were waiting for automatic retrofire—nothing. Belyayev reported the failure to mission control in Baikonur, which after hurried consultations authorized the crew to try a manual burn. They made it, but forty-six seconds late. As they went through re-entry, the spherical spacecraft failed to separate cleanly from its instrument module. (The same thing had happened on a couple of the Vostok flights.) So here were two masses swinging around at the end of some steel straps, eliminating what little lift the Voskhod had, and ultimately subjecting the cosmonauts to ten Gs at least. (Both suffered burst blood vessels in their eyes because of this.) They got down safely, thanks to the Voskhod soft-landing system of parachute and solid-rocket braking engine. But they were so far off course thanks to the late retrofire that no one in the Baikonur or Moscow control centers had any word for four hours. Eventually, a rescue pilot flying an Mi-4 helicopter reported seeing a red parachute and the two cosmonauts in deep snow and woods thirty kilometers south of the village of Berezniki in the Ural Mountains, 180 kilometers northwest of Perm, and almost 400 kilometers from the primary landing zone. The cosmonauts had no idea where they were.

With all the trees and deep snow, it was impossible to get a chopper down to them or to reach them by ground before dark, so Leonov and Belyayev spent a long, cold night huddled in the Voskhod. Wolves howled around them. They only had a few survival rations and a couple of shots of vodka that Belyayev had managed to smuggle aboard. On the morning of March 21, they were finally flown out of there and returned to Baikonur late that afternoon. They got to Moscow on the twenty-third for a gigantic reception and a press conference, where nothing was said about any of the numerous problems. Eventually there was some publicity about the manual re-entry because it was obvious that the crew had landed one orbit later. ("Have a go at it," Gagarin was reported to have told the crew, as if they were taking turns behind the wheel of a car.) But to all of us at the Cape, Voskhod 2 looked like another gigantic set of firsts for the Soviet manned program, and here we were still trying to get Gemini off the ground for three orbits.

On March 22, the day before the Gemini 3 launch, Wally and I stopped at Wolfie's Deli at the Ramada Inn in Cocoa Beach. We were both irked by the fact that Gus and John weren't going to have real food on their flight, so Wally had a corned beef sandwich made up. (Gus loved those sandwiches at Wolfie's.) The next morning, launch day, I was in the spacecraft in the white room at Pad 19 setting up switches inside the cockpit, when Wally slipped the sandwich bag into one of the leg pockets on John Young's pressure suit. He zipped the pocket and said, "Give this to Gus to eat at lunch."

The suiting took place in a medical trailer parked at Pad 16, a few hundred yards from Pad 19 as the crow flies but a mile or more if you followed the original roadways. This morning, however, there was a direct path from 16 to 19, courtesy of a mysterious Air Force chief warrant officer named "Gunner" Barton. Wally showed up in the most beat-up old Mercury pressure suit he could find, laughing as he told Gus and John it was their last chance to back out, that he and I were ready to step in. "No way," they said.

I helped Gus and John into the spacecraft, then wished them luck and rode down the elevator. My job was to serve as their blockhouse communicator, known in NASA slang as "Stony," watching for confirmation of liftoff. At that point Gordo Cooper would take over as the capcom in Gemini mission control, which for this mission was the refurbished Mercury center. Wally, Jim McDivitt, and Ed White were with Gordo.

The countdown was proceeding smoothly toward a 9 A.M. launch time when, at T minus thirty-eight minutes, we got an indication of a leak in a propellant line feeding the Titan. It was fixed, but it forced a twenty-four minute hold in the count. That was all, though: At 9:24 the Titan lit up. "You're on your way, Molly Brown!" Gordo radioed. (Gus had given Gemini 3 that name, to the annoyance of NASA headquarters.) Five and a half minutes later, Gus and John were in orbit, with a perigee of 87 miles and an apogee of 125, a little higher than planned, thanks to the overperformance of their booster.

No sooner had they passed the Canary Island tracking site than they got their first unpleasant surprise: John saw a drop in the oxygen pressure system that fed both the spacecraft and the suits. Gus flipped down his visor while John, figuring the problem was not in the system itself but in the read-out, switched to a backup electrical converter. Things proceeded more smoothly from that point. Gus and John tested the orbital maneuvering thrusters over Australia, and at the end of their first orbit, fired the main translation thrusters for seventy-four seconds, dropping both apogee and perigee, and becoming the first astronauts to maneuver their spacecraft in orbit.

They did another maneuver on their second orbit, firing both forward and aft thrusters to change their orbital speed and inclination. Finally, on their third pass, four hours and twenty-one minutes after launch, they did a 109-second burn that lowered their perigee so far (to what was called a "vacuum perigee" of fifty-two miles) that they were going to re-entry whether their retros fired successfully or not.

The equipment module separated with a loud *crack!* that startled the crew. A few moments later, the four solid-fuel retros lit up, one by one, louder and more forcefully than they expected. With another *crack!*, the retro-module separated. As Gemini 3 began its long fall to earth, a plasma sheath built up around it, blocking communications. Flames and small chunks of the ablative heat shield went flying past the astronauts' windows.

The plan was to let the computer fly the landing, maneuvering the re-entry module ever so slightly to create lift, and steer it to a target point. But Gus wanted to hand-fly Gemini. Had he trusted the computer, he'd have come down pretty close to the carrier; instead he landed fifty miles short. (That was one of the lessons we hit in the debrief at the Cape that night: *fly on the needles!*)

After the main chute had deployed, the crew got a big surprise. Mercury splashed down heatshield first, with the impact on the astronaut's back. But thanks to the original designs for a possible Rogallo-wing landing, Gemini slipped over to a horizontal attitude with the spacecraft suspended from the parachute harness at two points. While the Gemini 3 was traveling heatshield down, the drogue and main parachute came out—and by design flipped over to a forty-five-degree angle. But the maneuver was so violent it slammed both Gus and John into their windows. John's helmet faceplate cracked, and a knob on the control panel punched a hole in Gus's faceplate.

And then they hit the water. Gus had a bad moment there. His left-side window was supposed to be looking at nothing but sky, but he was under water. Shades of Liberty Bell 7, Gus's Mercury capsule that sank. Then he realized that the chute was still attached and dragging them. He punched the release, and Molly Brown bobbed to the surface. Where it kept bobbing even after the pararescue guys attached a flotation collar to it. Gus and John both got seasick before a chopper hauled them out of there and off to the carrier.

For all that, Gemini 3 was a good flight.

The mission wasn't all serious test work. Listening to the tapes later, for example, we were all amused by Gus and John's language. It was as if they had spent nearly three orbits cursing. *Goddamn this, where the hell is that, son of a bitch.* And when they had their electrical problem, it really got blue.

Then, when the crew was scheduled for a meal break, and Gus complained about the space snacks, John saw his chance. "Hey, Skip," he said to Gus, "how about this?" He held out the corned beef sandwich. Gus took a bite then wrapped up the remains, not wanting to set crumbs flying inside the cockpit. It was too late to stop the smell, however. The pungent odor of corned beef and pickles filled the place.

seven
Hold Kill

$\mathbf{W}$hen we were officially announced as the crew of Gemini 6 on April 15, 1965, Wally and I had known for a year that we would be flying a very exciting mission, with the world's first rendezvous, and I would be taking the first American spacewalk (EVA). Well, that's how it started out. Leonov's EVA in March 1965 spooked NASA into making a rapid response, so they moved the EVA up to Gemini 4. And to try to get another "first," mission planners started talking about having Gemini 4 "rendezvous" with the second stage of its Titan. It looked as though we weren't going to be left with *any* new challenges, though I was puzzled by the claim that station-keeping with an upper stage was a "rendezvous."

Wally was adamant about scaling down the mission, too. He had a very conservative approach to space flight, wanting to take one well-thought-out step at a time. Rendezvous was the step he wanted to take. Let someone else worry about EVA. I tried not to think of what a disaster it would be if we couldn't make rendezvous work; the whole concept of the Apollo lunar-landing program depended on it.

But in early summer 1965, it was looking pretty difficult. Our understanding of the best rendezvous technique was still evolving, with various methods under consideration, each with its own virtues and drawbacks. In late 1962, however, a Russian engineer published a paper titled "The Con-

60

centric Technique of Rendezvous in Concentric Orbits," and Ed Lineberry, a
trajectory expert, saw a translation. (Oddly enough, the Russians still used
the basic Hohman transfer technique, not the concentric one, for Soyuz rendezvous with Mir and the International Space Station. The only place they're
known to have used their concentric process is in their antisatellite program
of the late 1960s and 1970s.)

Using the concentric technique as a starting point, we eventually came
up with the M = 4 method, a procedure developed by a team of people from
MSC and McDonnell, including Dean Grimm (our flight crew support engineer) and Paul Kramer. The idea was to put your target vehicle (Agena) in
a circular orbit. Then, after the Agena passed over the Cape on its first revolution, you'd launch Gemini into an elliptical orbit, same inclination, with
an apogee lower than the Agena's. Two-hundred and seventy degrees behind
the Agena, you'd make a series of maneuvers that would eventually raise the
orbit of the Gemini to a circular one below the Agena. Then you'd glide up
below the Agena on the fourth revolution. At that time the crew would make
a series of maneuvers to an intercept trajectory, then break to stationkeeping
and docking. Buzz Aldrin, one of the astronauts selected in 1963, had been
given rendezvous as his technical support assignment, a logical move, since
he had a Ph.D. in the subject. He worked with us and the mission planning
team, and in spite of occasionally going off on tangents of his own, he made
significant contributions.

Gus Grissom and John Young, our backups, were part of this process, too,
taking their turns in the simulators along with Wally and me. Well, John did.
Gus was often absent, racing cars and boats. Having helped with Gemini development for three years, he had little interest in spending long hours in
simulations. He also knew he was headed for Apollo, whereas John could
expect to command a later Gemini. I probably spent more time there than
anyone: It was my first space flight and I was very serious about it. Wally,
having gone through this before, was a little more relaxed.

On June 3, 1965, Jim McDivitt and Ed White launched in Gemini 4 on a
planned four-day mission, triple the longest American flight to that time.
Gemini 4 was to be the first flight controlled from the new mission operations control center in Houston, so the focus of our activity shifted from the

Cape back to what had become our hometown. It made the work easier and gave us the sense that what we were doing was a little more operational, not some one-time event.

Aside from flying for four days, Jim and Ed had two other goals: A rendezvous with the upper stage of their orbiting Titan 2 booster and then a spacewalk. Actually, the "rendezvous" was stationkeeping—turning around and coming back to the booster. They were pretty much in the same orbit to begin with.

First problem: The booster had never really been prepared to serve as a target. A couple of running lights had been rigged on it, but even so, when the stage and Gemini 4 passed into night soon after launch, it was invisible. Further, the stage was tumbling, so Jim and Ed didn't want to get too close. When they emerged into daylight, the booster was below and ahead of Gemini 4. Jim's instinctual move was to thrust toward it, as though he were flying formation in a jet airplane. By doing so, of course, he increased his speed—and moved into a higher orbit even further behind the booster. The only way to get even close to the Titan, in these circumstances, would have been to fire thrusters retrograde—*against* the direction of travel—slowing the Gemini down and dropping its orbit. After about a half hour of this, not to mention the expenditure of a lot of fuel, the crew gave up. They had to prepare for Ed's EVA.

After the flight, our rendezvous support team, especially Buzz Aldrin, complained loudly about Jim's ignorance of basic orbital mechanics. We had all been through the classes. But going through class is one thing; flying a vehicle is another. Unfortunately, Jim and Ed had received almost no rendezvous training and very little in the business of stationkeeping.

For the EVA, Jim and Ed found that unpacking the tether and zip gun, which had been relatively easy on the ground, was a whole different challenge in the zero-G environment of the Gemini cabin. They were an hour behind schedule when they finally got depressurized and opened Ed's hatch. He floated outside, aimed himself one way, then the other, until his little gun ran out of gas. Then he just floated in front of McDivitt's window, so Jim could take some of the most famous photos in the history of manned spaceflight.

After about fifteen minutes, Gus Grissom, who was capcom in Houston, could be heard telling Jim to tell Ed to "Get back in!" It sounded more tense than it was: During the EVA, Jim had to hit a switch to allow mission control to be heard on the spacecraft, and he had gotten too busy to do so. The real challenge wasn't talking Ed back into Gemini 4—it was closing Ed's hatch. The hinge seemed to have stiffened, and Ed's suit had ballooned slightly, so the ingress maneuver in zero G was far more difficult than it had been in the 1-G trainer. It took every bit of Ed's strength (with Jim holding onto him) to pull that hatch closed and get it dogged down and locked. The process took fifteen long minutes, so clearly that was one area we were going to have to improve.

But given Ed's experience and what we'd heard about Aleksei Leonov's, EVA sounded like fun to Wally and me, as we listened there in the new mission control that day. A piece of cake.

Rendezvous was another matter. At the time of Gemini 4, Wally and I were already deep in rendezvous training. With Jim's misadventures in station-keeping with the Titan, we had to take a refresher course in the basics, whether we needed to or not. Paul Kramer went over the whole theory and practice for us in minute detail.

We were still faced with the problem of getting everyone involved in Gemini to understand the importance of rendezvous so that they would put the resources and money behind it. When Wally and I began our training, our procedures trainer and simulator at the McDonnell plant was rudimentary. The cockpit was nothing but plywood and cardboard. We had a few basic instruments: three-axis attitude indicator, radar display, computer, and a few switches. As in a real spacecraft, we also had maneuver and attitude controllers to make thruster inputs by hand. So we would feel as though we were in space, we had a movie screen outside our windows showing points of lights as stars that would move as our orbit progressed.

We needed three pieces of guidance and navigation equipment to do a rendezvous: onboard computer, inertial guidance platform, and radar. If they were all working, then rendezvous, starting in a nominal trajectory, should be a relatively straightforward task. But what if one of the three failed? Lose the radar, but still have computer and platform? Could you visually locate the Agena? What if you had the radar and the computer, but lost the platform? That was a real tough situation. We had to develop our own backup procedures for each possible equipment failure and make up our own charts.

What really killed us during that early training was lack of computer time. This was long before the days of personal computers, of course, and even big mainframes were pretty rare. McDonnell Aircraft shared its mainframe with a bank in St. Louis called Boatman's, where Mr. Mac's brother was chairman. Every working day at 3:30 P.M. we had to shut down our work so the computer could be reconfigured to handle financial records.

Fortunately, one night Wally and I were invited to Mr. Mac's house for dinner, and he happened to ask us how our training was going. I couldn't keep quiet. I told him that unless we got more of that mainframe computer time to develop procedures, we couldn't guarantee we'd be ready to fly in October. Mr. Mac tended to stammer when he got worked up, and he stammered away as he made some notes in his famous little black book.

The next morning, David Lewis, the president of McDonnell, walked up to Wally and me and told us we could have all the computer time we needed. Boatman's Bank would just have to work around our schedule. Mr. Mac was always behind the program and was one of my heroes.

Gordo Cooper and Pete Conrad were scheduled to fly the first "complete" Gemini spacecraft, one that not only incorporated modifications from the two previous flights but also carried rendezvous radar and the long-awaited GE fuel cells. Gordo and Pete would launch a small rendezvous pod called the Little Rascal and use it as a target for limited rendezvous practice. Mostly, though, they would try to gut it out for the eight days, which would be tough in the cramped Gemini.

Training for the flight didn't go smoothly. Gordo and Pete really didn't have time to absorb all the lessons from the Gemini 4 flight. Neither did the flight control team. Facilities were still a problem. Gordo also had a fairly casual attitude toward training, operating on the assumption that he could show up, kick the tires, and go, the way he did with aircraft and fast cars. So Deke went off to headquarters and asked George Mueller to slip the launch back by a couple of weeks.

Launch finally took place on Saturday, August 21, 1965. Wally and I joined the crew for breakfast then watched from the blockhouse as they took off. The Gemini 5 Titan developed some pogo, giving Gordo and Pete a rough ride, but they achieved orbit just fine. We jumped into our T-38 to head home to Houston, and got there in time to see the electrical power output from the fuel cells dropping before the crew had completed two orbits. The crew launched the Little Rascal, but before they could get into their tracking exercise, the pressure in the oxygen tank feeding the fuel cells ran down to its minimum level then fell below that. Chris Kraft and the flight control team had the crew conserve electrical power by shutting down all kinds of non-critical systems, including the rendezvous radar. There was some urgency about making a decision to continue the mission or not: While the crew had sufficient backup battery power for thirteen hours of flight, each successive orbit put them further and further away from recovery forces. No one wanted to have them come down in the ocean and have to wait hours for rescue. And no one wanted them to have to put their jungle or desert survival skills to the test, either.

But Kraft's team, seeing that the fuel cells were still putting out power even at this critically low pressure, decided to wait and see. And the next morning, surprisingly enough, the fuel cells still seemed to be working and putting out a little more power. So the crew brought some systems back on-line and even had time to go through a rendezvous exercise with a "phantom" Agena, an idea cooked up by Buzz Aldrin and the mission planning engineers. (The Little Rascal's batteries had died.)

The mission proceeded smoothly from that point on. Sitting there in those bulky suits in a spacecraft that was either too cold or too hot, Gordo and Pete were bored out of their minds. Gordo wasn't the most talkative guy around. Pete was, but he got tired of carrying the conversation by himself. He told me later he wished he'd taken a book along.

Their landing should have been perfect. Now that we had some hard data on the lift you could get from a Gemini in re-entry, Gordo and Pete were supposed to let the computer fly the whole thing. They did, up to the point where they could see they were going to land 250 miles short of their target. Gordo took manual control and made up some of the shortfall, but they still missed the carrier by a hundred miles. It turned out that some of our mission planners had forgotten one key thing in their calculations of orbits and trajectories: The earth continued to rotate after Gemini 5 had fired its retro-rockets. So the program was correct, and the crew had done what they were supposed to do, but this figure called the theta dot had been wrong to begin with.

Gordo and Pete were wobbly (who wouldn't have been, after sitting in the front seat of a Volkswagen for eight days), but they were still in good shape.

And they had taught us about fuel cells, one of the systems that had to work if we were going to get to the Moon.

By September Wally and I had run through at least fifty rendezvous and dock-ing simulations at St. Louis. Now we had a genuine Gemini simulator at the Cape and a second one on-line in Houston. Houston also had a large mo-tion-based docking simulator that was housed in a six-story building and was quite impressive. There was an inert Agena mockup and an active Gemini, both of them mounted on a "frictionless" surface, a floor polished so smooth it was like being on ice. When we fired the little air thrusters on our Gemini, the craft would move forward and back, left and right, plus roll, pitch, and yaw, just as it would when we were stationkeeping. We used it to rehearse a slow, 0.2 to 0.3 foot per second approach and docking with the Agena. Any faster than one foot per second, and it would slide away.

While we were in intensive training, Gordo and Pete took a foreign post-flight trip, with Deke Slayton, to an international astronautical conference in Athens, Greece. There they met two Soviet cosmonauts, also riding the hero trail after their 1965 mission—Pavel Belyayev and Aleksei Leonov. Al-though there had been some brief encounters between astronauts and cos-monauts before, this was the first time the two teams had any extended time together. The five of them had breakfast where a significant amount of toast-ing took place, including one from Aleksei to Deke Slayton: "May we meet in orbit someday."

That didn't seem at all likely in September 1965.

Wally and I invited Mr. Mac to dinner the night before our scheduled launch, to thank him for all of the support he had given us. The next morning, Mon-day, October 25, 1965, Al Shepard woke us. We had breakfast in the crew quarters then headed out to the suiting trailer at Pad 16. On the trip, Wally lit up a Marlborough. He had not yet given up smoking, figuring he could survive a twenty-four-hour flight without getting the shakes.

We got zipped into our pressure suits, complete with our own patch, which showed the number 6 on a field of black surrounded by stars. Since we were the first Gemini-Titan to fly with an Agena, Wally had decided that the patch should read "G-T-A 6," with the Arabic numeral rather than the Roman numerals NASA officially used. The 6 rested in the constellation of

Orion, since that would be the background of our target Agena vehicle at the time of the final phase of rendezvous and docking. Then we headed down the Barton FREEWay to Pad 19 where John Young and Gus Grissom were setting up the switches inside the cockpit.

Our Atlas-Agena was proceeding through its final count on Pad 14, a mile to the south of where our Gemini-Titan was stacked. We had already been buttoned inside Gemini 6 when we heard the Atlas light up at 10:00 A.M. and roar off the pad. I took that as a good sign. Everything seemed to be going great until fourteen minutes after Agena's launch, when it should have appeared in the sky over Bermuda—and didn't.

"Maybe it's the tracking station," Wally said. "Let's wait for Ascension Island." That was the next station in the net.

No joy at Ascension Island. We kept sitting there, waiting, our countdown held at T minus forty-two minutes. Finally we passed the time when the Agena should have appeared over Australia. Still nothing. At 10:54 we were told the Agena was lost and the launch of GT-6 was scrubbed. Later investigation concluded that the Agena had exploded, thanks to an oxidizer feed sequence that had been changed.

It seemed to take a long time to get the erector raised so we could get out of the spacecraft. Then we rode back to the crew quarters, where we sat around for a few moments asking ourselves, "Now what do we do?" We all felt disappointed in the Agena failure. Al Shepard appeared at that point. "Boys," he said, "what we need is a good scrub party." So Wally and I headed off with Al, Gus, and John.

What we didn't know was this: Even before Wally and I were extracted from Gemini 6, Frank Borman and Jim Lovell had been watching the Atlas launch, and our scrub, from the blockhouse. With them were Walter Burke, John Yardley, and Raymond Hill of McDonnell. It was Burke who started talking to Yardley about having Gemini 6 rendezvous with Gemini 7. The Titan and 6 would be destacked and stored. Gemini 7 and its Titan would be erected on Pad 19 and launched on schedule. Since 7 was planned to last two weeks, there might be time to bring 6 *back* to the pad and launch it in time to do a rendezvous. Apparently Martin had done some studies about shortening the turnaround time between Titan launches and Burke thought it would work.

Pretty soon all five of them were playing with the idea. Burke and Yardley pitched it to Chuck Mathews and George Mueller, who were at the Cape,
too. Then to Lt. Col. Jack Albert and the rest of the Titan 2 launch team, a
group of about thirty-five people from the Air Force, Martin, Aerojet, Mc-
Donnell, and the Aerospace Corporation. Burke and Yardley next flew to
Houston to sell their double-Gemini flight to Bob Gilruth, George Low, and
Chris Kraft. By late afternoon, Tuesday, October 26, all of the key depart-
ments in Houston were behind the idea. The next morning George Mueller
presented it to Bob Seamans, one of the top three people in NASA, who laid
it out for Jim Webb and his other main deputy, Hugh Dryden. Webb approved it.

So less than forty-eight hours after the Agena had blown up, ruining the
launch of Gemini 6, Wally and I were ticketed for a flight called Gemini 6-A,
scheduled for launch in December 1965 after Gemini 7—our rendezvous (not
docking) target. Deke told us the new plan upon our return to Houston the
following day. Gemini 7 would have a radar transponder and docking lights
added and would serve as our rendezvous target in December. We would
have preferred to dock with an Agena, but we knew that the investigation
would keep Agenas grounded until at least December or January, so that
wasn't an immediate option.

There was also a possibility I might do an EVA from 6 to 7, swapping
places with Jim Lovell. We talked about that for some time, until it became
clear that Frank didn't like the idea and that it would require Jim to wear an
EVA suit on a long-duration mission. Wally was disappointed. Even though
he had worked hard to get EVA thrown off the original 6, he had worked
just as hard to get it back, once we lost the Agena. But without success.

Wally and I had considered ourselves trained for rendezvous and docking before our scrub. We didn't need to do anything extra to get ready for a rendezvous with Gemini 7, so we gave Frank and Jim priority on the simulators.
Meanwhile, I found myself with two new jobs. First was to serve as astronaut office liaison to the mission planning group for the last three Gemini
missions. The mission planning team scheduled an astronaut's daily routine
in space. They would have big meetings with sometimes a hundred attendees,
hammering away at each other for hours and filling blackboards with numbers and diagrams. Deke and Al wanted me to make sure the flight crew's

perspective was part of the discussion. If there was a battle for the blackboard, I was empowered to get to the chalk.

My other new job was a flight assignment. I had known for some weeks that Neil Armstrong and Dave Scott were going to be the prime crew of Gemini 8. This made sense, since Neil had been Gordo's backup on Gemini 5. But his pilot on that crew had been Elliot See, and now Elliot was being replaced by Dave Scott. Dave was a very capable pilot and deserved a chance to fly, but Elliot was good, too, and had seniority. I didn't want to see him left out. So I had asked Al what was going on.

Al reassured me, "We've got that squared away." Elliot was going to command Gemini 9, with Charlie Bassett as his pilot. And in early November, I learned from Deke that I would be Elliot's backup for Gemini 9, that I would go on to command Gemini 12, the last manned flight in the series. "How about Gene Cernan for your pilot?" Deke said.

Gene had been the astronaut representative for the Agena and had worked "tanks" (monitoring fuel pressure in the Titan) on several Gemini launches. I didn't know him as well as some of the other astronauts in that third group, like Charlie Bassett or Donn Eisele. But Charlie was on the prime crew for 9, and Donn was working on the Apollo program. So I said, "Sure," and went to Gene's office, two doors from mine, to give him the good news that we'd be flying together. I couldn't spend much time on 9 at the moment. But the prime crew, Elliot and Charlie, were already at work. Gene would join them now, and I would catch up in a month.

Gemini 7 with Frank and Jim launched at 2:30 P.M. December 4, 1965. The afternoon liftoff was chosen so the crew could keep to a work and sleep schedule that was "normal." Wally and I watched the liftoff with Gus and John. No sooner were they in orbit than the pad crews, plumbers, electricians, welders, swarmed over Pad 19, doing their damage assessments, and getting to work on clean up.

Fortunately, there was relatively little damage to the pad. The next day the tractor pulled up with the Titan 2. First stage was erected, second stage on top of that, followed by the Gemini spacecraft, all by sundown. Meanwhile, up in orbit, everything was going so smoothly that Houston canceled a phasing burn Frank and Jim were to have made. It looked as though Gemini 6-A would be able to launch as early as Sunday, December 12.

Wally and I went through the breakfast and suiting routine (no cigarette for Wally this time) on the twelfth feeling confident that we would soon be in orbit. For one thing, our target, Gemini 7, was already up there. We were all buttoned up, ready for launch at six seconds after 9:54 A.M., listening to Al Bean counting down those last few seconds. "Four . . . three . . . ignition! . . . two . . . one!" I could feel the Titan come alive—

And just as quickly, at T = 0, *shut down*. The sound of the engines died even though the clock started and the computer light came on, both indications that we had lifted off. But I could feel that we hadn't moved. And most important, there was no word from Al Bean confirming liftoff, which was critical. Frank Carey, the test director called, "Hold kill," a missile-testing term meaning the bird had shut down, and Wally confirmed, "Roger, hold kill." It was a tough few seconds. Had we lifted off the pad at all? If so, we had to get out of there before the booster settled back and blew up! But Wally didn't pull the D-ring that would have fired us out of the spacecraft on our modified SR-71 ejection seats, good from zero altitude up to seventy-thousand feet.

I'm glad he didn't. Given that we'd been soaking in pure oxygen for two hours, any spark, especially the ignition of an ejection-seat rocket, would have set us on fire. We'd have been two Roman candles shooting off into the sand and palmetto trees.

Not long before the first manned Gemini launch, back in February 1965, Gus, John, Wally, and I had observed a live-fire test of the ejection seats from a boilerplate spacecraft at the China Lake Naval Air Station. It went fine, but then I happened to say to Gus, "I wonder if they have pure oxygen in there?" "Hell, no!" Gus said. "It's purged with nitrogen." I wondered then why they hadn't made the test more realistic by using oxygen. I wasn't specifically thinking that the spacecraft or dummy astronaut would burst into flame, but they might have. And Gus might not have died in the Apollo fire.

It wasn't as though we were all safe and snug sitting in that spacecraft. We were told that a fire had broken out at the base of the Titan. "Well, put the damn thing out," I said. Or maybe something a little stronger.

Wally asked Al Bean to read us the egress procedures. "Since we're just sitting here waiting."

It took ninety minutes to raise the erector and get us out, a lot longer than it should have. Although he had kind words for Guenter Wendt and the pad crew, Wally was furious. But by the time we returned to the crew quarters, he had calmed down.

Meanwhile, Faye, Dionne, and Karin had remained home in Houston for the launch and were watching on television when we shut down. They saw the smoke and flame and heard someone say, "Hold kill," and understandably got scared. Fortunately, someone at mission control telephoned to reassure them, and from that time on, it was standard procedure to have an astronaut present with the crew's families during any launch.

Back at the Cape, the problem that had caused our "hold kill" turned out to be relatively easy to fix. Actually, there were two problems, one minor and one major. The minor one was an umbilical plug that simply shook loose from the base of the Titan at ignition, starting the various timers. The plug was *supposed* to require forty pounds of pull before it separated, but it had just rattled out of its housing. At first the engineers thought the plug was the cause of the whole shutdown. But Ben Hohmann of the Aerospace Corporation, looking over the telemetry traces, discovered that the thrust in one of the two Aerojet engines was dying even *before* the plug fell out. The teams on the pad started investigating around seven that night; it took them until nine the next morning to discover a small plastic dust cap still in place, covering the fuel inlet port of one of the gas generators.

Normally, when the engine starts up, a pyrotechnic device is fired into a turbine that in turn spins up a turbo pump. The pump feeds the hypergolic fuel into the gas generator combustion chamber, where it ignites on contact. The cap had prevented the fuel from entering the gas generator. It should have been removed before the launch vehicle left the factory in Baltimore, because once the bird was assembled, the cap was impossible to detect. So the Titan's malfunction detection system—the same MDS that had shut down Gemini 2 earlier in the year—did the same thing here. With about a second to spare. Any slower, and the Titan would have lifted off the ground without enough power to fly. It would have fallen back, and we wouldn't have had enough time to eject, even if we'd wanted to.

By Wednesday, December 15, we were back on Pad 19. There had been some worries about the weather when we went to bed on the previous evening, but the morning was perfect, blue skies, warm temperatures. I rode out to Pad 19 convinced that the third time was the charm. And this time everything went as planned. At 8:37:20, the count reached T minus three seconds . . . the engines lit up as they had on Sunday, but no shutdown. Buttoned up inside the suit, I couldn't hear much noise, but I did feel a slight pressure on my back, and a little shaking and vibration, which dropped off as the Titan rose.

Al Bean called, "Liftoff," and we moved right out. "We have a big, fat 'go'!" Wally radioed. I kept my eyes on the pitch indicator and the needles throughout. I glanced out the window twice: There wasn't much to see except sky, especially since we were going straight up. We shot through a layer of clouds—*whoosh!*

G-levels on the first stage built up to five and a half, no discomfort at all. As the first stage started to shut down, however, the second stage did its "fire in the hole," igniting before separation. Suddenly it looked as though we were flying through a fireball that left a thin layer of soot on our windows. I had been expecting it, but it was still pretty startling.

Then the first stage dropped off and we rode the second stage into orbit. As the Titan continued to pitch over, I finally saw the earth's horizon appear in the lower part of my window. What a sight! The earth's atmosphere, from sea level up to a hundred thousand feet (twenty miles) was a slightly curved, pale-blue line. The clouds below were small and racing past. G-loads were climbing now to over seven, and I felt some pain in my gut and pressure on my lungs. I took short, sharp breaths and waited for shutdown at five minutes, thirty-five seconds.

Wham! In a tenth of a second we went from nearly eight Gs to zero. Immediately after cut-off, I punched address 72 on the computer, which gave me a value of 25,690 feet per second, more than enough to ensure that we were in orbit and staying there. Our immediate task was to separate from the second stage, ideally within twenty seconds. There had been instances in Air Force missile tests where the stage had blown up in what they called a Green Man situation. We wanted to avoid the Green Man. I pushed the separation switch while Wally thrust the spacecraft away. Then we rolled to local vertical (on Gemini-Titan you rode into orbit rightside down) and started in on our checklist, aligning our guidance platform and unstowing equipment before losing communication with mission control.

Within twenty minutes we had moved into darkness, and here was an amazing sight. Below us the nighttime surface of the Earth was alive with thunderstorms and the flash of meteorites. You could even see the lights of cities—not many of them, though, since we were over Africa. The night sky from orbit was the real surprise. I could see perhaps ten times as many stars as on the clearest night. The Milky Way truly was a gigantic puddle of stars.

Aside from a few glances out the window, though, I was busy. We had to go through a series of maneuvers to reach the co-elliptic trajectory. At the end of our first revolution, we made a short burn to correct a slight under-performance of the booster. At 2:18 into the mission we made a phase-adjustment burn, raising the perigee of our orbit. Thirty minutes later we had to make a slight change of our orbital plane, shifting it to the south. Then we had to make another tweak—less than a second long—to trim our apogee by a few hundred meters.

Wally and I hadn't unstrapped. We had merely raised our helmet visors. After a bit, we took off our gloves, then the helmets, too, stowing them below our knees. We had a snack of juice but I didn't feel especially hungry, not after that huge prelaunch breakfast. The only discomfort I noted was that our suits were a little warm; they would stay warm for most of the flight.

Gemini 7 was above us in a nearly circular orbit of 183 by 187 miles. After two revs, we were 250 miles behind and 17 miles below them, close enough for a radar lock. It was as if we were two horses on a racetrack: The one on the inside travels faster and gains ground on the one to the outside. We turned on the radar at three hours, ten minutes mission elapsed time, and got our first, sporadic lock on Gemini 7 three minutes later.

With the radar data, we were in position to make the normal slow rate (NSR) burn at 3:47, for a total duration of fifty-three seconds. From that point on, our onboard computer was the primary source of data. I kept watching the figures, calling them out to Wally, who spotted Gemini 7 when it was still seventy miles away, reflecting the rays of the sun. It was near the belt of the constellation Orion and, at first, appeared to be the star, Sirius. But then Wally realized it was in the wrong position. (Frank and Jim saw us before we saw them, since we were below, against the earth.)

When Gemini 6 reached a point thirty-four miles behind and fifteen miles below the target, 5:16 into the flight, it was time for the initial terminal phase maneuver. We had already briefed Frank and Jim to pitch their spacecraft fif-teen degrees below the horizon, nose toward us. Gemini 6 would be fifteen degrees above the horizon, nose toward them. That way our radar would have the best chance to stay locked onto them. As we moved closer, I called out new pitch angles and Frank pitched Gemini 7 down in response. Wally was flying as I read the backup charts. I got the final solution from those charts before we received one from our onboard IBM computer or mission control.

At the precise moment, on my count, Wally fired the thrusters, boosting us out of our circular chase orbit on an intercept trajectory. Nose down, Gemini 7 broke into daylight above us. We closed in, and at 5:56, as I radioed to Houston, "We are 120 feet apart and sitting." We could hear clapping and cheering from mission control.

"You guys sure have big beards," Wally said to Frank and Jim, since we could see them in their windows.

"For once we're in style," Frank said.

As Wally flew us around Gemini 7, I had the Hasselblad camera in hand and was taking pictures like crazy, including one that made the front page of the *Washington Post* a few days later—the first spacecraft-to-spacecraft photo ever made. I shot movie footage, too. My first surprise was seeing all the thin flaps and streams of material hanging off the back of 7—and, according to Frank and Jim, the same stuff was hanging off ours, too. It was tape that had been used to protect the pyrotechnic devices that separated the Gemini adaptor from the upper stage of the Titan.

Frank reported that he had seen the plumes of our thrusters firing out to forty feet. And when we flew around the backside of Gemini 7, we saw that even our smallest thruster firing would cause the gold insulation blanket on 7 to flap—an important thing to know for future spacewalks. You didn't want an astronaut to get shoved around and hit by the toxic fumes.

"Jim," I said, "the doctors have been worried about your vestibular function since you've been up here longer than any other crew. Why don't you take a picture of this and tell us what you see, so they can correlate." As Jim Lovell raised his camera, I held up a blue-and-gold piece of cardboard the size of my window. It said, "Beat Army," a little taunt from three Annapolis graduates (Wally, Jim, and me) to Frank Borman, West Point '50.

We kept station with 7 for over five hours, through nighttime passes, which were very different, with 7 sitting out there with its docking lights. Our closest approach was within a couple of feet, though most of the time we stayed an adequate distance away. I took my own turns flying, having convinced the Gemini program managers to add a second maneuver controller to the pilot's side of 6 (and all subsequent Geminis).

Finally, however, it was time to make a small burn and start drifting apart. Wally and I were headed home soon, but Frank and Jim had three long days to go. Jim later said they had quite an emotional letdown when they saw us leave.

After we separated from Gemini 7, I worked for a short time with an Air Force experiment, using an optical sextant. We had another meal, then tried to get some sleep. It wasn't too comfortable; the suit was still warm, though it cooled down once we powered down the spacecraft. I probably slept a total of four hours, waking up at least once an hour, looking at one of my two Omega watches to see what time it was. (We wore one watch for mission elapsed time, and one for Houston time.)

On December 16, 1965, Wally and I were over the United States on our next-to-last rev, when I called down to Elliot See, our capcom: "Houston, we have an object, looks like a satellite going from north to south, probably in polar orbit. Looks like he's heading in a descending trajectory, with zero angular bearing rate." In other words, he was on a collision course. "In fact, it looks like he might be closing in on us."

You could practically hear the sudden tension in Elliot See's voice. They must have wondered what the hell was going on. What was this, some Russian satellite? I went on, "It looks like he's trying to signal us."

The next sound anyone heard from Gemini 6 was Wally Schirra playing "Jingle Bells" on a tiny harmonica, while I rattled some tiny bells.

"You're too much!" Elliot said.

Well, it was almost Christmas.

We ran through the re-entry procedures very smoothly. SEP ON, SEP ELECTRIC, SEP ADAPTOR, ARM AUTO RETRO. That was the sequence of steps in the checklist; I could have done them in my sleep.

The retros fired automatically. I backed them up by pushing the RETRO FIRE button again. Then I pushed the SEP RETRO section button. Wally was keeping the spacecraft oriented; Gemini had no autopilot for retrofire attitude. You had to control it manually. I saw yellow flames briefly outside my window. Then we started the long fall through the atmosphere. I cross-checked the computer display with the needles. They seemed to be squared away, so I watched the coppery ionization cloud build up outside the spacecraft. The thin layer of soot on the windows seemed to crack, ball up, and peel off as the fireball engulfed the spacecraft. We were going backwards, heads-down, so I had a great view of the horizon and the cloud-covered Gulf of Mexico, and a clear sense that we were really moving fast. Wally was flying the space-craft, rolling left and right as needed.

At thirty-five thousand feet we deployed the pilot chute, which really jerked the spacecraft around. Wally pushed the button to deploy the main chute, which came out at ten thousand feet. In spite of the improvements in the system shifting the vehicle to two-point suspension, which had cracked Gus Grissom's helmet faceplate, we still got a pretty good jerk. Wally, in fact, cracked his faceplate because he had braced it against the arm of his suit, and it hit the metal ring for the glove attachment.

We plopped down to a calm ocean about seven miles from the carrier USS *Wasp*. Wally had insisted that we stay with the spacecraft until it could be lifted aboard the carrier, which is what we did. I was dehydrated, tired, but happy as hell. We had proved that rendezvous would work, one of the key goals of the Gemini program and a major step toward landing on the Moon.

eight
Lambert Field

I returned to Houston for the usual debriefing, then a postflight news conference with Wally, and with Frank Borman and Jim Lovell, who had splashed down safely on the eighteenth of December. I was able to take Faye and the girls back to Weatherford for a short Christmas vacation, then it was back to work for me as backup commander for Gemini 9.

Well, there would be a couple of ceremonial postflight duties, including a parade back home. And there were rewards: a NASA Exceptional Service Medal, plus a promotion to lieutenant colonel. I had Gus Grissom to thank for that. Shortly after the Gemini 3 flight, a reporter happened to ask Gus about the differences between the Soviet cosmonauts and American astronauts. "Yeah," Gus snapped. "They get promoted, and we don't." President Johnson heard about the exchange, and though he took no immediate action, he included Gus and John Young when Jim McDivitt and Ed White received spot promotions after Gemini 4. The new policy was, you got bumped one grade after your first flight. At the time of Gemini 6 I was already on the list for early promotion to lieutenant colonel: The postflight bump merely helped me on date of grade by six months.

Gene Cernan, the pilot on my crew, had already been training for Gemini 9 on his own, supporting the prime crew who would fly the mission, Elliot See and Charlie Bassett. Elliot was one of my group of nine, and I had gotten to know him fairly well in the three years since we had been selected. He was a short, quiet individual, very religious. A capable pilot, if a little shaky on instruments. (He hadn't had the advantage of spending two years flying in cloud-covered Europe, as I had.) Like Neil Armstrong, he was a civilian test pilot, but where Neil had spent years flying for NASA at Edwards, Elliot had worked on the corporate side with General Electric.

I knew Charlie Bassett somewhat better than Elliot, even though he had been selected with the third group of astronauts in 1963. Charlie had been one of my students at the Test Pilot School at Edwards, where he'd won the Honts Award for best flying and academics in Class 62-A. He had stayed at Edwards after graduation and gone through the space school. He was like Elliot in that he was quiet, very disciplined. He was also an outstanding pilot.

Elliot and Charlie's mission was to rendezvous and dock using three different methods, beginning with an $M = 3$ rendezvous, linking up with their target Agena one revolution earlier than Wally and I had reached Gemini 7. (This would become the standard mode for the lunar missions.) Then Elliot and Charlie would back off a distance of fifteen miles and come back to the Agena in what we called an "equi-period orbit rendezvous," to test to using a future Apollo command module to find an orbiting lunar module. Finally, the Agena would be maneuvered to a point below and behind the Gemini, simulating an aborted lunar landing. In this mode, the Gemini would be standing in for a lunar module. During the docked phase of the mission, Charlie was going to make a two and a half hour spacewalk using a rocket backpack developed by Ling-Temco-Vought for the Air Force's Space Systems Division. Launch of Gemini-Titan 9 was scheduled for May 17, 1966.

I was already thinking beyond Gemini 9 because Deke Slayton had told me that Gene and I could logically expect to fly Gemini 12, the last manned mission in the series. I was really looking forward to it; being commander of a backup crew was one thing; commanding my own mission was my real goal. But first we had to get Gemini 9 flying.

As the Gemini program proceeded from one milestone to another—first flight, first EVA, a four-day, eight-day, then fourteen-day flight, and finally success with rendezvous—there was, strangely, no response from the Soviets. When we caught our breath long enough to think about it, we wondered why. Where were their long-duration flights? What about more EVAs? What about rendezvous and docking? We knew something must be in the works, but where was it?

Years later I would learn that the Soviet space and missile programs were strained for cash and torn by competing managements. Another factor was the death, on January 14, 1966, of Sergei Korolyov, the most powerful and capable individual in the Soviet space program, the one man who had the clout to overcome most, if not all, of these problems. Cosmonauts like Aleksei Leonov, who had by now gotten to know Korolyov, were shocked and saddened. Aleksei, I learned later, had spent a fascinating evening at Korolyov's home not long before that ill-fated surgery, hearing stories about the chief designer's imprisonment as an "enemy of the people" back in the 1930s. Now his bureau was thrown into chaos as various forces fought for control of it.

On February 3, 1966, the Soviets accomplished the first soft landing of an unmanned probe on the Moon, Luna 9. It would be the last triumph they would have for some time.

Our first trip as a group up to Mellow Old St. Louis to get our hands on spacecraft number nine was set for Monday, February 28, 1966. Both crews would travel together, Elliot and Charlie in one T-38, Gene and I flying formation in another. When we all showed up at Ellington early that morning, the pre-flight briefing told us the ceiling at Lambert Field, St. Louis, was fifteen hundred feet, broken to overcast, three miles visibility, with occasional rain or showers. Nothing to get worried about.

When we checked in the NOTAMs (advisory items to pilots concerning the airport), we were told that the glide slope indicator for the instrument landing system at Runway 12—the main runway—was out. This meant we'd have to perform our own manual calculations on descent, but that wouldn't be a problem for either of us. I'd been flying in and out of Lambert for almost two years by this point. Elliot had been going back and forth for the better part of 1965, as backup on Gemini 5.

At 7:35 A.M., Elliot and Charlie took off in NASA 901, Elliot flying. Gene and I followed on their wing in NASA 907. I was in the front cockpit, at the controls. En route we checked the St. Louis weather and found that the ceiling was lower than advertised. At our altitude, the soup really got thick, so I took up a position just a few feet off Elliot's right wing. As we let down for final approach, after a flight of about ninety minutes, Elliot reported that he had the outer marker and called "Gear down." I lowered our landing gear.

First problem: The blinking green light of the outer marker was barely visible in my peripheral vision. And we weren't feeling any of the buffeting you get with a T-38 as you slow to the normal approach speed of 165 knots. I had been so busy trying to stay on Elliot's wing that I hadn't paid attention to my own airspeed. I quickly glanced at it now, and saw that we were trying to land at 225 knots, about 60 knots too fast. I realized that Elliot must have lowered full flaps. Now, my experience with the T-38 at Edwards had taught me to only lower flaps to sixty percent, since it was obvious that the difference in lift coefficient between the two settings was minimal. All you got was more drag and buffeting—if you were at the right speed to begin with.

We kept sinking through the soup toward the runway, and then I noticed a flashing green light—the inner marker. "What the heck happened to the middle marker?" I asked Geno. It was confusing, but the cloud layer was so thick, I could barely see Elliot and Charlie's T-38 a couple of feet to the left of my canopy.

Suddenly we broke out of the overcast, and I was amazed to see that we weren't at the approach end of the runway, but at the far end, still several hundred feet in the air, and headed for a hill. I radioed Elliot, "We've missed the runway!" I expected him to abort the landing and make a slow, climbing turn. Instead, *zoom!*—Elliot banked to the left and disappeared into a cloud. I tried to follow, but when he made a second sharp turn, I lost him completely. "Missed wingman approach!" I told him, and turned the standard ten degrees to the right.

Gene and I broke out of the clouds again, and saw that we were directly over McDonnell 101, the building adjoining Lambert Field where the Gemini spacecraft were assembled. Then we flew over Mr. Mac's office in the corner building of the headquarters. Shaped like funnels and reaching nearly to the ground, columns of clouds drifted across the field, spraying snow, sleet, and rain. Elliot was snaking between those columns, trying to turn the aircraft left yet again and line up on one of the runways. But he was too close and missed. Nevertheless, it was obvious he was trying to keep the field in sight.

Not me. One look at snow showers above and around us, at five hundred to a thousand feet, and I radioed the tower, "NASA 907 is making a missed approach." I added power, pulled up the landing gear, raised the flaps, and headed out to try this again. As I did, I switched radio frequencies.

I looked around for Elliot and Charlie, and saw their plane banking tight again and trying for the runway they'd missed the first time. I could see that they were too close, and they missed it again. With their gear and flaps still down, they passed behind the control tower on the west side of the field. I lost sight of them at that point, and because my radio was now tuned to a different frequency, I heard nothing more from them.

Lambert approach control kept us in a holding pattern until our fuel got dangerously low. Finally I had to tell them, "Any further delay and I'm going to declare an emergency. I need to land now!"

They gave me a vector to the outer marker. On my own, this time, I checked the time-and-distance and altitude on the approach chart. Squared away, I flew down the localizer, slowed to 160 knots (feeling the buffeting), and came to the outer marker right on altitude. We passed the middle marker, then broke out of the clouds at three hundred feet, with snow falling. I set us down without incident, rolled out, and turned off onto the taxi-way, radioing, "NASA 907 on the ground."

"Roger, 907," Lambert tower said. Then there was a pause. "Who was in NASA 901?"

That was odd. "See and Bassett," I said. "Why?"

"McDonnell Aircraft has a message for you."

I taxied toward the McDonnell ramp, where I saw a large group of people waiting for us. The expression on their faces told me something was wrong. I shut down, raised the canopy, and said, "What happened to 901?"

A McDonnell crew chief said, "A plane just crashed into Building 101, where they build the Geminis!"

Mr. Mac himself appeared as Gene and I got out of the plane and headed inside. He waited until we were in the ready room before telling us, "They're both dead," meaning Elliot and Charlie. "Some people were injured in the building."

Elliot's last attempted approach had taken him too low and too close to Building 101. Either he or Charlie had tried to hit afterburner at the last moment, to gain altitude, but it hadn't worked. The T-38 pancaked into the asphalt roof, then flipped into the parking lot, where it exploded. Elliot and Charlie were killed instantly. Thirteen people were injured by falling debris inside the building. None of them was seriously hurt, however. And the Gemini spacecraft were undamaged. Had they hit a couple of hundred feet earlier, they would have hit the side and roof of the building instead of just the end of the roof, and wiped out the whole Gemini program.

I went off to call Deke Slayton with the bad news. Deke appointed Al Shepard head of the investigating committee, and he flew to St. Louis from the Cape late that afternoon.

The following Thursday, a cold, cloudy, miserable day, Elliot and Charlie were both buried at Arlington. Gene and I attended both ceremonies, of course. Gene was particularly stunned by Charlie's death: They had been working together for two years, and Charlie was the second member of that 1963 astronaut group to die in a span of sixteen months. The member of our group who took Elliot's death the hardest, though, was Neil Armstrong. Not only had he and Elliot shared the distinction of being the first two civilian astronauts, but they had also been teamed together for almost a year on the Gemini 5 backup crew and had become good friends.

Right after the funeral Deke Slayton took Gene and me aside and said we would be moving from backup to prime crew for Gemini 9. Jim Lovell and Buzz Aldrin would be our backups. So I would be going back into space less than six months after my first flight. I hated to have it happen this way.

Launch of Gemini 9 was targeted for May 9, 1966, ten weeks away. It really didn't leave much time for training. My role on 9 would be overall command, plus flying the rendezvous and docking with the Agena. Fortunately, I had already been through the Gemini cycle twice, as backup for Gemini 3 and prime crewman for 6, so I was able to tell Gene, "I know all the systems. You'll have to learn some of them, but I want you to concentrate on doing your spacewalk, and on operating the onboard computer."

The first few Gemini spacecraft carried an onboard computer with a memory of 4096 words. Starting with spacecraft number eight, the one Neil and Dave would fly, we would have an upgraded computer with a tape-drive memory of five hundred thousand words, which seemed like a huge amount. Gene was to become an expert on knowing what data had been stored and how to call it up.

The spacewalk would be another challenge. Gene had already been working himself into good physical condition. He would need to be because his

EVA was very ambitious. The plan was to have him exit the Gemini hatch, go forward to test his ability to control his motion, then crawl back to the adaptor section, where a rocket-powered backpack called the astronaut maneuvering unit was stored. He would back into the AMU, strap himself in, then detach the whole thing from the Gemini and, secured by a 125-foot tether, go jetting around. Because the AMU jets used hot gas (as opposed to the cool, inert gas in Ed White's handheld zip gun), Gene's EVA suit had a special layer of metal mesh added to the legs and arms—just in case the hot jets happened to impinge.

The AMU was an Air Force experiment studying the possibility of having future military astronauts inspect hostile satellites. The project officer for the backpack was Maj. Ed Givens, the same Ed Givens who had graduated from Annapolis when I did, and who had served as my instructor and friend at the Test Pilot School. Ed had transferred from Edwards to Space Systems Division in Los Angeles in 1964 then moved to Houston with the AMU project.

This was a lot of work, given our short schedule. It helped that our backup command pilot, Jim Lovell, had been through the Gemini training cycle twice. And Buzz Aldrin had worked rendezvous for Gemini 6. Buzz was very smart, but he tended to go off on tangents. I had to remind him to stick to the things he needed to learn for the mission and encouraged Jim Lovell to keep Buzz focused, too. "You have to treat him like a full-choke twelve gauge shotgun. You can't let him ricochet around."

Before Gemini 9 could fly, Neil Armstrong and Dave Scott would fly Gemini 8, scheduled for launch on March 16, 1966, on a mission that would essentially repeat what had originally been planned for Gemini 6: an $M = 4$ rendezvous and docking with an Agena, and a spacewalk. Because spacecraft number eight had fuel cells instead of batteries, it could stay up longer than number six. Dave Scott's spacewalk would be far more ambitious than anything previously planned, lasting up to two hours and using a handheld cold gas gun that was much more capable than the one used by Ed White.

The Atlas-Agena took off beautifully on March 16, followed a little over an hour later by Neil and Dave. Gene and I watched on television from mission control then returned to the Gemini simulator in Building 5 to continue our training.

We heard that Neil and Dave had made a smooth set of burns, coming right up to the Agena, with Neil slowly nudging the nose of the Gemini into the docking collar six and a half hours after launch. "Flight, we are docked," he radioed.

Gene and I kept running through our own rendezvous sims, when suddenly we got a call from mission control to get over there: "Gemini 8 has already used up one ring of re-entry fuel and half of the second. They're coming down!"

We climbed out of the simulator and hurried to Building 30. There we learned that less than a half hour after docking, Neil and Dave had noticed an unexplained roll and oscillations in their attitude. At the same time, they had problems getting the Agena to respond to commands. So, figuring that there was some problem with the Agena, they switched off the system giving command back to their Gemini and undocked, which turned out to be the wrong thing to do. Their Gemini started rolling faster and faster, up to one complete revolution *per second*. Realizing that they had an attitude control thruster that was stuck in the on position, they eventually shut down all sixteen thrusters and activated the re-entry control system. Neil fired those until the Gemini stopped spinning and came under control.

They were stable again, but they had used much of their precious re-entry maneuvering fuel—one-and-a-half rings out of two. Mission rules said they had to come down, right now. They splashed down in the Pacific about six hundred miles south of Yokohama, Japan, in one of the backup landing zones. The destroyer USS *Leonard F. Mason* was standing nearby to pick them up.

Neil and Dave had accomplished a rendezvous and docking, but obviously there were still problems with the Agena and the Gemini. And, worst of all, we had lost Dave's EVA.

As Gene and I gave Gemini 9 our total concentration, the Apollo program moved center stage. Even before that fateful flight to St. Louis, the first unmanned Block 1 Apollo spacecraft, 009, had been launched from the Cape atop a Saturn 1B, making a successful heatshield test. And within a week of the splashdown of Gemini 8, on March 21, Gus Grissom, Ed White, and Roger Chaffee were named as the crew for the first manned Apollo mission, scheduled for launch by the end of 1966. Jim McDivitt, Dave Scott, and Rusty Schweickart would be their backups.

My good friend Donn Eisele was disappointed by the announcement. He had been told months before that he would be on the first Apollo crew. But he had banged up a shoulder during a zero-G flight at Wright-Patterson in early 1965 and had subsequently aggravated it playing handball, so badly that in January 1966 he had to have surgery. That cost him the crew assignment. One night he actually cried on my shoulder. I told him he would get another chance. For Apollo 1, however, Roger Chaffee took Donn's place.

NASA also expanded the astronaut team, selecting nineteen new pilots on April 4, including my friends or ex-students Ed Givens, Jack Swigert, Joe Henry Engle, and Jim Irwin. Added to five scientist-astronauts hired the previous June—a move that struck me as premature, given the state of the program—there were now almost fifty astronauts. That was more than we were likely to need for several years. The reason for the expansion was that James Webb had been burned by Mercury astronauts like John Glenn and Al Shepard throwing their weight around. What better way to dilute astronaut power than to select more of them?

During the spring of 1966, I was too busy to think about Apollo, fellow astronauts, or anything but Gemini 9. Looking back, it was an insane schedule. I had been in active flight training for two years straight by this point and had spent more days in St. Louis than I had at home in Houston. Add to that the time at the Cape and at contractor sites, and I was living the life of a traveling salesman. Home on weekends, gone during the week. Faye kept the household together, taking care of the chores I couldn't. She was the one who helped Dionne (eleven years old, in fifth grade) and Karin (eight, in second) with their schoolwork.

By and by, as the neighborhood built up, I did get to know the families around us. We lived among MSC doctors such as John Gordon and John Billingham, and engineers, including Cal Bennett, Gordon Heard, and Chet Vaughan, as well as astronaut families like the Eiseles and the Youngs. In fact, the whole area was Manned Spacecraft Center people, except for an airline pilot who lived at the end of the street. And everyone was working the same schedule, from the trajectory people to the simulator staff to the engineers. The motivation at NASA was unbelievable: You'd look out at the MSC parking lot at 4 P.M. and nobody was going home.

But it was damaging to marriages and to the serious business of parenting. Still, nobody looked back. We were in a race.

nine

"If He Dies, You've Got to Bring Him Back!"

On the morning of Tuesday, May 17, 1966, Gene Cernan and I suited up and rode out to Pad 19, climbing into Gemini 9 to wait for the launch of our Agena docking target over on Pad 14. After a short hold in the Atlas-Agena countdown, we heard it take off at 10:15 A.M. A little over two minutes later, we heard that a problem with the number two engine on the Atlas caused the vehicle to go out of control and off trajectory. The range safety officer sent a shutdown signal that "inhibited" the ignition of the Agena upper stage. Though the Agena separated from the Atlas right on time, it had no propulsion, so it nosed over into the Atlantic. Tired, sweaty, and disappointed, Gene and I climbed out of the cockpit.

Given the failure of another Atlas-Agena back on Gemini 6, my personal record with the system was now 0 for 2. That night an Air Force lieutenant colonel at the Cape recited a poem in my honor:

I think that I shall never see
An Agena out in front of me.

The poem turned out to be prophetic. Our backup target vehicle wasn't an Agena (the next one wouldn't be ready until Gemini 10), but a bare-bones unit called the augmented target docking adaptor, or ATDA, that had been developed by McDonnell because of the lost Agena on Gemini 6.

Two weeks after the Agena failure, by June 1, NASA and the Convair crew had the Atlas-ATDA stacked on Pad 14. Gene and I suited up again. A few seconds after 10:00 A.M., the Atlas lifted off, and within ten minutes the ATDA was safely in orbit. There was, however, one disturbing bit of telemetry: It appeared that the shroud covering the docking collar on the ATDA had not separated and that one ring of the attitude control system had depleted nearly half of its fuel.

But we were too busy to worry much about that issue. Our Gemini-Titan countdown was in its terminal phase. Then, just three minutes before scheduled liftoff, the Titan launch vehicle suddenly refused to accept updates from mission control, data we would need for a successful rendezvous. Controllers tried to fix the problem in the brief time we had for the launch window but couldn't do it. Gene and I were out of luck. By this time, counting Gemini 6 with Wally Schirra, I had been up and down the elevator at Pad 19 five different times for only a single launch. Gene was beginning to think I was a jinx, but I straightened him out: Schirra and Cernan were the jinxes. I was fine.

During our two-day recycle for a third try, I happened to ask how long the ATDA would be able to maintain its orbit. It didn't have a propulsion unit, just a Gemini re-entry attitude control system—the very same re-entry hardware used on my Gemini 6, refurbished and installed on the ATDA. John Yardley, the Gemini program manager for McDonnell Douglas, assured me that the ATDA had enough fuel to operate for a month, maybe longer.

But that didn't make sense. Each of the attitude control rings on the ATDA only held about twenty-five pounds of fuel. These little thrusters didn't burn much, but even so, fifty pounds of total fuel was nowhere near enough for several maneuvers every day for thirty days. I told Yardley that, but he assured me that one of his engineers had done the precise calculations.

After the mission was over, I did my own, using the same number of predicted attitude control firings and came out with a figure thirty-six hundred times *lower* than Yardley's engineer. It turned out that in converting the amount of time from minutes to hours, the unnamed engineer had *multiplied* by sixty instead of *dividing*. Oops. (I couldn't help teasing Yardley for many years thereafter.) Unfortunately, the real figures meant that we would have time to make one attempt to reach the ATDA.

Gene Cernan's spacewalk was very ambitious: Wearing his beefed-up pressure suit, he was going to strap himself into the astronaut maneuvering unit, then go flying around, connected to Gemini and me by only a 125-foot nylon tether. I got a reminder of the risk when Deke Slayton took me aside the morning of our first launch attempt, when Gene and I were suiting up in separate rooms in the trailer on Pad 16.

Deke told the suit tech that he needed a private word with me, then closed the door. "Look," he said, "NASA management has decided that if Cernan dies up there, we can't afford to have a dead astronaut floating around in space. You've got to bring him back."

I just stared at him for a few seconds as I absorbed this statement. Then I said, "Jesus Christ, Deke, have they thought about the ramifications of that? To bring him back, the hatch is going to be left partially open because the attachment point for the umbilical is inside the spacecraft near the attitude hand controller." I really started to warm to the subject and went on to point out that if I was bringing a dead astronaut back, the spacecraft would have to be depressurized during retrofire and re-entry, and all I'd be wearing was this relatively flimsy one-layer suit, which had to be pressurized. Now, without Gene I would have to reach over to the right cockpit to reprogram the computer and then manually fire the retros while controlling the spacecraft, all of them difficult maneuvers in a pressurized suit.

"And what about the dynamics of the spacecraft during retrofire, with the mass of that body and the AMU out there, just slinging back and forth?" The Gemini didn't have a large margin of stability during re-entry. I mentioned the three-thousand-degree plasma on the heatshield that would be coming right into the spacecraft through that open hatch and probably burning through my single-layer suit. And, assuming I came through re-entry, would the parachute be able to deploy properly with the tangled mass and a tether flapping around above the spacecraft? Oh, and if I managed to splash down, my hatch would be open, and I would be in the same situation Gus Grissom was on his Mercury mission, when his capsule sank in the Atlantic.

As I ran through these points, Deke just kept nodding. When I was finished, he said, "What do I tell management?"

"Tell them when the bolts blow, I'm the commander, and if something goes wrong, I'll make the decision."

"Okay." With that I finished putting on the suit and snapped on the helmet.

When Gene and I were finally hooked up in the spacecraft, he asked, "What were you and Deke talking about for so long?"

All I could say was, "He said he hoped we had a good flight."

We finally launched successfully at 8:39 A.M. on June 3, winding up in an orbit that ranged from a perigee of 99 to an apogee of 166 miles, about 675 miles behind the ATDA. Since we had lost our Agena and gone to a backup plan, our flight was now officially known as Gemini 9-A. There was barely time to look out the window because we had to perform a burn to reshape that orbit forty-three minutes after launch. It went great, raising the low point of our orbit by forty-three miles.

We carried out a second maneuver at 116 minutes into the mission, on our second revolution, which actually did three things at once: It reshaped the orbit again, corrected our orbital plane, and changed the rate at which we were closing in on the ATDA. Exactly half an hour after that second burn, we did a third one at our second apogee, putting us into a circular orbit, 14 miles below and 124 miles behind the ATDA. From that point on, orbital mechanics would allow us to catch up as we started our third revolution. By this time we also had a radar lock on the ATDA, even though the yaw and pitch needles on our indicator were oscillating, suggesting that the ATDA was changing its attitude. As we crept closer, we saw a blinking light on the target, which was good news: It meant that the shroud had separated. (The light was mounted inside it.) The light, however, would fade out, then reappear. Troubling.

We closed in on the ATDA over the coast of Brazil. A few minutes later we passed into darkness, where we were supposed to stationkeep until moving back into sunlight. Right behind the ATDA I could see the constellation Scorpio, just like those summer nights in Oklahoma. That night there was a bright Moon, and its light gave us our first good look at our target. It turned out to be a depressing sight. Yes, the beacon was visible, but only because the shroud had opened just enough to let it be seen. The shroud was still attached, its two halves partly open. "We have a weird-looking machine here," I radioed. "It looks like an angry alligator."

McDonnell Aircraft had built the adaptor ring, but Douglas Aircraft had built the shroud. We found out later that the wife of the Douglas technician working checkout and assembly was having a baby. When the tech ran off to the hospital, he'd told his McDonnell counterpart to "secure the disconnect lanyards." But rather than simply connecting them, the McDonnell tech had *taped* the lanyards around the firing wires.

Flight controllers in Houston tried everything they could, including extending the docking cone with the shroud still attached, hoping to knock it free. That didn't work. The ATDA was slowly rotating. Mission control would send a command to stop the rate, and we could see the thrusters rapidly firing. I told them to turn off the attitude control system because it was obviously using a lot of fuel.

Since we couldn't dock, we decided to press ahead with the different types of rendezvous maneuvers that had been scheduled for the second day of the mission. The first called for us to back the Gemini away from the ATDA, stopping when we were above and behind it, then going below it to make an approach using eyeballs only, with the computer simply as backup. That worked pretty well: The sun reflecting off the shroud made the ATDA a nice, bright target against the blackness of space. After we had finished that maneuver, we burned away again, putting ourselves into a more leisurely approach to the ATDA that would take several hours. Gene and I were worn out by now, so we tried to get some sleep. It turned out to be difficult, with all the noise in the spacecraft.

The next morning, June 4, we initiated maneuvers to bring us back in on the ATDA, and here's where things got hairy. NASA wanted to demonstrate the feasibility of approaching a target from above—that is, with the Earth as background. This maneuver was preparation for potential Apollo aborts, where a command module might have to descend from a high lunar orbit to rescue a stranded lunar module in a much lower one.

So there I was, moving in on the slowly spinning ATDA, listening to Gene call out range and range-rate data but still having to calculate, in my head, how much thrust in the Y and Z axes to add to the Gemini. We were pointed straight down at the Earth and the ATDA was moving across terrain features at 25,799 feet per second. Instead of black space and stationary stars, the background looked like a video recorder on fast forward. I had no visual references to keep a constant inertial angle for the braking and approach phase to the stationkeeping position. I broke out in a sweat and nearly started to feel vertigo but managed to maneuver to a distance of five feet, close enough to prove that this kind of eyeball, seat-of-the-pants maneuver could be done.

Then Houston came back on line with this idea: Have Gene go ahead with his spacewalk while we were still within reach of the ATDA. But before moving back to the maneuvering unit, which was mounted at the rear of our Gemini's adaptor section, he was supposed to take a pair of surgical scissors from our med kit and try to cut the shroud loose! I didn't like that at all. That shroud had two three-hundred-pound separation springs on it that were preloaded and ready to go off. We could see the sharp edges where half of the adaptor had separated by explosive cutting devices. Suppose one of them popped and hit Gene in his suit? "No way," I told them.

What Gene and I did instead of the spacewalk was place a small movie camera in my window, match the Gemini's roll rate with that of the ATDA, and shoot some film from a few inches away. This film was one of the tools McDonnell would use to figure out what went wrong with the shroud in the first place. Since we hadn't slept much and had completed three different rendezvous, I didn't think we were in shape for any kind of spacewalk, so with flight's agreement I postponed it to the next day, and we said good-bye to the Angry Alligator.

The plan was for Gene to exit the spacecraft, perform a few simple tasks near the nose section to get acclimated to working outside, then climb back to the adaptor, and put on the astronaut maneuvering unit (AMU). He would then separate and go jetting around, just like Buck Rogers in the comic strips I used to read as a kid in Weatherford.

We depressurized the cabin and opened the hatch 185 miles over the Pacific between Hawaii and California. In his suit, Gene stood up and slowly floated out. He pulled in a micrometeorite experiment, then mounted a sixteen millimeter camera and a rearview mirror on the docking bar, so I could see him when he was working back in the adaptor. He pulled himself around with his snakelike tether, just to see how that felt.

Within minutes, however, it was clear that this spacewalk was going to be tougher than we thought. Under full pressure, Gene's suit became a rigid balloon, restricting his movements. The suit kept forcing his arms out in front of his body; he had to exert a lot of effort to get them back to his sides.

Whenever he tried to stabilize himself by grabbing the docking bar on the nose of the Gemini, he torqued the whole spacecraft around. Since I had to keep us stabilized, I was firing thrusters—and warning Gene not to be too close to them when I did.

Gene was huffing and puffing with exertion before he even got back to the adaptor, his heart beat ranging from 155 to 180 beats a minute. As we approached the day-night terminator and passed into darkness, Gene got himself back to the AMU, where he was supposed to back himself into the unit, sit on a saddle, pull down the arms, then strap himself in. Still attached to his umbilical, which provided communications and oxygen, he would unlatch the AMU and start using its hydrogen peroxide jets for attitude and maneuver control.

Gene was in trouble right from the start. Standing in the foot restraints, he couldn't get one of the unit's arms to fold down. Then he started complaining that his back was "burning up." (His pressure suit's super insulation had a long tear near the zipper, which ran from the crotch up his back and allowed the intense heat flux of the sun to burn through.) The moment the sun went down, Gene got so cold that his visor fogged up, and he couldn't see out.

Right about then we developed a communications problem, too. The only sound I could hear from Gene was a garbled squawk. I had to work out a signaling system. "Geno, if you can hear me, try to say 'yes.'"

Squawk.

"Now, say no by giving me two squawks."

Squawk, squawk.

"Can you hear me okay?"

Squawk.

We still had twenty minutes of darkness, so I told him to hang tight. There were only three more steps on the checklist before I was to activate a switch that would set him free on the AMU, but I sure as hell wasn't going to do that with his visor fogged and communications all broken up. It was night, we were 185 miles up, over the Pacific Ocean, out of range of tracking ships. As I sat there in my own pressurized suit with the hatch open and Gene hanging on the back of the spacecraft, I spotted the Southern Cross through my window and thought, Damn, it's lonely out here!

Finally we flew back into sunlight. "Geno, can you see?"

Squawk, squawk. No.

"We're going to call it quits," I told him. "I want you inside the spacecraft before we come around to night again." He had already been out there for over an hour.

It took a long time for him to disconnect from the AMU. He just couldn't see due to the fogged visor. Fortunately, he had practiced the disconnect many times with his eyes closed, so he was able to perform the task, however slowly. The rearview mirror gave me some visibility, so I was able to guide him to the handrail. Eventually Gene got back to the hatch area, swung himself around, and put one of his legs inside. I then reached over and pulled Gene's feet down to his seat, helping him wedge himself in, and I started reeling in the tether—all 125 feet of the snake—shoving it down under my legs so Gene would have some room on his side. The poor guy had to pull down against a bar below the instrument panel to force his ballooned suit into his seat. He had practiced this maneuver many times in the 1G mockup on the ground and for a few seconds in the zero G KC-135 aircraft, but in real zero G it was far more difficult. I couldn't do much, since I was also operating in a rigid pressure suit on my side of the spacecraft.

Eventually we got him far enough inside that I could pull down the cable and bar mechanism, which literally jammed Gene down into the seat, though the top of his helmet was flush with the sill. He dogged the handle to lock the hatch in place, and I turned on the air flow. He was wedged into his seat, his legs beneath the instrument panel, unable to move until pressure built up in the cabin and allowed his suit to relax. When he raised his helmet visor, I saw that his face was hot pink, like he'd been baked in a sauna too long. I used the water gun to give him a drink and then squirted some in his face. He had been out there for two hours and five minutes, and he had lost over ten pounds. He faced a miserable cold environment for a day inside that suit, too. After it got back to Houston, the technicians would pour a pound and a half of water out of each boot.

"Boy," he said, huffing and puffing, "there's a lot we don't know about EVA."

Our third day in space, June 5, was free of major mission tasks. What we had to think about was our landing on the sixth. Three weeks before launch I had telephoned Capt. Gordon E. Hartley, USN, skipper of the carrier USS

Wasp, which was our prime recovery ship, currently stationed three hundred miles east of Florida. Hartley and the *Wasp* had done the same duty for Gemini 6, so we had gotten to be friends.

I alerted him to the possibility that we might put Gemini 9 "down on the carrier's deck. I'll land right on the target point if you can get your ship there."

Hartley laughed and said he would try. This was years before the existence of inertial navigation systems on surface ships and the satellite-based Global Positioning System; it was still very challenging for naval commanders to navigate their ships to a precise point on the open sea using sextants and the stars alone.

I was joking, of course, but not entirely: We had finally developed a new software program that, given a good platform, would fly the Gemini (using its lift) to just about any spot you wanted. It had taken us a few off-target landings (Gemini 3, Gemini 5) to fine-tune both the software and the procedures. The last few weeks, Gene and I worked out a milligraph to help us out even more in the final bit of re-entry. If we were too rapidly approaching a particular longitude, we would roll into a "split S" and dive faster. If we were approaching too slow, we'd roll a "lift vector up" and go farther downrange.

Prior to launch I had suggested a late-mission burn to John Llewellyn, one of the retro officers in mission control. We knew that the more elliptical our final orbit, the more accurate our entry and splashdown would potentially be. But making a final burn depended on our fuel margins. Fortunately, I had used as little as possible during the various burns and rendezvous maneuvers. We had enough for the burn and just before we went to sleep on our third night we got approval to make the maneuver from Chris Kraft, head of flight operations, John Hodge, the flight director, and Ben Krong, our trajectory specialist.

Next morning, we packed up and I went through the now-familiar retro sequence as we flew over Australia. The experience of having flown Gemini 6 gave me a whole new perspective on what we faced. I had been there and done it. So I told Gene, "When we fire those retro-rockets it's going to feel like someone kicks us in the butt and shoves us all the way back across the Pacific Ocean." We fired near Hawaii—received four good jolts, one for each retro-rocket—and started our descent toward the atmosphere. We separated the retro-module.

I warned Gene about the fireball that was going to engulf us. Sure enough, there it was—like being the head of a comet. We shot over the coast of California at an altitude of ninety miles, dropping fast and lighting up the sky. Coming out of the maximum part of fireball, I knew we could expect our heaviest G-load. It would feel worse than usual, because we had been in zero-G for three days. The pressure built up to five Gs. Then it began to slack off.

I flew the entry manually, following the computer outputs. At the end of its program, the computer gave us a full lift vector up to reduce the final G load. Using the milligraph, Gene was rapidly reading out longitude from the computer and calculating the rate of approach to the final one. "Tom," he said, "roll over and split S! We're approaching fast." I rolled the Gemini to full lift vector down the rest of the descent trajectory as we fell in.

Time for the drogue chute deploy, to stabilize us for main chute. I punched the button at thirty-five thousand feet, and out it came, rattling in the wind. We waited anxiously for main chute deploy, because without it we were left only with the option of using our ejection seats, not a great choice. At ten thousand feet, I punched the main chute button. Sure enough, it deployed, reefed so its opening wouldn't slam us around. We kept falling like a stone. I knew Gene was thinking, Why is it taking so long to open fully?

I started to get impatient myself. "De-reef, you mother! De-reef!"

Wham! Out it came, slowing us for the final few thousand feet of the mission. Then the usual two-point suspension maneuver, where we braced for the huge forward jolt.

Back on the *Wasp*, which had acquired us on radar, Captain Hartley had to come about: He had put the ship right on the aiming point, and now it looked to him as though we really were coming right down his smokestack! We were so close that television cameras and the whole world saw us descending, the first time that had happened.

Gemini 6 had slipped into a calm sea with hardly a ripple. Not so Gemini 9. The wind was blowing strong and the seas were rougher, and we happened to hit on the face of a wave that gave us a surprisingly strong jolt which bent several shingles on the skin of the spacecraft and practically dazed us. We went under the water, then bobbed to the surface. I realized we had water in the cabin and wondered if we had sprung a leak. That would have been a tough situation, trying to get out of that spacecraft in those conditions.

But after a few hairy moments, we realized that Gemini was floating, not sinking. It turned out that the violence of the splashdown had ruptured a drinking-water line inside the cabin. We sat back to wait for the flotation collar to be attached. Like Wally, I wanted to be taken aboard the *Wasp* inside my spacecraft, and I was. We had landed .38 nautical miles from our aiming point—the closest-to-target landing of any manned spacecraft in history through the second Shuttle flight in November 1981. My old friend John Young, piloting the first one, had landed just long enough on the dry lakebed at Edwards to leave Gemini 9 as the record holder.

After our welcoming ceremony and a medical check, Gene and I were flown to the Cape. It was only when we were back in the crew quarters and having a drink that I finally told Gene what Deke had really said in the suit-up room.

"Tom," Gene said, "would you really have left me out there?"

"Geno," I told him, "how could you give a shit? You're already dead."

ten

Chariots of Fire

After Gemini 9, with no new flight assignment for the first time in more than two years, I was finally able to take part in a full set of ceremonial activities. I joined Gene Cernan and his family on a three-day trip to his hometown of Bellwood, Illinois, a suburb of Chicago. There we shook hands with Mayor Daley and were honored with a parade. Gene and I then visited my hometown of Weatherford, where we had a far smaller but no less heartfelt ceremony.

In early July, Faye and I took Dionne and Karin to Acapulco for our first major family vacation since 1964. An American named Brandy Brandstetter ran the Las Brisas resort there; he loved the astronauts and went out of his way to make us welcome. It was fun to relax with my family. When we got back I spent several weeks loafing around the house or visiting my mother in Weatherford.

I had my ongoing technical assignment, of course. My work as astronaut office liaison to mission planning now shifted from Gemini to Apollo. I attended classes in geology, and basic training on Apollo systems. Finally, in mid-September, Deke Slayton told me I was going to be command module pilot on the backup crew for Apollo 2. Frank Borman was going to be commander, and Mike Collins would be the lunar module pilot.

Deke didn't let us in on his thinking when it came to crew assignments, but he had made one thing clear: The command module pilot on any Apollo mission involving a lunar module would have to have rendezvous experience.

The Apollo 2 prime crew consisted of Wally Schirra, Donn Eisele, and Walt Cunningham. Their mission was the second manned flight of a Block 1 Apollo spacecraft, number 014, scheduled to spend two weeks in orbit in summer 1967.

Aleksei Leonov, now a lieutenant colonel in the Soviet Air Force, not to mention a Hero of the Soviet Union, resumed active flight training in the summer of 1966, after spending more than a year carrying out the extensive ceremonial and political duties required of cosmonauts. The USSR had only one cosmonaut group, numbering about fifty military pilots, navigators, and engineers, but it had several different programs. In addition to Soyuz and the manned lunar missions, there was a new military space station. General Kamanin didn't need a new selection for these programs. He simply divided his team into squads, one for civilian programs, one for the military.

On June 25, 1966, while he was still doing graduate work at Zhukovsky Air Force Engineering Academy, Aleksei was named deputy commander of the first or civilian squad under Vostok 3 veteran Andrian Nikolayev, and he began training for a possible lunar landing. He also qualified as a helicopter pilot and learned to fly Mi-4s and Mi-8s.

From September 1966, I put Gemini out of my mind, quit traveling to St. Louis, and started spending time in Boston, where the MIT Instrumentation Lab was developing the Apollo guidance and navigation and related support systems, and in Downey, California, where North American Aviation was building the Apollo command and service modules.

Like most Air Force pilots, I had great respect for North American's aircraft, which included the P-51 Mustang, the B-25 Mitchell bomber, the F-86 Sabre, the F-100 Super Sabre, and the X-15 rocket plane. I had personally flown their T-6 and T-28 trainers, the F-86 and F-100, too. Their Apollo program manager was Harrison Storms, a big, smart, tough individual. They had strong political connections in Washington with a great lobbying team. North American was a slick, big-time bunch of Washington operators compared to the mom-and-pop operation at McDonnell.

Or so we thought. I hadn't made too many trips out there with Frank and

Mike Collins before I began to see all kinds of problems. The first was that North American had placed the Apollo program at its instrumentation division in Downey, the one that made the T-28 trainer and the Hound Dog missile, not their main plant in Los Angeles, where the hot fighters, the X-15 and the B-70 bomber were put together. North American had several first rate engineers and managers on Apollo, like Charlie Feltz, George Jeffs, Dale Myers, Joe Cuzzupoli, Jim Berry, and John Healey. My impression, however, was that the Downey team ranked below the L.A. group.

The larger problem was that most of North American and a lot of the NASA Apollo program office seemed to think that the lessons we had learned on Gemini were of no value. Granted, Apollo was an entirely new spacecraft, much larger and more complex than any built up to that time. And North American had been forced to redesign its spacecraft thanks to the late decision to use the lunar orbit rendezvous mode. But we had learned hard lessons on Gemini about quality control in manufacturing, about organizing a factory shop floor for the intricate business of building a spacecraft, as well as basic nuts and bolts issues involved in laying out a cockpit or designing environmental systems. The McDonnell team had been a bunch of square, Midwestern engineers and technicians who came to do the job. My first exposure to North American's Downey team made me think that some were more interested in what they were going to do off the job than on it.

It wasn't just North American that was struggling, however. NASA's Apollo program office (ASPO) was making its own mistakes. ASPO had been headed since 1963 by Joe Shea, a brilliant engineer from the electronics world. Joe was also a protégé of George Mueller's. Unlike Mueller, though, Joe was the same age as most of us in the astronaut office, which made him very competitive. We'd play handball with him, for example. But whenever issues or problems came up, he was no longer Joe Shea, the other guy on the handball court, but Mr. Shea, the program manager.

We would become close friends years later, but during Apollo, Joe and I had some real head-knockings. For example, based on my experience flying rendezvous on two Gemini missions, I felt that the Apollo command module desperately needed to have a means of giving the flight crew a reference to the earth's local horizontal of the orbit. I went in to talk to Joe about it, and he just dismissed it. "Tom, this is Apollo. You must think inertial."

"Inertial reference is fine for certain phases of the mission," I said, "starting in posigrade attitude with inertial attitude. When you're 180 degrees around the world, however, that's retrograde. It makes a hell of a difference how you apply that thrust with respect to the rotating radius vector." In other words, without some local horizontal, the pilot could easily become disoriented by the many maneuvers he was required to perform.

Joe not only didn't see my point, he practically threw me out of his office. Unlike most of the NASA engineers we worked with routinely, Joe had almost no experience with aircraft. He had worked with systems, electronics, and guided missiles—machines that didn't talk back to program managers. So I persisted, and went to see both Deke Slayton and Chris Kraft, who helped me prevail in getting a torquer into the attitude reference system, giving the crew their local horizontal at any instant. But that was just one battle of many.

The command and service modules were only one piece of the gigantic puzzle that was the Apollo program. You had the Saturn 5 booster, for example, managed by Wernher von Braun's team at Marshall and built by a team of contractors: Boeing, Douglas, Rocketdyne, IBM, North American. Another large puzzle piece was the construction of Saturn launch facilities at the Cape, a major civil engineering effort. Finally, the lunar excursion module (LEM) was being developed by Grumman.

Like North American, Grumman, based on Long Island in the city of Bethpage, had a reputation for building terrific aircraft. In Grumman's case, it was Navy carrier fighters from before World War II. Their planes were so rugged the place earned the name, "The Grumman Ironworks." Despite their skill and reputation, however, they faced a major challenge in creating the LEM, the first manned vehicle designed to operate exclusively in the vacuum of space. The first new concept Grumman (and NASA) engineers had to learn was that the LEM could be any shape it needed to be. It didn't matter whether it was smooth or square, whether it had ninety-degree edges or boxes sticking out of it at odd angles. Aerodynamics and airflow were irrelevant here. The LEM only had to fit inside the conical shroud connecting the Saturn 4B upper stage and the Apollo service module. And, of course, it also had to be able to land itself on the surface of another planet, then take off again, and it mustn't weigh more than twenty-five thousand pounds.

What ultimately emerged, after five years of hard development, was a bug-like contraption with thrusters and antennas sticking out wherever they needed to be. Designed to operate in zero-G, it was so flimsy that its landing gear would break if you happened to load it with fuel while still on earth. The outer skin was so thin a dropped screwdriver could poke a hole in it.

With Grumman we had fewer quality control issues than we had with North American. But the LEM was coming together very slowly. We originally hoped to have it flying by summer 1967, but by the time I joined Apollo, no one thought that was realistic. On our first trip to Grumman as a crew, just before Christmas 1966, the assembly line carried mostly panels and wires, and a small amount of structure. Instead of spacecraft, what they had was spaghetti.

In late August 1966 Spacecraft 012, the one scheduled to be flown by Gus Grissom's Apollo 1 crew, was shipped to the Cape, even though over a hundred items remained to be finished or fixed. (A few hundred others would show up once 012 spent some time at the Cape). On August 25, Spacecraft 011 made a good unmanned test flight aboard a Saturn 1B.

Through the month of October, the Apollo 2 crews tried to check out 014, which was difficult because the spacecraft was still being put together. We were still hoping to fly a few months after Gus, Ed, and Roger, however, possibly around May 1967. The delays forced Mueller, Phillips, Shea, Gilruth, and other managers to start taking a hard look at the Apollo schedule.

In the middle of this, Wally Schirra pulled another one of his high-G maneuvers. He had always thought that the Apollo 2 mission was redundant. What was the point in flying another Block 1 spacecraft on a mission that would essentially duplicate the one flown by Gus and his crew? What would we learn? Wally wanted to fly an all-up, Block 2 mission, with his own lunar module. So one weekend late in October, he, Donn and Walt came up with a list of demands regarding their mission. Without consulting the rest of us (we had relatively little contact with Wally's crew), they turned it in to Joe Shea.

I never heard the precise details of what happened, but I assume the shit hit the fan, because in mid-November, during the Gemini 12 mission, I was called into Al Shepard's office. Deke was there, too, and they got right to it: "Look," they said, "we're swapping crews around. The Apollo 2 mission is cancelled. The new Apollo 2 mission, on two Saturn 1Bs, is going to be flown by McDivitt's crew. You're the commander backing them up, with Cernan and Young. Young for command module pilot, Cernan for lunar module pilot."

This sudden cancellation and shifting of crews left Wally, Donn, and Walt assigned as backups to Gus's crew. They weren't happy. In fact, when I saw Wally at a party at Dr. Chuck Berry's house a couple of nights later, he was still unglued, complaining that Deke and Al had "screwed him," that they had "destroyed" his career.

Wally's crew had gone from having their own mission to a dead-end backup job; that was tough to take. On the other hand, the move made all the sense in the world, since two of the three individuals on the crew were fairly inexperienced, and all of their training had been on the Block 1 spacecraft. Wally's relaxed work habits had caught up with him, too. Deke and Al just figured those three were not as ready for more challenging assignments as the other crews.

I was elated, of course. Here was my Apollo command. I went looking for Gene, to tell him the good news. We were backing up a very ambitious flight, and given the experience of our crew—five flights between us, including several rendezvous and an EVA—we would be certain to rotate to a downstream Apollo mission, possibly the first lunar landing. (Knowing that John Young was likely to be a little unhappy about having to work for me, however, I let Deke and Al tell him.) Deke still insisted that the command module pilot in every Apollo crew had to have experience in rendezvous.

That all assumed we would get Apollo flying at *all*, of course. Gus got so fed up with the command module simulator at the Cape that he hung a lemon on it. The team in Florida was so busy trying to keep up with a flood of changes North American was making in the flight article that they just couldn't get the simulator and spacecraft to match.

Spacecraft 012 finally got stacked atop its Saturn 1B booster in early January 1967. Launch was scheduled for the morning of February 21, on a fourteen-day mission.

On Friday afternoon, January 27, 1967, John, Gene and I were in Downey, California, at North American, where 012's sister spacecraft, 014, was undergoing similar tests, even though it would never fly. The newer Block 2 spacecraft were incomplete, so if we wanted to train as a crew in a real vehicle, we had to use 014.

It wouldn't have been easy to get 014 ready for flight, in any case. The spacecraft's cooling system had leaks, spilling a nasty water glycol mixture onto the floor. After the water evaporated you were left with a flammable glycol residue. We had all kinds of electrical and communications problems. We hated the new pressure suits built by ILC, which made our shoulders, wrists, and backache. The suits did nothing to enhance our mood as we worked through a day filled with computer alarms, electrical shorts, and delays. By four in the afternoon we had yet to get through a single successful countdown, and I called off the test. "Go to the Moon, hell," John Young snapped. "This bucket of bolts won't reach Earth orbit."

We struggled with the hatch—another Apollo monstrosity, a two-piece job that seemed to weigh a ton. Getting both open involved inserting a ratchet handle in half a dozen spots and cranking away, then pulling the pieces apart. It never took less than a couple of minutes. Today, when John got the inner hatch off, it fell on his feet. He called the hatch and its designers every name he could think of, and he knew quite a few.

As soon as I got out of the spacecraft and onto the workstand, a tech came up to me and said I had an emergency call from Al Worden. Al was an astronaut selected in April 1966, a West Point graduate and Air Force test pilot who was one of our support crew members. He was calling from the test control room of the large 290 Building at Downey. "Have you heard anything about a fire on the pad at the Cape?" he said when I answered the phone.

I knew that Gus, Ed, and Roger were doing a plugs-out test that day inside spacecraft 012. They were sealed in, and the spacecraft was operating on its own systems, just like a real launch. I was afraid the booster had caught on fire. "Are they all right?"

"It looks like the crew is dead."

At first I didn't understand what Al was telling me. "What the hell happened?"

"We don't have the details yet."

I was still thinking about a booster fire. "Al," I said, "are you sure the crew is dead?"

He spoke very slowly and seriously. "Yes, I'm sure. The crew is dead."

Shaking my head, I bent down and put my head back into the spacecraft, where John and Gene were still doing the final shutdown procedures and starting to slowly extricate themselves from the spacecraft. I said, "Come on, get out of there, quick!" They wanted to know what was going on. "I can't tell you here. Come on."

I led them down the steps to the main floor, and off to one side, where we could have some privacy. And I told them. Obviously they were both shocked. John had worked very closely with Gus for the better part of two years. He was friends with Ed White, too. And Gene had been good friends with Roger Chaffee. They lived next door to each other.

We skipped our showers and got into our street clothes, then went up to the office, where Al Worden was waiting. All he was able to tell us was that a fire had broken out in the Apollo spacecraft at 6:31 Eastern Time—3:31 where we were in L.A.—with the countdown held at T minus ten minutes. The crew was sealed inside the spacecraft, plugs out, pressurized to sixteen pounds per square inch, pure oxygen. When the hatches were finally opened, five minutes after the fire, the pad team found that Gus, Ed, and Roger were dead.

We needed to get back to Houston, so we just walked out to our rental cars and drove through rush hour traffic to Los Angeles International airport, where we changed into our flying suits. Gene and I got in one of our T-38s, and John and Al Worden got in the other, and we all took off. It was a clear night that gave you a lot of time to think. I wondered how we could have been so gung-ho that we overlooked fire, especially since we used pure oxygen.

After a refueling stop in El Paso, we landed at Ellington after midnight, Houston time. Since it was too late for a condolence call, I went straight home. Faye was upset, of course, but she had no more details than I did. I was exhausted, physically and mentally, so I went to bed.

First thing the next morning I went over to the Whites. Ed's two children, Eddie III and Bonnie let me in. Pat was still in the bedroom, sitting on the bed, devastated, but I went in to see her and give her a hug. Jim McDivitt, who was probably Ed's closest friend in the group, was also at the house, and so were Neil and Jan Armstrong, who lived next door. A little while later, Ed's father, a retired Air Force major general, and mother arrived from Florida. Ed's brother flew in from the Air Force Academy. The family gathered.

Ed and I were both Methodists and attended the same church in Seabrook. That's where a memorial service was held on Sunday, January 29. All seven of us from the second astronaut group chipped in for a bouquet of yellow flowers in the shape of the astronaut pin on a field of white flowers. The pastor, Reverend Connie Winborn, delivered the sermon.

Given Ed's love for West Point, the White family wanted him buried there. This caused a momentary problem with HQ and the White House, who had thought all three Apollo astronauts should be buried at Arlington on the same day. Ed's family insisted: West Point. John Young, who had worked so closely with Gus, went to Arlington, and so did Gene Cernan, who was escorting Roger's widow, Martha.

I flew to West Point with Pete Conrad in a T-38 for the ceremony on Tuesday, January 31. James McDonnell donated his corporate Jet-Star to fly the wives to the service. Neil Armstrong and Buzz Aldrin (who had graduated from West Point a year before Ed) decided to make it nonstop. They took off after Pete and I did, and we were on our second leg after refueling in Memphis when we heard them discussing their fuel situation. Finally, they had to declare an emergency and come straight in, landing at Stewart Air Force Base on fumes.

Apollo was on hold, all crew assignments suspended, while the accident investigation ramped up. Deke and Al told us we were likely to be assigned to various parts of the process. A board had been convened, headed by Floyd Thompson, the director of NASA Langley, an engineer from the old school. The astronaut representative was Frank Borman—a good move, given Frank's independence and honesty. He wasn't going to let anybody snow him.

The investigating board took Spacecraft 012 apart piece by piece and prepared a thousand-page report on what they found. At the same time, 014 was disassembled beside it. They weren't able to find an obvious, inescapable cause for the fire. The best they could do was pinpoint a possible electrical short in the lower left forward bay, near Gus Grissom's legs. The short had caused bare wires to burn and melt; in the hyperflammable, pure oxygen atmosphere, flames had quickly spread to the Velcro and netting inside the spacecraft, turning it into an inferno within seconds.

The one thing we knew already was that the spacecraft was full of flammable material. The original specifications required anything in there to be nonflammable up to temperatures of four hundred degrees Fahrenheit at five psi pure oxygen, the pressure used in orbit. But everyone seemed to forget that the center of a tiny electrical spark could reach six thousand degrees Fahrenheit.

The crew had put patches of Velcro all over the consoles, to hold pens and flight plans. There was Raschel netting, too, and nylon covers on the suits, and even things like a large block of Styrofoam the crew had brought in to help relieve the pressure on their backs during long hours of tests. The Styrofoam exploded like a bomb in that environment.

Worst of all, the crew had no means of quick egress. Within a few days of the fire, John Young and I sat down with Charlie Feltz, North American's chief engineer for the Apollo command and service module or CSM. Feltz had worried about the pure oxygen atmosphere from the very beginning and had even worked out a design for an explosive, outward-opening hatch back around 1962. But both issues had been pushed aside.

Among the three of us, we were able to come up with a concept for a hatch that could be opened by the crew within a few seconds. That's all it would have taken. Gus, Ed and Roger died of asphyxiation from carbon monoxide, not from burns. The intense fire had smothered itself, and then the wall of spacecraft 012 had ruptured. If the crew had been able to open that hatch within a few seconds, they would have suffered some burns, but probably would have been able to get out alive.

The issues of flammability and the hatch were among the most important, but the review board ranged far and wide, into North American and NASA decision-making, safety procedures, and quality control and documentation (a small socket wrench turned up inside the charred 012 spacecraft, and no one seemed to know how or when or why). There wasn't even a fire extinguisher inside 012 that day, and the test hadn't even been classified as "hazardous."

Within a month, Congress was holding hearings, and Jim Webb got blindsided by Senator Walter Mondale, who had gotten hold of a 1965 report by Gen. Sam Phillips on problems with North American. Webb had never seen it, so he was embarrassed and unhappy. Heads started to roll. Joe Shea, who seemed to be taking the deaths of the crew very personally, was moved out of the ASPO job to a holding place at headquarters. (He left NASA a few months later.) At North American, Harrison Storms was replaced by Bill Bergen, formerly the Titan program head at Martin. There were other changes, too.

Shea's replacement as head of the Apollo program office in Houston was George Low, and going to work for Low as his executive secretary was George Abbey, a former Air Force pilot who had come to the Manned Spacecraft Center in 1964 as a flight controller. Low's style was completely different from Joe Shea's; for example, he communicated better with Robert Gilruth and other center directors, including them in a spacecraft change control board. He would also listen to input from the flight crews.

And there were a lot of changes to be discussed, beginning with a redesign of the Apollo command module. There was an immediate fix-it list of a hundred-plus items, along with a larger wish list of about fifteen hundred. Simply coordinating all these changes—especially those originating with the astronauts—became Frank Borman's job. Eventually 1,697 changes would be suggested, and 1,341 would be implemented, ranging from redesigning the Apollo pressure suits to new procedures requiring the use of a mixed nitrogen-oxygen atmosphere in the spacecraft when it was on the pad.

Low asked me to deal with the troubled Apollo software, which was being developed under the famed Charles Stark Draper at the MIT Instrumentation Lab in Boston. Pete Conrad would be my deputy. For most of 1967, Pete and I lived in Boston, flying from Houston to Logan Airport, checking into the Sonesta Hotel, then walking to the Instrumentation Lab. They hated to see us coming.

The largest problem with the software was the sheer number of commands the crew was expected to enter during a typical flight. By the time you reached the Moon, you'd have been worn out from punching the buttons on the keypad. Just as seriously, the X-axis of the inertial measurement unit wasn't aligned with the X-axis of the spacecraft. It was offset by nearly thirty degrees because some designer noted that if the axes were aligned (as they should have been) and then the spacecraft had an off-nominal trajectory returning from the Moon, it *might* miss its landing point by as much as seven miles. That was just stupid, and we got it changed.

When the Apollo program came to a screeching halt, the Soviet manned space program was gearing up to resume manned launches. Soyuz 1 was to be launched on April 23, 1967, carrying Vladimir Komarov, a veteran of the first Voskhod mission in 1964. A day later, Soyuz 2 would be launched, with a crew of three—Valery Bykovsky (from Vostok 5), Aleksei Yeliseyev, and

Yevgeny Khrunov. Soyuz 1 would dock with 2, and then Yeliseyev and Khrunov would do an EVA, returning to earth with Komarov. So the Soviets would demonstrate the ability to maneuver, rendezvous, dock, and do EVA, half a dozen Gemini flights rolled into one.

Things went wrong, however, shortly after Soyuz 1 reached orbit. One of the solar power panels on the spacecraft failed to deploy, sharply limiting the amount of energy available. There were problems with the orientation system, too, and they made the power problem more acute because Soyuz didn't get to the right attitude to use the remaining solar panel. With Soyuz 1 running on batteries, flight controllers decided to cancel the second launch.

They also had to bring Komarov home on the seventeenth orbit because the batteries' lifetime was not much more than that. With failing guidance systems, Komarov couldn't get the Soyuz properly aligned for the first pass on the seventeenth, and ground control wasn't ready for another attempt until the nineteenth. With great difficulty, Komarov managed to get himself lined up for retrofire.

He made it that far, but when his main parachute deployed to slow him down, it failed to come out of its container properly. A reserve chute got tangled up with it, and Soyuz 1 hit the ground at over a hundred miles an hour, instantly killing Komarov. After several hours' delay, the Soviets reported the accident. Now their manned program was as dead in the water as ours was.

I heard very few of the details, even by the standards of the time, since I was representing NASA and the American space program in Montreal, Canada, at Expo '67. All I knew about Komarov's tragedy was what I read in the newspapers.

Shortly after I returned from Montreal, Deke Slayton called a meeting in the small conference room in Building 4. This was not a full pilot's meeting—aside from Deke, only eighteen astronauts were present, and with the exception of Wally Schirra, all were from the 1962 and 1963 groups.

The first thing Deke said was, "The guys that are going to make the first lunar landing are here in this room." I looked around. Here was Wally, the last of the Mercury guys on flight status. Not a great bet for the first landing, given his outbursts with Deke and Al over the Apollo 1 shuffle. But he, Donn Eisele, and Walt Cunningham already knew they would have the first manned

Apollo, now called Apollo 7. John, Gene, and I were assigned as backups for Wally's crew. That made sense; we had been backups for the second Apollo, and we just moved up a notch. Apollo 8, the first manned test of the lunar module, would be flown by Jim McDivitt, Dave Scott, and Rusty Schweickart, with Pete Conrad, Dick Gordon, and C. C. Williams as backups. The crew for Apollo 9, a manned test of the CSM and LM in a high Earth orbit, looping four thousand miles out, would be Frank Borman, Mike Collins, and Bill Anders, with Neil Armstrong, Jim Lovell, and Buzz Aldrin as backups.

Still to be assigned were the missions that would take the CSM and LM into lunar orbit and the big prize of the first lunar landing. I figured my crew as a good bet for one or the other. Deke went out of his way to tell us, "Be flexible. This stuff will change." We knew that. Apollo 7 wouldn't be flying for at least a year.

Congressional hearings into the Apollo fire ended in late April. Shortly afterward, the assignment of the Apollo 7 prime and backup crews was announced, and Frank, Wally, and I were invited to appear on the NBC News program, *Meet the Press*. We all flew to Washington with our wives for the taping, which took place on a Sunday morning. Afterward, Jim Webb invited us all to lunch at his house.

Webb spent a few minutes congratulating us on our television appearance and how we had supported the program then devoted the next half hour to complaints about Al Shepard and Al's investments, his arrogance, and, most of all, about the time Al went around Webb to JFK to try to get approval for Mercury-Atlas 10. I can still hear Webb's North Carolina voice saying, "That boah, Alan Shepudd."

It was a strange day.

On the afternoon of Friday, June 6, 1967, I was in my office in Building 4 when Ed Givens stopped by. My old friend from Annapolis, test-pilot school, and Gemini 9 was headed off to a meeting of the Quiet Birdmen's Club in Houston and wanted to know if I wanted to come along.

I couldn't, so we went our separate ways. Early the next morning about three-thirty I was sleeping so soundly I didn't hear the phone ring. Faye practically had to shout in my ear and shake me with the news: "Ed Givens is dead."

He was giving two other pilots, Bill Hall and Fran Dellorto, a ride back

---

to Ellington from the Birdmen's meeting. There was no alcohol involved; Ed was trying to find a way onto the Gulf Freeway in a poorly lit and badly marked part of Pearland when his Volkswagen slid into a ditch. Hall and Dellorto were injured, but Ed was killed. This was terrible news. I hurried over to the Givens house, just two blocks away, to see what I could do for Ada, Ed's wife.

There was a memorial service at our Methodist Church in Seabrook on June 8. Afterward, in a NASA-chartered C-47, I accompanied Ed's body to burial in his hometown of Quanah, Texas. Ed's death was especially tragic for his parents, Bill and Helen Givens. Their only other child, Ed's younger brother, Donald, had died in the crash of a Navy patrol aircraft in 1952. Ada, who faced raising three young children alone, was devastated, too, and I tried to help her receive the appropriate veteran's benefits and other support.

But we weren't through with funerals. Pete Conrad and I were in Boston at the MIT Draper Lab one day a few months later, on Thursday, October 6, when I got a call from Penny Study, our secretary. "Colonel Stafford," she said, in tears, "C. C. Williams has been killed." He had been flying from the Cape back to Houston, encountered some problems with his T-38, and tried to bail out. He hadn't made it.

C. C. had been assigned to Pete's crew as lunar module pilot, and Pete thought the world of him. I had the sad task of finding Pete to tell him. We made what calls we could from Boston then flew back to Houston the next day. C. C.'s wife, Beth, was pregnant at the time, too, though only a few individuals knew it.

On September 27, 1967, the first big Saturn 5 was ready for the start of countdown tests, which were supposed to be complete in six days; they took seventeen. The problems were understandable. NASA was trying to launch a vehicle the size and mass of a Navy destroyer, one with eleven new engines powered by new fuels, new pumps, and using new guidance.

It wasn't until November 9 that von Braun's baby was finally ready to take its first steps. John Young, Gene Cernan, and I were standing at the viewing site three and a half miles away, when the five first stage engines lit up. As the Saturn 5 slowly rose, we could feel the sound waves on our chests and had to shield our eyes against the glare. The vibration was so intense that Walter Cronkite's CBS News trailer practically shook apart.

That first Saturn carried a Block 1 command module, 017, atop an S-4B. They were placed in a perfect Earth orbit, and several hours later the S-4B fired to send the CM into the atmosphere at twenty-five thousand miles an hour, the speed it would attain on a return from the Moon. Everything about the flight went great. In spite of that triumph, though, 1967 was a tough year for manned space flight.

eleven

Steps to the Moon

With the new year, 1968, it felt as though things were starting to get back on track. The first new Block 2 command module, number 101, was taking shape in Downey under the supervision of John Healey. And the first lunar module had completed months of checkout at the Cape and on January 22 was finally ready for launch unmanned atop a Saturn 1B.

LM-1 was successfully placed in orbit and its descent engine was fired by remote control, testing its throttle and its shutdown capability. There were some computer glitches, but nothing we didn't think we could fix. The flight—known as Apollo 5[1]—went well enough that George Mueller and management scrubbed the second unmanned LM flight.

Aleksei Leonov and nine fellow cosmonauts from the first group completed their long years of study at the Zhukovsky Air Force Engineering Academy and officially graduated in January and February, 1968. This meant that they were free to resume full-time training and flying. Aleksei was put in charge of a group of ten military and civilian cosmonauts in the lunar program. The earth-orbital Soyuz program was recovering, too, preparing for a pair of unmanned launches that would rendezvous and dock automatically.

On March 27, 1968, a typical gloomy, cloudy day in the Moscow area, Aleksei and his group were making parachute jumps at a small airfield in the village of Kirzhach. While they were on the ground, they heard a MiG-15 roar overhead through the clouds. It seemed low and off-course, but other than that it was just a momentary incident. But when they returned to the Chkalov air base near Star City, they learned that Yury Gagarin and his flight instructor, Col. Vladimir Seryogin, were missing. The wreckage of their MiG-15 was found hours later. Both men had been killed.

Just in case we were thinking about getting arrogant, along came Apollo 6. This was the second unmanned launch of the Saturn 5, and it had problems shortly after liftoff. A violent fore-and-aft shaking (pogo) in the vehicle caused two of the five engines in the S-2 second stage to shut down prematurely. The three remaining second stage engines were able to extend their burn long enough to get the S-4B and Apollo stack to Earth-orbit velocity, when the S-4B would perform a final burn. But a crew would have had a wild ride and possibly an abort long before that. The viciousness of the pogo, which knocked off pieces of the service launch adaptor (SLA), could have damaged the lunar module. And the S-4B upper stage failed to relight for its second maneuver. I was at Downey the day of the Apollo 6 launch, and while I was disturbed by the reported problems, I knew von Braun and his very capable team at NASA Marshall would deal with them. Which they did.

Not long after this, Deke and Al called me in and confirmed that John Young, Gene Cernan, and I would be flying Apollo 10. They wanted us to get a jump on the training by tracking the assembly and checkout of LM-5 at Grumman. Gordo Cooper was assigned as my backup commander, Ed Mitchell backup lunar module pilot for Gene, and Donn Eisele as backup command module pilot for John. I asked Joe Engle, Jim Irwin, and Charlie Duke to start working as our support team. By May 1968 I had my own team of nine astronauts.

And the Air Force promoted me to full colonel. I received the word while working in the command module at Downey. The North American Rockwell customer relations team led by Walker "Bud" Mahurin, a World War II ace, threw a promotion party for me at the Tahitian Village, a motel close to the Rockwell Downey facility where the astronauts always stayed. Since the insignia for full colonel is a pair of silver eagles, as a joke Bud and his able deputies, Had Dixon, Ted Finnerman, and Beverly Gresham, presented me with two parrots in a cage. I took the birds home with me.

It was a quite a promotion party.

My old commander, Wally Schirra, was very tense as the launch of Apollo 7 approached. He clearly felt the full weight of the program riding on a successful mission and as a result became more openly critical and more sarcastic. At a crew equipment review one time, rather than give an analysis of the problem, he simply threw some of the support gear on the table and said, "This is a bunch of junk." Personally, he and I got along fine. We had worked together through most of 1964 and all of 1965. But he was having a tough time.

Two weeks before the scheduled launch, he announced that he was retiring from the astronaut corps, NASA, and the Navy. He felt this announcement freed him to comment openly on any issues. For example, he got unhappy that Deke was going to be at the Cape rather than in Houston and that Al Shepard wasn't going to be in Houston, either. So instead of having me at the Cape, my normal post as his backup, Wally wanted me in Houston mission control as his "personal representative," to consult on any decisions regarding the flight.

On the night of October 10, I had dinner with Wally, Donn, and Walt, then headed to Patrick Air Force Base and my T-38, returning to Houston and leaving John Young and Gene Cernan to do the prelaunch checkout of the spacecraft on the pad.

The morning of October 11 arrived with high winds from the east gusting to between twenty and twenty-five knots, beyond the abort envelope of eighteen. (If you aborted at a low altitude, the winds would blow the command module back onshore and force a painful, possibly injurious touchdown on land.) Everything was going so well, at the Cape and in Houston, however, that no one wanted to call off the launch just because, for a few seconds here and there, we might be violating one of our abort criteria. George Low was part of the group discussing the situation in mission control. It was his view, shared by Glynn Lunney, the ascent flight director, that the Saturn's record of reliability made it unlikely we'd be faced with an abort in the first few seconds.

Everything was looking good, and at 10 A.M., the largest rocket ever to carry astronauts into space roared off Pad 34 as Apollo 7 climbed safely into orbit. Over the next few days, Apollo performed beautifully. Its fuel cells worked well, producing electricity and potable water. The service propulsion system got a good workout. We even shot the first series of television shows from orbit, using a new black-and-white camera.

The only thing that wasn't working smoothly was the crew. Wally had been quite adamant about how he wanted his mission run, and even when he had lost battles prior to launch, he hadn't given up. The television camera was one. The crew was supposed to turn it on for the first time on day two of the mission, but Wally scrubbed it, annoying NASA management and public affairs.

Making matters worse, Wally developed a cold, which he passed on to Donn and Walt. All three crew members discovered an unpleasant fact of space flight: Mucus doesn't drain in zero-G. So they were sick and cranky, and it showed in their dealings with Glynn Lunney and Gene Kranz's flight control teams. Wally was never one to be shy about letting people know how he felt, and Walt followed his lead. The slight surprise to me was Donn, usually fairly easygoing. When he started snapping, "I'd like to talk to the man, if that's the word, who developed this procedure," I knew conditions aboard Apollo 7 must be ugly.

Chris Kraft, the head of flight operations, was getting angrier with each incident. He wanted Deke or Al or me to get the crew to behave. But none of us could. The biggest argument came prior to re-entry. Mission rules called for the crew to be buttoned up in their pressure suits, helmets sealed. But Wally, who still had a stuffed-up head ten days after launch, was afraid that the expected rapid changes in pressure during the final descent might rupture his eardrums. He announced that the crew were going through re-entry *without* the helmets.

Deke got on the line and tried to talk him into it. "Sorry, Deke," Wally said. "Unless you can come up here and put them on for us, we're coming home with the helmets off." That was the whole problem with a crew in revolt: You were on the ground, and they were in orbit. There wasn't anything you could do.

That is, not until they returned. Wally had already announced his plans to retire from the space program after Apollo 7, so he was immune to punishment. (Deke did have a few choice words for him on the carrier after splashdown, though.) Donn and Walt were a whole different matter. Chris Kraft said quite openly that they shouldn't fly again. Donn was rotated to a previously assigned backup job on Apollo 10, but clearly it was a temporary step into oblivion. Walt Cunningham was shuffled off to the Apollo Applications Program.

On November 12, 1968, NASA made official what John, Geno, and I had known for six months: We would fly Apollo 10 in May. Suddenly a lot of behind-the-scenes maneuvers broke into the light of day. Back in late July 1968, George Low, looking at the lagging lunar module delivery schedule, had concluded there was no way McDivitt's crew would be flying LM-3 before late February 1969. That left a three-to-four month gap in the Apollo schedule. And here we had the Soviets breathing down our necks. George Low was cleared for CIA recon materials that showed the Soviets getting ready to launch circumlunar missions and building launch pads for their gigantic N-1 manned lunar booster (American analysts called it either the Type G or, for those who thought the administrator was crying wolf, "Webb's Giant").

Georgy Beregovoi, the first Soviet cosmonaut who had a background as a test pilot, was launched aboard Soyuz 3 on October 26, 1968. The next day he rendezvoused with the unmanned Soyuz, but his docking attempt failed. Nevertheless, he returned safely after four days in space, requalifying Soyuz for manned missions.

Low figured, rightly, that the Soviets were in a race to send cosmonauts on a free-return trajectory around the Moon. So why not send an Apollo command and service module there in December 1968 and beat them? The lunar module wouldn't be ready, but von Braun's team could possibly have the third Saturn 5 ready for launch by then. (All of this was predicated on the assumption that Apollo 7 would be a success.)

Low had run the idea past Gilruth, Faget, Kraft, Slayton, and the other decisionmakers at MSC. Once they were on board, the contractors were informed. Almost everyone thought it was a great idea. Frank Borman was summoned back from Downey one weekend in August and offered the choice: Would you rather fly the second manned lunar-module mission in May 1969, or go to the Moon in December 1968? Frank didn't hesitate. He said he and his crew, which was Jim Lovell and Bill Anders, could be ready.

The only parties who seemed hesitant were Jim Webb and George Mueller.

Finally, on the recommendations of his senior advisers, including Gen. Sam Phillips, Mueller and Webb agreed to Low's proposal. But Webb seemed disturbed by it. Maybe it was fallout from the public beating he took over the Apollo fire. But even before Wally's crew took off, while the around-the-Moon decision was still being debated privately, Webb announced he was stepping down as NASA administrator. Thomas Paine, who had replaced Robert Seamans as Webb's deputy in January, took over on an acting basis.

On November 15, 1968, the unmanned Zond 6 looped around the Moon. Three days later, it landed inside the Soviet Union. Western analysts could see that the next favorable window for a Soviet circumlunar launch was December 6—more than two weeks before the window opened for Apollo 8. *Time* magazine ran a cover showing an astronaut and a cosmonaut racing toward the Moon. But there was no launch in December or in January 1969 or the following March. The Soviets never even attempted a manned circumlunar mission, though they had the hardware and it seemed to have proven itself.

Well, that was the problem. The hardware *hadn't* proven itself. Zond 6 had suffered a catastrophic depressurization before re-entering the atmosphere. This caused sensors to malfunction, and its recovery parachute opened too early. So Zond 6 piled into the ground about ten miles from the same pad it had launched from. The Soviets had managed to recover a couple of beat-up film canisters from the wreckage, but a crew would have been dead. The state commission, and Vasily Mishin, head of the Korolyov Bureau, insisted on another unmanned launch.

This was a bitter decision for Aleksei Leonov and civilian flight engineer Oleg Makarov, two of the candidates to fly that circumlunar flight. "We could have done it," Aleksei would tell me years later. "We could have beaten the Apollo 8 crew. But Mishin was a blockhead."

Gene Cernan and I watched Apollo 8 like most Americans, on television. We were at Grumman on Long Island, getting familiar with our new lunar module, having switched from LM-5 to LM-4 with the shuffle of the McDivitt and Borman crews. The big Saturn 5 put Frank, Jim, and Bill into a good orbit, where they lit up the S-4B and headed for the Moon. The only glitch was that Frank got a bad case of vomiting and diarrhea. Fortunately, though Jim and Bill had brief moments of discomfort, they didn't catch whatever affected Frank.

They arrived at the Moon on Christmas Eve 1968, passing out of sight of mission control and everyone on planet Earth as they swung around the farside and made a very lonely burn into lunar orbit. For the next twenty hours they took photographs, including the famous one of the earth rising over the lunar landscape, and discovered that the Moon had a few surprises in store for us: Something was perturbing Apollo 8's orbit. Every time it came around the Moon, it was in a slightly different place than our trajectory people would have predicted. It turned out this was due to previously unknown mass concentrations (mass cons) inside the Moon. One of the crew's biggest contributions was simply learning how to identify lunar features from an altitude of sixty miles, how to correlate what they saw with what our Lunar Orbiter photos showed.

Finally, after a wonderful reading, by the crew, of passages from Genesis as they flew over the seas and craters of the Moon, Frank, Jim, and Bill fired their service propulsion system and launched out of lunar orbit. As Apollo 8 came around the Moon and headed home, Jim Lovell told mission control, "Please be advised, there is a Santa Claus." It was quite a moment in a mission that had been full of great moments.

Our management was so pleased with Apollo 8 that we started getting a little arrogant. I was down at the Cape shortly after the Apollo 8 crew returned, when I ran into George Mueller at a restaurant and club. I was with Pete Conrad and Gene Cernan. "Hey, Tom," George said. "We'll launch McDivitt next month, then have you make the first lunar landing a month after that."

All I could do was laugh. "George," I said, "I'm all for a rapid schedule, but our lunar module is too heavy, and we don't have the procedures worked out for a rendezvous around the Moon. They're different from earth orbit, you know. Show me a handbook where they're completed." The software for the LM's powered descent was also still being written. "I would love to land on the Moon, but it's going to take quite a few months."

"Oh, we can still do it," he insisted.

I couldn't tell if he was serious or not. I finally said, "George, you may launch Apollo 10 for a lunar landing in two months, but the flight crew won't be on it."

There was just so much to do.

During the first week in January, Deke assigned Neil Armstrong, Mike

Collins, and Buzz Aldrin as the crew of Apollo 11. Neil and Buzz had been on the backup crew for 8; Mike Collins had originally been assigned as command module pilot on Frank's crew, only to lose out when he developed a bone spur in his neck that required surgery. He had lost out on the first flight around the Moon only to get what could be—depending on how Apollos 9 and 10 went—the first lunar landing.

But Apollo 9 and 10 were big ifs at that point. The lunar module had only made one unmanned test, in January 1968. It was successful, but just barely. Now Jim McDivitt and Rusty Schweickart, who had been living with the LM for almost three years, were finally going make the first flight of a manned spacecraft that could not return you to Earth. Rendezvous and docking were essential, and here the responsibility fell on Dave Scott, the command module pilot. He had to be able to fly the command module (CSM) himself, in case Jim and Rusty ran into problems. One other major mission objective was to have Rusty do an EVA using the new ILC suit for Apollo.

Because the CSM and LM would be flying separately for a while, they needed separate radio call signs. So Jim's crew was the first since Gemini 3 (a.k.a. "Molly Brown") to officially name its spacecraft. The CSM became "Gumdrop" and the LM became "Spider."

John and Gene and I watched the Apollo 9 launch, which went fine, at the Cape, then headed for Houston. We wanted to be in mission control for the LM separation and testing. The crew spent most of their first two days doing checkout on Spider, much as you would in an Apollo lunar mission, during the climb to the Moon. They also tried to deal with the fact that Rusty was sicker than hell, so sick they had to postpone the EVA. Jim didn't want his lunar module pilot throwing up inside a pressure suit. When they were finally able to clear him for a limited EVA, Jim and Rusty climbed into Spider, sealed it off, depressurized it, and opened the front hatch. Rusty crawled out on the front porch and proved that the suit worked well.

On day three, Jim and Rusty buttoned up Spider again, this time to maneuver to a point a hundred miles away and behind Gumdrop. Then they came back and made rendezvous, docking safely after six hours of solo flight. The LM had performed well, and Jim had found no problems flying it standing up.

Now it was our turn.

twelve

"Houston, Tell the World We Have Arrived!"

No sooner had Apollo 9 splashed down than some of the NASA managers started talking—again—about moving the first landing forward to Apollo 10. After all, they reasoned, we had flown around the Moon and tested the lunar module. Did it make sense to fly a quarter million miles again, get to within fifty thousand feet of the surface, then come home without landing?

Gene Cernan and I would have loved to be the first astronauts to walk on the Moon. But there were still too many unknowns to make it feasible for our flight. The computer procedures that had worked for Jim and Rusty in Earth orbit had to be redone for lunar orbit, and all kinds of communication and trajectory matters had to be resolved. The software for the powered descent and landing did not yet exist, and the procedures were incomplete. I hadn't flown the lunar-landing training vehicle, which was still grounded, following Neil Armstrong's crash the previous May.

And there was one basic practical obstacle: LM-4 was *too heavy* to take off from the surface of the Moon and reach lunar orbit. It had not been subjected to Grumman's Super Weight Improvement Program (SWIP), in which NASA paid a bonus of ten thousand dollars for every pound removed from the vehicle. LM-4 had always been scheduled for testing in Earth or lunar orbit. Our former LM, number 5, *was* light enough, but wouldn't be ready for flight until July 1969. No. The Apollo 10 "close encounter" was necessary if Apollo 11 were going to make a landing. And that's what we trained to fly.

Between us, John, Gene, and I had made five previous space flights. We had experience in rendezvous, docking, and EVA. We were, in fact, the most experienced astronaut crew ever sent into space until the Shuttle era started to mature. Knowing we had a good knowledge base already, I was able to let John "José" Young deal primarily with command module 106, while Gene and I concentrated on LM-4. As the next crew in line, we now had priority on simulators at the Cape, and that's where we spent March, April, and May 1969, mastering our flight plan and rehearsing the split-second timing needed for the execution of hundreds of different tasks. We also rehearsed procedures for every possible contingency.

Part of the preparation for missions involving both command and service modules was the selection of call signs. McDivitt's choice of Gumdrop for the CM and Spider for the LM had seemed a little frivolous to NASA HQ, but the names had the virtue of being descriptive.

John, Gene and I didn't make HQ any happier when we selected "Charlie Brown" for the CM and "Snoopy" for the LM. In our defense, however, NASA had for years given out Snoopy pins for outstanding quality work by members of its team. I had personally handed out a few dozen myself. So the choice of Snoopy was a way of acknowledging the contributions of the hundreds of thousands of people who got us there. Once you had Snoopy, Charlie Brown couldn't be far away.

One thing that always surprised me about Deke Slayton and most of the Mercury astronauts was their indifference—or animosity—toward the public affairs side of the manned space program. It was clear to me that the American public was paying for Apollo and deserved as much access as it could get. They should see the wonders we saw. Hasselblad photos and 8 mm movies were great, but nobody saw them until after a mission was over.

What better way to take viewers along to the Moon than by using color television? But Deke and Wally had resisted the inclusion of a black-and-white camera on Apollo 7, though Deke eventually came to accept and even embrace the idea. Borman's crew carried the same fuzzy camera as Wally's did. Apollo 9 had nothing. I thought we could do better.

After proposing the idea to George Low, I got together with a small team of NASA engineers in Houston, and we designed a color television camera that would be small enough and light enough to carry aboard Apollo 10. The color imaging system was the same one originally developed (then discarded) by CBS-TV back in the early 1950s, using a spinning wheel of blue, red, and yellow colors to encode signals, which would then be decoded by a synchronized wheel in mission control. We obtained two low-light-level TV camera tubes originally developed for use by the military in Vietnam (and still classified), two lenses from a French camera, and an actuating motor from a Minuteman missile and put the new unit together. We didn't know if it would function, or even if it would be finished on time. But the skunk works team came through, and the camera was installed on Apollo 10 only ten days before launch.

A tanking problem during tests on the first stage of our Saturn 5, number 505, reminded us that we were breaking new ground every day. Our Saturn 5 was going to be the first launched from Pad 39B—the four previous Saturn 5s had been launched from 39A. NASA wanted to have two pads functioning in case of an accident. A new pad also meant a new firing room. So we faced several "firsts" on just the launch phase. That gave me some second thoughts early the morning of March 11, 1969, as I watched 505 being rolled from the vertical assembly building or VAB to the pad, knowing that workers were still rushing to finish the paint job on the umbilical tower

The workload for Apollo 10 was so intense, it wasn't until I was down at the beach house, looking toward our Saturn 5 on Pad 39B as the support structure was pulled away, that it really hit me that *tomorrow* I was going to be riding on top of that monster to the Moon! That was exhilarating.

That night John, Gene, and I had a private dinner with James McDonnell and Vice President Spiro Agnew as our guests. The vice president to lead a task force to lay out the future of the United States in space—a job I would find myself repeating twenty years later.

Also present at dinner was Gordo Cooper, my backup commander, who then, according to our new Apollo procedures, got into a T-38 and flew to Houston, to serve as the crew representative in mission control. Even though he was doing his second backup job in a row, Gordo had been very supportive all through the year he had served in that capacity for me. I had no complaints about his attitude. Which isn't to say he was ready to step in for me. Deke Slayton had to encourage Gordo to work harder. And some weeks prior to launch, Deke had said to me, "Damn it, Tom, you'd better not get sick on me."

I had no plans to do that.

With our launch scheduled for lunchtime, we were awakened at a relatively normal hour. We had the usual big breakfast of steak and eggs—really a necessity, given the unpredictability of our next opportunity for a meal—then headed off for suiting.

Buttoned up in our bubble helmets, carrying portable air conditioners, we walked down the hallway to the bus. Waiting by the door was Jamie Flowers, one of our secretaries, holding a giant stuffed Snoopy dog. I patted him on the nose for luck, John gave him a little swipe. Gene Cernan put his arm around Jamie and Snoopy and tried to take them both with us.

Saturn 5 number 505 ignited on Pad 39B at 12:49 P.M., May 18, 1969. It was very different from the Titan 2, which got off the pad fairly quickly. The Saturn sat as the thrust from the five first-stage engines built up, then slowly started climbing. After two seconds, it literally started to lean away to get clearance from the tower. In fact, it took eleven seconds just to clear the structure.

The ride on the S-1C first stage was smooth, nothing but a guttural roar you felt rather than heard. We pitched and rolled as planned, heading out over the Atlantic for over two minutes. Then it was time for staging. Jim McDivitt had warned me to expect a sharp jolt when the first stage shut down, and he was right: We went from nearly five Gs to zero in a fraction of a second, flying toward the control panel. But unlike McDivitt, who got what he described as a solid jolt, we got a sharp, nasty ripple, no doubt exaggerated by the fact that we were no longer pressurizing suits once we got into the command module. (McDivitt's crew had re-pressurized, so their straps were looser). The shutdown felt like being in a train wreck.

I was trying to hold on as the S-1C shook us back and forth. It turned out there were two reasons for that: The Marshall engineers had shaved twenty-thousand pounds of metal out of that stage, making the booster walls more flexible and more prone to pogo. Also, there was a ground stabilization bar inside the cockpit that connected our crew couches to the rear bulkhead. It was supposed to be removed before launch, but somebody forgot. The bar magnified the pogo.

The S-2 second stage lit up its five J-2 engines, pinning us back in our seats. At the proper time, John activated the switches and the escape tower and shroud fired off one second later, giving us our first view out the windows, where we saw flames from the rocket exhaust of the launch escape system.

Another *wham!* We felt another, smaller ripple as the second stage shut down after five minutes. More spiked vibrations, but fewer and for a shorter time than the earlier shutdowns. Then the S-4B third stage fired its single J-2.

Eleven minutes after launch, we were in orbit.

Glynn Lunney and the team in mission control were concerned that our rough ride to orbit might have damaged the LM, but nothing showed up on their telemetry, so we were cleared for the translunar injection maneuver on our second revolution. As we approached night-darkened Australia, our cap-com Charlie Duke radioed the "go." John, Gene, and I, flying with our heads down, felt the S-4B ignite. Within moments we had burst back into the day side of Earth, which was already getting rounder and smaller below. As we climbed, Australia and the South Pacific quickly drifted out the tops of our windows.

As our speed rose, however, so did a disturbing sensation from the S-4B, a kind of flutter. The vibrations grew so strong we could not read dials on the control panel. I had my hand on the abort handle, but couldn't bring my-self to turn it. "We're experience frequency vibrations," I radioed, literally having to spit out a syllable at a time. It felt like flutter, though there were no aerodynamic forces that could cause such a phenomenon. In any case, an abort would leave us in a giant, looping orbit. There would be no visit to the Moon, no test of the LM, just a two-day wait for re-entry. I told myself, If she's going to blow, she's going to blow.

Then, shutdown. We'd made it in one piece. I did ask mission control to check their telemetry. (It turned out that the helium vent valves used to pres-surize tanks in the S-4B had caused the oscillation, and the problem was fixed for future missions.) While the engineering teams in Houston and elsewhere looked into that, we headed for the Moon.

Our next mission milestone, four hours after launch, was to separate from the S-4B stack, move off, turn around and come back for the lunar module. José flew the maneuver, which was called transposition and docking. I took this opportunity to fire up our TV camera, giving the world their first color look at the earth falling away beneath us—and, more importantly, allowing Houston to watch over our shoulders. This was the first live color television picture ever transmitted from space—certainly from a manned spacecraft. And our little skunk works camera was so good you could see the rivets on Snoopy's metal skin as we closed in for the docking.

The docking mechanism on the Apollo command module was an unheralded engineering marvel. It allowed us to lock together two spacecraft massing over fifty tons, yet it could also be disassembled quickly, allowing us to pass from one vehicle to the other. And then it could be reassembled and still function. Imagine a Swiss watch that was able to withstand the impact of an eighteen-wheel semi truck. The Soviets were unable to duplicate this technology at the time: Their Soyuz and lunar spacecraft could dock, but they had no tunnel. Cosmonauts had to move from one to the other by space walk.

In fact, I spent more time worrying about the docking mechanism than I did about the recovery parachutes. Fortunately, it all worked very well. John slipped the probe on the end of the adaptor into the drogue atop the LM, giving us a soft dock. "We have a capture," I radioed to Houston. "We haven't fired yet." That is, the twelve latches around the rim of the probe hadn't immediately fired.

Then they did, *bam-bam-bam-bam.*

Four and a half hours after we had lifted off from Pad 39B, we separated Charlie Brown and Snoopy from the S-4B stage. As we moved off, Houston commanded small rocket motors on the stage to fire, sending it off on a trajectory away from us. By now we were thirty thousand miles out from Earth and slowing down. Only now did we finally get a chance to catch our breath and take a look back. Blue and white, the size of a basketball, Earth was still literally shrinking before our eyes. For the first and only time in my space flights, I felt strange. It was a long, long way from the windmill on that farm near May, Oklahoma.

Living aboard Apollo, especially with the lunar module attached to it, was far easier than living on Gemini. It was almost like having an apartment in space. We were able to eat, sleep, and do television shows with relative ease. During our broadcast showing the Earth receding into space, I had radioed, "You can tell the members of the British Flat Earth Society that they are wrong: The Earth is round." Their president had a message for me the next day: "Colonel Stafford, it may be round, but it's still flat, like a disk."

On our second day in space, Geno Cernan got his chance to open up Snoopy. When he came back a few moments later, however, his hair and eyebrows were full of white flecks of insulation. He looked like a hound dog who'd been in a chicken coop. A Mylar cover on the outside of the command module's tunnel hatch had torn, releasing a cloud of white fiberglass. The particles itched like hell and it took us hours to clean up what we could. Most of the stuff got swept up by the command module's circulation system and deposited on the filters. Of course, that meant we were breathing the particles, too. It could have been worse, I suppose: Instead of fiberglass, it could have been some kind of asbestos.

By Tuesday morning, May 20, we had climbed to a distance of 150,000 miles from Earth, our speed dropping to a poky twenty-five hundred miles an hour. As we approached the point where the Moon's gravity was greater than Earth's, our speed began to pick up, reaching fifty-seven hundred miles an hour as we fell toward the Moon. Our trajectory had been so accurate that three of our four planned mid-course correction burns had been canceled. We were, in fact, only 1.15 miles off course.

At a distance of nine thousand miles from the Moon, we did another telecast for viewers at home. I noted that now the Earth appeared to be between a grapefruit and an orange in size. And it was now half an Earth. But I couldn't describe the Moon because we hadn't seen it yet. During the entire mission we had been facing its nighttime side, which was almost totally black. Peering through his navigation equipment, John Young had been able to find a place in the sky where the stars were occluded, so we were pretty sure the Moon was out there. But it was still a little unusual. I told Houston, "We'll take your word for it that it's there."

It wasn't until we were preparing for the critical engine burn that would put us in lunar orbit, after we had dipped around the limb of the Moon, losing contact with Earth that the surface suddenly appeared to us—bright and rocky, and only sixty miles below. "God, that Moon is beautiful!" Geno said.

"We're right on top of it!" I told him to get his head back in the cockpit. If for some reason the service propulsion system (SPS) failed to light, we would swing right around the Moon and head home. More worrisome was the possibility that it might fire but for less than the programmed time. That could be bad.

Right on time, we fired the SPS, which slowed us to thirty-seven hundred miles an hour and put us in orbit sixty miles above the surface of the Moon. I pitched the spacecraft over so we could get a good view of the surface. We were looking at the so-called farside of the Moon, the tide-locked side facing away from Earth. It was full of unfamiliar mountains and craters and seemed pretty chewed up. Here was the giant crater Tsiolkovsky, named by the Soviets because it was one of the few features that showed up on the first pictures taken of the farside back in 1959.

It was early morning, lunar time, and the colors ran from white to black to gray to light tan to very pale yellow, with slightly reddish peaks on the craters and mountain tops. Then we saw our first Earthrise, a little blue and white ball, two-thirds the size of a baseball, that popped up from the horizon very quickly. We could recognize Baja California and the polar ice cap.

Mission control was awaiting word, Joe Engle calling, "Apollo 10, Houston, over." They had tracking data, of course, so when we emerged from behind the Moon on time, they knew our burn had gone as planned.

"Houston," I said, "tell the world we have arrived."

All too soon, we entered the darkness of nighttime and saw earthshine, which rendered the rocky surface a beautiful pale blue. Then we saw our second sunrise and Earthrise. It was every bit as inspiring as the first. We also did another television transmission, and Gene moved over to Snoopy to make sure the lunar module had come through the LOI burn in good shape. He told Houston, "You watch Snoopy well tonight and make him sleep good, and we'll take him out for a walk and let him stretch his legs in the morning."

After a solid night's sleep and breakfast, I joined Gene aboard Snoopy the next morning, running through the checklist in preparation for the day's work. Right away, we ran into problems with the docking adaptor and tunnel. After closing the LM tunnel hatch, John unlocked each CM docking-tunnel latch so the two spacecraft were held together by three small latches on the end of the docking probe. This had to hold the force of five pounds per square inch acting over the door of the docking tunnel, well over a ton of force.

Then the pressure in the tunnel between command and lunar modules wouldn't bleed down, probably due to a clogged vent somewhere. We needed to lose that pressure to know whether our hatches were secure. I finally checked it by slightly reducing the pressure inside Snoopy.

After that we had an unexplained twist of 3.5 degrees in the alignment between the two spacecraft. That wasn't an immediate issue, but it might portend a problem on recapture. We postponed the undocking for a whole revolution trying to figure that one out. Finally, with Houston's agreement, we just decided to take the chance.

When we disappeared around the Moon on our eleventh orbit, Charlie Brown and Snoopy were still docked. When we appeared on the other side, we were fifty feet apart, flying formation. "You'll never know how big this thing gets when there ain't nobody in it but one guy," John told us.

"You'll never know how small it looks when you're as far away as we are," Gene replied.

We were running through our preburn checklist very smoothly, until we got to rendezvous radar. There was no signal from Charlie Brown, which mean that we couldn't rendezvous and couldn't even proceed with a descent burn. Houston suggested that John recycle the switch, which seemed to solve that problem. Then we lost the communications link between Charlie Brown and Houston. A quick check of the system showed that a breakdown had occurred in the line between Houston and the tracking station in Goldstone, California. I was getting testy. "Tell them to get with it!" I said.

They did, and we were given a go for DOI—descent orbit insertion. "Okay, José," I radioed to John Young. "Say 'adios,' and we'll see you back in about six hours."

"Don't accept any TEI updates while we're gone," Gene joked. That is, don't leave the Moon without us.

We fired a small burst from the descent stage propulsion system to put us in an elliptical orbit with an apolune (high point) of 195 miles and a perilune (low point) of only nine. That perilune would occur right over the proposed landing site for Apollo 11, in the Sea of Tranquillity. The elliptical orbit also caused Snoopy to fall well behind Charlie Brown.

As we began to descend, the rocky surface of the Moon loomed closer and closer. Distances were hard to judge. We were only thirty-five thousand feet above the highest peaks, not much more than a commercial airliner cruising above the surface of the earth, but since the Moon had no atmosphere, and thus no clouds, smog, or other distortion, and no cities or highways, you lacked the usual visual cues. We had another brief communication problem, which prevented Houston and capcom Charlie Duke from talking to us, but it cleared up. "We is down among 'em, Charlie!" Gene radioed.

"I hear you're weaving your way up the freeway," Charlie said.

Working with geologists, who had created maps of the Moon using data from unmanned lunar orbiters, we had given names to the features along that "freeway," including a rill that paralleled our flight path. We called it "US 1." A range of low mountains to the left of the proposed landing site earned the name "Oklahoma Hills." A second rill eventually split into two craters; since the structure looked like a snake's head, one crater was dubbed "Diamondback" and the other "Sidewinder." Scientist-astronaut Jack Schmitt, a key member of the geology support team, named a ridge near the site for my wife, Faye.

Knowing that, with luck, Neil Armstrong would be flying this same approach in a couple of months, I tried to give him, and the rest of the world, some idea of what we were seeing. (The color TV camera was still aboard Charlie Brown.) "It looks a lot smoother than some of the orbiter photos show," I said. "I estimate twenty-five to thirty-five percent to be a semiclear area, so if the LM has enough hover time, based on what we can see from fifty thousand feet, it should not have a problem. But if you come down in the wrong area and don't have enough hover time, you're going to have to shove off."

Observations aside, one critical milestone was a test of the LM's landing radar, built by Teledyne Ryan. If it didn't lock onto the lunar surface by a certain point, you had to abort the powered descent and go back up. Fortunately, the radar worked beautifully, locking on well in excess of the altitude demanded by the specs.

I was snapping pictures of the pass over Tranquillity, a shot every three seconds. Just as we were starting to climb out, the camera jammed, and I saw a puff of smoke emerging from it. "Goddamn Hasselblad," I said, frustrated. (After the mission, I apologized to Victor Hasselblad, whose company made great cameras, for taking his name in vain.) The sheer size of the features below was so amazing that I had forgotten I was broadcasting to the whole world.

At one point, I was so impressed that I said, "There's Censorinus," referring to a large crater with dramatic black striations and gigantic boulders on its rim, "just bigger than shit."

Down in mission control, Jack Schmitt was asked by a reporter, "*What did Colonel Stafford say?*"

He said, "Oh, there's Censorinus . . . bigger than Schmitt."

We flew into the dark side, climbed out to apolune, then began coming down again for our second and last pass in Snoopy. Gene and I prepared to jettison the descent stage and fire the ascent engine to shape our orbit for rendezvous with Charlie Brown. We were upside down in relation to the surface of the Moon, flying backwards and heading into night time when the thrusters began to fire. My attitude indicators showed a slight yaw rate. But looking out the window and at the main attitude indicator, I knew we didn't have one. Telemetry suggested we might have an electrical anomaly, so I started to troubleshoot the problem.

Gene and I had taken off our helmets and gloves for a brief time during our flight in Snoopy, but we had them back on now. It was hard to reach and even harder to hit the right switch, and I got the wrong one, flipping the AGS—abort guidance system—to AUTO when it should have been left in HOLD ALTITUDE.

Whoop! The whole lunar module, ascent and descent stage, flipped end over end. "Son of a bitch," Gene said, not knowing we still had a hot mike, "something's wrong with the gyro."

Something was wrong, though not with the gyro. By activating the AGS, I had, in effect, told Snoopy's radar and the LM's X-axis to start looking for Charlie Brown *right now.* The AGS was causing the lunar module to flip around. My immediate concern was our attitude indicator, which was going toward the red zone, meaning we were in danger of tumbling our three-gimbal inertial platform—screwing up our guidance system.

I grabbed the attitude controller, switched to manual, and blew off the descent stage to give my hundred-pound thrusters more effect. (They would only have to maneuver a ten-thousand-pound ascent stage, not a combined thirty-thousand-pound vehicle.) Within a few seconds, I managed to get

Snoopy's ascent stage under control. We still had forty seconds before the scheduled shaping burn.

John Young, meanwhile, had heard our momentary excitement. "I don't know what you guys are doing, but knock it off. You're scaring me."

With good reason. Any delay in the burn or mistake in attitude or trajectory would have been greatly magnified in the one-sixth gravity. But we made it right on time, giving ourselves another noticeable jolt. (The ascent engine was, essentially, right in the cabin of the LM itself. There was no avoiding it.)

As we rose toward a rendezvous with Charlie Brown, our only lingering concern was the docking probe mechanism. Had it been damaged by our abrupt separation under pressure? If we couldn't redock, we would have to maneuver the two spacecraft into close formation. Gene and I would have to seal our pressure suits, depressurize Snoopy, and open the front hatch while John did the same with Charlie Brown. We would then have to crawl out of Snoopy and over to Charlie Brown—without having the spacecraft docked together and without any bridging handrails. We weren't anxious to try that.

Charlie Brown loomed closer and closer, a welcome sight. From John's point-of-view, we were upside down, our feet in the air. Our goal at this point was to get to the right attitude and let him come to us. (The command module, with its greater mass, had finer control than the LM in maneuvers like this.)

Just then Earth came back over the horizon. Joe Engle was now our capcom, and he asked for our status. "Houston," I said, "we're only about three feet apart. Stand by. We're about ready to dock. Everything's good. Don't call us, we'll call you."

Then, *boom!* We got the soft dock. John retracted the drogue, and we heard the rapid bangs of the latches as we got a hard dock. I said, "Houston, Apollo 10. Snoopy and Charlie Brown are hugging each other." Both of us ran through our checklists. John equalized the pressure in the tunnel and took out the CM hatch and the probe while we took out the drogue. As soon as I saw John, I hugged him. I was glad to see him.

As if the day hadn't been busy enough, we still had one major task ahead of us—jettisoning Snoopy. Knowing our LM was headed for an eternal orbit around the Sun, we placed a United Nations flag and a package of all fifty U.S. state flags aboard. We also loaded the LM with the docking probe, since we wouldn't be using it any more, along with empty food bags and some other garbage. John had taken advantage of his relative privacy on Charlie Brown to perform his first bowel movement of the flight, so that got left aboard Snoopy, too. We joked that Snoopy would have food, water, oxygen, organic material, all the ingredients for the creation of life. Maybe a few billion years from now some kind of Snoopy monster (distantly related to John "José" Young) will emerge from somewhere in the solar system.

Once the hatches were buttoned up, we tried to depressurize the tunnel, and failed. (We didn't know yet that the problem was due to a manufacturing error: The vents for depressurization had not been drilled. They were solid metal.) With the tunnel still under pressure, we knew were in for a jolt when Snoopy let go. Just in case, we put on helmets and gloves and strapped in. When John fired the switches, we got banged backwards so hard we felt G-forces. Snoopy took off like a dingbat.

After a night of almost exhausted sleep, we spent the better part of a day in lunar orbit, photographing potential landing sites. It wasn't just a matter of snapping pictures: I manually flew Charlie Brown in the local horizontal mode while John picked out the sites and Gene took stereo photographs. After each pass I would roll the spacecraft 180 degrees so John could realign the inertial platform by star sights, and we would send the data to mission control. Then I would roll back to pick up the local horizon.

We were continuing that specific task on the farside of the Moon when a red warning light came on. One of our three fuel cells, those necessary but intricate devices that mixed hydrogen and oxygen to create electricity and water, had simply up and died. The command and service modules could operate with two fuel cells; they could even operate on one, though certain systems had to be shut off. But we were a long way from home. As soon as we reacquired contact with Houston, I told them about our problem. They began to look into it. John said, "Just wait until we get to night on the back side, then another one of those SOBs will start out on us."

I thought John was just being cynical. Imagine my reaction when, halfway through the next nightside pass, the readouts on a *second* fuel cell began to flicker. This time I was a bit more urgent in telling Houston, "We could have some major problems." It was time to update our vectors for an early transearth injection burn. But Houston calculated that we had enough power in our remaining good fuel cell and a partially operating second to make the trip home. So we stuck with the flight plan and its schedule. Ours was the only fuel cell to fail on any Apollo mission.

As we made our last farside pass, 137 hours after launch from the Cape, over 60 hours after arriving in lunar orbit, John punched the command that ignited the service propulsion system motor. We got a perfect two-minute, forty-four-second burn, and were on our way home.

Our trajectory was designed for the fastest return possible, allowing us to cover the 238,000 mile distance in forty-two hours, rather than the usual fifty-six or more. This meant that at one point we reached a speed of 24,791.4 nautical miles (28,547 statute miles) an hour, the fastest human beings have ever flown, or ever will fly, until astronauts return from a trip to Mars.

The two days gave me time to reflect on what we had just accomplished, the sights we had seen, the distance we had traveled—not just from the earth to the Moon, but from the first Mercury to the threshold of a lunar landing. It was an incredible accomplishment, one that I was proud to have helped in, and one that has stayed with me all these years. John and Gene were feeling the same way. There was no letdown once we left the Moon. We stayed happy all the way home.

My enthusiasm finally got the better of me in a conversation with capcom Jack Lousma, who read a message from the Governor of Samoa that inviting us to a reception in Pago Pago, complete with dancing girls. "Will that be top hat or top-less?" I said. The next day's news summary noted a frosty message from the governor to Colonel Stafford that these dancers were "sophisticated ladies." Oops.

Even with the greater volume and comfort of Apollo, hygiene was always a problem on space missions. There was hardly room to turn around, much less take a sponge bath and clean up properly. On longer missions, astronauts and cosmonauts had returned to Earth looking pretty scruffy. I wanted to look sharp when I arrived aboard the carrier.

Shaving was another one of those problems—like the television camera— that was relatively easy to solve, once you decided to solve it. Some crew systems people had experimented with various kinds of electric razors that would vacuum up whiskers so they wouldn't float around inside a cabin, but this was unnecessarily complicated. Apollo 10 carried a lightweight Gillette Techmatic rollable razor blade and a tube of brushless shaving cream. The whiskers would wind up on the blade or in the cream, where they could be easily contained with a towel. And so the crew of Apollo 10 treated the world, on live TV, to the first space shave.

Three hours before entering the earth's atmosphere, we made one minor burn to correct our trajectory, reducing our speed by three feet per second and giving us the perfect angle in that narrow re-entry corridor. Earth was now a growing crescent that showed only one-sixteenth of the surface.

As we hit the upper atmosphere, we created a plasma sheath that caused the sky outside our windows to grow lighter. Gene asked, "Is it daylight?" (We were re-entering just before dawn, local time, over the South Pacific.)

"Hell, no," I told him. "This is re-entry!"

I trained a movie camera on the flames and molten matter spewing off the heat shield as we blazed across the sky. Our descent was caught on a video camera in American Samoa, where we looked like a huge comet with a long trail of fire. Our drogue chute opened as scheduled, followed by the three big main chutes. Splashdown was seven-tenths of a mile from the target point, within sight of our prime recovery ship, the carrier USS *Princeton,* on station three hundred miles east of Samoa. The whole world saw us floating down live on color TV.

We were hoisted out of Charlie Brown into a recovery helicopter, and ferried to the carrier. After a brief welcoming ceremony—where, as promised, we were clean-shaven and sharp—we were flown to American Samoa for a polite, but cool reception by the ambassador and others. Then it was back in the air, aboard a C-141 for a twelve-hour flight back to Ellington. Thanks to some tailwinds, we made it all the way, nonstop.

thirteen
Chief Astronaut

In February 1964 Al Shepard had been grounded because of Ménière's syndrome, and he had been trying to find a cure ever since, reading everything he could find on the subject and visiting specialists all over the country, but nothing helped. About the time Al got grounded, I visited Dr. James Crabtree, a high school friend from Weatherford, who now practiced at the prestigious Otological Medical Clinic in Los Angeles, under Dr. William House. Through Jim I learned of Dr. House's pioneering work on Ménière's, a technique for implanting a tube into the cranial cavity to shunt excess fluid from the inner ear down the spinal column, relieving the pressure.

I told Al about it then, in 1964—a little apprehensively. Al was a Christian Scientist and, I thought, not interested in surgery. I don't know that his religious beliefs had anything to do with it, but he didn't take the surgical option until four years later, when his Ménière's got worse. Finally, in the summer of 1968 he flew out to Los Angeles in secret and had the procedure under Dr. House. None of us in the astronaut office had any idea he was doing this. But suddenly, in April 1969 Shepard was recovered, requalified for flight, and angling for the next available crew assignment.

The next unassigned mission was Apollo 13, scheduled for launch in March 1970. Apollo 13 was then planned to be the third lunar landing, but who knew? A problem on Apollo 11 or 12, and 13 could become the second.

Or the first. Apollo 13 was the mission Al wanted. And that's what Deke gave him. Deke took the position that Al had been bumped off a prime crew for the first Gemini. Therefore, he should go back on the first available prime crew.

Deke and Al selected Stu Roosa, who had impressed everybody with his support work on Apollo 9, as command module pilot. And Ed Mitchell, from my Apollo 10 backup crew, as lunar module pilot. In June 1969, the names were sent to HQ for routine approval and announced to the astronaut office. Al, Stu, and Ed started training—and then the shit hit the fan.

The first problem was Gordo Cooper, who felt that Apollo 13 was supposed to be his. He had flown two orbital missions and toiled through two backup jobs in a row while Al sat on the sidelines tending his investments. Gordo complained to HQ.

Then there were the rest of us in the astronaut office. I respected Al's intelligence and skill, and I supported his move back to flight status. But I thought Apollo 13 was too early and that he needed more time to train. And so did almost everyone else who had commanded missions—Pete Conrad, John Young, Jim McDivitt, and especially Jim Lovell.

And so, as it turned out, did George Mueller at NASA HQ. For the first time since 1962, one of Deke's crew selections got overruled. Mueller would *not* approve Shepard for Apollo 13.

I found myself a new job. Al Shepard had been chief of the astronaut office since July 1964, supervising the day-to-day activities of a team that had now grown to sixty-five astronauts. With Al's return to flight status, that position was now open. And within two weeks of my return from Apollo 10, as we were finishing our lengthy debrief, Deke called me into his office and offered the job to me.

I could have stayed in the flight rotation, of course. But I wanted management experience. And Deke was offering something similar to a promotion from squadron operations to wing command. So I took it.

Neil Armstrong, Mike Collins, and Buzz Aldrin were deep into training for Apollo 11. Since their mission would be identical to the one we'd flown on Apollo 10—with the small exception of actually landing on the Moon—John, Gene, and I made ourselves available for consultation. As nearly as possible, Apollo 11 would duplicate the mission model we'd used on 10, right down to having the same flight control teams and capcoms working the same phases of the mission. That's how Charlie Duke, our capcom during Snoopy's flight to within forty-seven thousand feet of the lunar surface, wound up as capcom for Neil and Buzz's landing.

The Soviets had been strangely quiet since January 1969. They seemed to be making no attempt to fly a manned circumlunar loop, probably because it would seem like a poor response to Apollo 8 and 10. It looked as though the Race to the Moon had been won. But there were still several opportunities for glory, or mischief, depending on how you looked at it.

Late on the evening of July 3, 1969, the second N-1 superbooster stood on its pad at Baikonur, ready to carry an unmanned L-1 toward the Moon. Aleksei Leonov was in the viewing area, along with fellow cosmonauts Oleg Makarov and Nikolai Rukavishnikov. Shortly after midnight, local time, the big booster lit up the night sky and rose two hundred meters before exploding in a gigantic mushroom cloud with a force of 250 tons of TNT, and falling back to earth, essentially right on the pad.

Debris landed up to ten kilometers away. The disaster damaged the launch support tower, tankage, and other structures at the pad so completely that it would be easier to build a new one than to repair it. Years later (long after Apollo-Soyuz) I would see Corona reconnaissance satellite photos of the damage—a black smear on the steppe, visible from orbit.

It just so happened that Frank Borman was in Moscow later that day, part of a two-week visit to the Soviet Union accompanied by cosmonauts German Titov, Georgy Beregovoi, and Konstantin Feoktistov. Rumors had sneaked into the press of Soviet plans to scoop up some lunar soil and return it to earth before the Apollo 11 mission, and at a reception at the American Embassy on the fourth, reporters pressed Titov and the other cosmonauts for information. They got nothing about any sample return and less than nothing about the giant booster failure. The next day, Frank became the first astronaut to visit Star City.

He was back in the United States on the thirteenth of July when a Proton finally succeeded in carrying a sample return craft into earth orbit and putting it on a trajectory toward the Moon. According to the Soviet press, the probe was called Luna 15, and its mission was to photograph the Moon, and to study circumlunar space and the Moon's chemical composition.

By this time the Apollo 11 launch was three days away, and we were concerned that Luna 15 might interfere with communications. Chris Kraft went to Frank, and the two of them composed a telegram, which they sent to Mstislav Keldysh, the president of the Soviet Academy of Sciences. To everyone's surprise, Keldysh responded with Luna 15's orbital parameters and assurances that the probe and its signals would not interfere with Apollo 11's operations. It was a small step toward communication between our two countries on space issues.

Launch day arrived for Apollo 11, July 16, 1969, and I found myself assigned as VIP escort at the viewing area, sitting between Vice President Spiro Agnew and former president Lyndon Johnson. Agnew had flown down to the Cape the day before and shared a dinner with Neil's crew. James McDonnell was there, too. All around us on that beautiful, muggy July day were a million people, including thousands of journalists from all over the world. As soon as Apollo 11 with Neil, Mike, and Buzz had rocketed into the sky and was safely in orbit, I disengaged and headed for my T-38, planning to be in mission control.

I had VIP duty again on Sunday, July 20, 1969, during the critical descent to the Sea of Tranquillity, this time sitting in mission control with NASA administrator Dr. Tom Paine on one side, and Wernher von Braun on the other. Since I had flown essentially the same approach to the Sea of Tranquillity that Neil and Buzz were flying that day, I was able to brief both Paine and Von Braun on the sights the crew would be seeing, and the actions they would be taking. It was a privilege to share that special moment with Von Braun, whose vision and leadership had been so important in making Apollo a reality.

There was some tense moments. I heard Neil and Buzz discussing computer program alarms, heard them receiving a "Go" from capcom Charlie Duke. Then . . . "Contact light?" And a few moments later, Neil said, "Houston, Tranquillity Base here. The Eagle has landed."

I was astonished. LM-5, better known as Eagle, had less than twenty seconds of fuel left when it finally touched down. But it had touched down. And four hours later, Neil stepped off the footpad at the base of the LM, followed by Buzz. There they were, walking on the Moon. We could see them in that fuzzy, black-and-white TV picture. (My color camera hadn't been approved for Apollo 11.) It was amazing just to see it. I was almost overwhelmed at the thought that I had been part of this adventure, that I had pioneered the rendezvous techniques and most of the procedures the crew would use to reach home.

And home they came, on July 24, 1969, fulfilling the pledge JFK had made eight years earlier, "before this decade is out, to land a man on the Moon, and return him safely to earth."

What about Luna 15? It burned successfully into orbit around the Moon on July 17, as Neil, Mike, and Buzz were headed that direction themselves. The probe spent three days in orbit as ground controllers made a series of burns, and tried to get a hack on its trajectory. Several hours after Neil and Buzz landed on the Sea of Tranquillity, Luna 15 attempted its own landing in the Sea of Crises. It never landed: The Soviet maps of the Moon were imprecise, and Luna 15 slammed into a mountain side.

The success of Apollo 11 cleared the decks in a lot of ways. We had met JFK's goal—now what? A team led by Vice President Spiro Agnew had mapped out various courses for the United States to take in space over the next decade, ranging from an ambitious (and extremely expensive) fast program leading to a manned Mars mission by 1984, down to a more modest proposal for a reusable spacecraft and a space station. But the Nixon administration certainly wasn't interested in picking up the tab for the fast Mars program, so the future was uncertain.

We did have nine more lunar landings, though, and at least three earth-orbit missions for the Apollo Applications Program. Pete Conrad's crew was the only one set was for the first of these, Apollo 12, scheduled for November. Al Shepard could not fly 13, but Jim Lovell, coming off the backup assignment on Apollo 11, was willing and able. Ken Mattingly would be his command module pilot, and Fred Haise the LMP. Deke gave the backup job to John Young, Jack Swigert, and Charlie Duke. Shepard, Roosa, and Mitchell would fly 14, with Gene Cernan, Ron Evans, and Joe Engle as their backups. We were confident there would be missions beyond these, perhaps as many as six additional lunar landings. Crew members would be drawn from astronauts already working Apollo backup or support jobs. Everybody else was assigned to the Apollo Applications Program.

Within a month of Apollo 11, we took on a new group of highly trained astronauts from the Air Force's Manned Orbiting Laboratory, which had been cancelled that May. Gen. James Ferguson, commander of the Air Force Systems Command, had immediately asked George Mueller and NASA to take all fourteen of them, and Mueller had been more than willing—looking at the Agnew reports and budget issues, he realized that NASA needed Air Force support if it hoped to have a vigorous manned space program in the 1970s. But Deke and I knew that we didn't have enough missions to fly all of the people already on board. Deke didn't want to take any of the MOL guys.

Which didn't make any difference. Mueller had us interview all fourteen in Houston. Thirteen of them were eager to join NASA, even if they wouldn't be flying until the mid-1970s. One of the group, Lt. Col. Robert Herres, opted out. But thirteen was still too many, so finally Deke came up with the idea of applying the usual astronaut selection criteria to the group—specifically the age limit. All those who were still under the age of 36 would be accepted; those who were older were out of luck.

That gave us seven new astronauts, including Bob Crippen, who would be pilot on the first Shuttle mission twelve years later; Bob Overmyer and Bo Bobko, future Shuttle commanders; and Dick Truly, who would fly two Shuttle missions and later become NASA administrator. All would work for me on Apollo-Soyuz. We took an eighth MOL pilot, Al Crews, into the aircraft operations division. We lost out on some outstanding individuals, however, including Greg Neubeck, and Jim Abrahamson (later a three-star general, head of the Shuttle program, and first director of the Strategic Defense Initiative Organization), and Herres, who eventually retired as the four-star vice chairman of the Joint Chiefs of Staff.

One of the issues that landed on me as chief astronaut was the Apollo Applications Program, which had been started back in early 1967 as a way to exploit the technology developed for Apollo. The original schedules were very ambitious, at one point calling for something like twenty manned earth orbit, lunar orbit, and lunar landing missions between 1969 and 1975. It was this sort of planning that had encouraged NASA to load up on more astronauts in 1966 and 1967. As the war in Vietnam ate up money, however, AAP began to shrink until, when I took over the astronaut office, it consisted of six Saturn 1B launches, only three of them manned.

The original concept had been to outfit the fuel tank of an S-4B upper stage so that once in orbit and purged of fuel, it could be converted into a habitable volume by a crew of three astronauts launched separately. Once I took a look at the plans, however, I was appalled. The wet workshop wouldn't have a real attitude control system or solar panels. I told Mueller that working in space was too difficult, that nobody would be able to install all the racks, electrical lines, and other equipment. Slayton, Kraft, and Gilruth were of the same mind.

A better proposal was a "dry" workshop—to convert an S-4B on the ground to a fully equipped lab and living quarters then launch the whole system atop a Saturn 5. Pretty soon NASA management agreed, and on July 18, 1969, in the middle of the Apollo 11 mission, Thomas Paine gave the dry workshop his approval. The bad news was that it took one of the ten remaining Saturn 5s away from the lunar landing program.

In October 1969 the Soviets flew three Soyuz spacecraft in earth orbit. On October 11, Georgy Shonin and Valery Kubasov were launched aboard Soyuz 6. A day later, cosmonauts Anatoly Filipchenko, Vladislav Volkov, and Viktor Gorbatko went up in Soyuz 7. And the day after that, Vladimir Shatalov and Aleksei Yeliseyev took off in Soyuz 8.

Three manned spacecraft! What was the purpose, other than to overtax the fairly rudimentary Soviet flight control and tracking system? It wasn't clear then and not for years later. Soyuz 7 and 8 were supposed to dock, and Soyuz 6 was supposed to photograph the whole business. Soyuz 6 also carried an experiment in space welding that Kubasov would operate.

Well, Soyuz 8 failed to link up with Soyuz 7. And I never saw any pictures from 6. The welding experiment worked to some degree, though we're still waiting for its applications to space construction. It seems that the only reason to fly three Soyuz at the same time was to gain some tiny bit of publicity for a dubious space "first."

During Apollo 12, our second lunar landing, Pete Conrad and Al Bean would set their LM (named Intrepid) down on the Ocean of Storms within walking distance of the unmanned Surveyor 3, which had landed there in 1967. We had come an amazing distance in just a few months, from the first lunar orbits by Apollo 8, and we approached Apollo 12 with great confidence. Maybe too much.

Apollo 12 was the first mission where I served as chief astronaut, waking Pete, Al, and their command module pilot, Dick Gordon, at 6 A.M. on the morning of November 14, 1969. They had a medical check, then a weather briefing. Weather was on our minds to a greater extent than usual that morning because thunderstorms and rain had pounded the Cape the day before, and now a cold front had moved into the area. Nevertheless, things had started to clear for the moment, and mission director Chet Lee had given a "go" for launch.

Suited up, Pete, Dick, and Al headed for the pad. I kept them company on the drive then returned to the firing room for Pad 39A. The weather was gray overcast with stratus clouds at twelve hundred feet. Radar showed no thunderstorms. So although the weather was marginal, it was still within limits. As we counted down, the weather team reported a thunderstorm on radar eighty miles to the northwest, too far away to affect our launch plans. We even got a weather update from Air Force One, which was bringing President Nixon to the Cape.

Pete asked about the clouds. I got on the line at T minus nine minutes and told him that we were looking at nothing but low-lying stratus, that the radar had no thunderstorms near the area, and gave him my "go" for launch. The launch director polled his troops, the count resumed toward zero, and the Apollo 12 Saturn 5 roared into the November sky. President Nixon was out there in the drizzle, the only chief executive to witness a manned space launch until 1998. Deke Slayton was with him.

Everything went perfectly for the first thirty-six seconds, with Pete reporting, with his usual enthusiasm, that they were "really going." After the call "tower clear," I looked up from my console and watched the giant Saturn as it rose. Suddenly, as it entered the clouds, two parallel lighting bolts crackled out of the clouds and hit the launch pad. *Bang!*

There was a rush of static on the speakers. When it cleared, we heard Pete saying, "Okay, we just lost the platform, gang. I don't know what happened here; we had everything in the world drop out." It was a tense few moments, until the crew got the fuel cells back on line for the ride into orbit.

What we learned later, and what Pete suggested almost immediately, was that Apollo 12 had been hit by lightning but not from the storm eighty miles away: Apollo 12 had created its own lightning when the huge, ionized gas plume from the first stage engines opened an electrical path to the ground. When the nose of the vehicle reached the clouds, it discharged static electricity all the way down to the launch pad.

Thanks to the hard work of Dick Gordon, taking star sightings and punching numbers into the guidance computer, Apollo 12 got its platform re-aligned just in time to burn toward the Moon. Pete and Al made a very successful landing within sight of Surveyor 3 four days later.

Meanwhile, we were rethinking our launch weather criteria. And I was wondering about the number of personnel changes that had taken place since Apollo 11. Almost the entire NASA management, from administrator (Tom Paine having officially replaced Jim Webb) to George Mueller to Gen. Sam Phillips to George Low to Rocco Petrone had turned over in the past few months. Had we lost something in all the changes? Certainly a lot of talent had moved, but the replacements were all capable. Apollo 12's close call was just another reminder of the unknown dangers of flying in space. My input to that "go" decision was the worst operational decision I ever made.

There were tough personnel decisions in the astronaut office that season. The surplus of astronauts meant that Deke and I could afford to unload anyone who didn't seem to want the job. One painful case was my old friend, Donn Eisele. Following his open conflict with flight controllers on Apollo 7, an unimpressive turn backing up Apollo 10, and a messy divorce that had caused him to neglect his duties on Apollo Applications, some managers (including Gen. Sam Phillips and George Low) decided it was time for him to move on. It fell to me to give him the news. Though this situation caused some tension between us for many years, we eventually patched up our friendship, I'm happy to say. When Donn died of a heart attack in 1987, Susie, his widow, asked me to give the eulogy at Arlington National Cemetery. Donn transferred to NASA Langley within a few months, later retiring from the agency and the Air Force to work for the Peace Corps.

We still had upcoming flights, of course, and new crews to assign. Fresh from Apollo 12, Pete made it clear he wanted another chance at a lunar landing. Apollo 20 hadn't officially been canceled, but we knew it was gone. The crews for 18 and 19 hadn't been named yet, and he had his eye on one of those. But I told him, "Sorry, old buddy. You only get one lunar landing."

Besides, we needed an experienced commander to take over Apollo Applications, which was shortly to be named Skylab. Pete jumped at the new job and took Al Bean with him.

Dick Gordon, however, having been within sixty miles of the Moon, wanted to walk on it. He chose to stick with Apollo, and was named backup commander for Apollo 15, with Vance Brand as CMP and scientist-astronaut Jack Schmitt as LMP. Dave Scott, Al Worden, and Jim Irwin, the Apollo 12 backup crew, were named to fly Apollo 15.

I had my own opportunity to leave NASA in 1970. Frank Borman, who was getting ready to retire and go into business, had been asked by President Nixon to evaluate the possible political futures of his fellow astronauts, and my name appeared at the top of his list. A political operative named Frederick Clifton "Clif" White, who had helped Barry Goldwater get the Republican nomination for president in 1964 and still served as an adviser to President Nixon, came to me, saying, "We need a good Republican base there in Oklahoma." The current senator, a Democrat named Fred Harris, had gotten increasingly liberal in a state that was and is very conservative. The White House was unhappy with him and was searching for a Republican to challenge him.

I had maintained my ties with business, political, and family interests in Oklahoma, so it was worth considering. But there was one major complication: Until this time I had been a registered Democrat, though of the conservative, Robert Kerr brand, and I usually voted as an independent. I also wasn't ready to leave NASA or the Air Force. After several months of consideration and investigation, I declined the offer. (From the 1972 national election on I became a solid Republican, though I did support some conservative Democrats.)

Jim Lovell, Ken Mattingly, and Fred Haise were in the final days of training for the next lunar landing, Apollo 13, when a problem arose: Charlie Duke, one of their backup crew members, had come down with German measles and exposed the prime crew. Jim and Fred had immunity because they had had measles as children. But not Ken. And now, five days before the scheduled launch, NASA doctors, led by Dr. Chuck Berry, were recommending that we remove Ken from the crew. They weren't just being arbitrary: German measles could be a serious illness for an adult, complete with fever. The incubation period suggested that if Ken got sick, it would be while the crew was in lunar orbit. Did we want to have a feverish Ken Mattingly trying to perform even a routine rendezvous with Lovell and Haise in their lunar module? No.

Deke and I first approached Jim Lovell, who wasn't too happy about the possible switch. Had it been Fred Haise who would be flying the lunar module Aquarius and working on the Moon with Jim, we probably would have delayed the mission by a month. But the CMP did much of his work on his own: Jack Swigert, Ken's backup, was superbly trained. Jim agreed to a trial with Jack, and I had to locate our bachelor astronaut in a hotel and tell him to cancel whatever plans he had made for mid-April 1970: He was going to the Moon.

Jack passed the test; Ken was replaced. And Apollo 13 was launched on the morning of Saturday, April 11, with no problems at all. These lunar flights were becoming more and more routine.

On the evening of Monday the 13th, I was attending a party at Ron Evans's house when we got a call from Deke in mission control: "Tom, we've had an explosion on board Apollo 13. They're losing oxygen. Get over here quick!"

Driving over to MSC, I found the flight control team still thinking of the situation as an instrumentation problem or an oxygen leak. I saw the oxygen readings dropping, and said, "We need to get them into the lunar module right away!"

When that didn't seem to sink in, I added: "This thing is going to shut down. You need to get that lunar module powered up and get its platform aligned!"

The situation was very tense. We had never simulated anything quite like this: We were looking at using the lunar module as a "lifeboat" for a crew that had a dead command and service module. Obviously, the LM couldn't return the crew to Earth, but it might keep them alive long enough for us to figure out the problem with the command module. (By this time, the lunar landing had been cancelled.) Ironically, the one astronaut who knew those lifeboat procedures best—because he had developed them—was Jack Swigert.

Glynn Lunney's flight control team had taken over from Gene Kranz's about an hour after the accident, and, like all of us, they were still trying to figure out what had gone wrong and how to help the crew. Glynn wanted them to power down the command module's inertial platform now and align the LM's later, using the optical telescope. When I heard that, I went right over to Glynn to warn him about the difficulties of doing an alignment like that in the LM, with thirty-one tons of command and service module hanging on it. Based on my experience on Apollo 10, I told him, "Maneuvering the docked vehicles with the LM's thrusters to get manual star sightings will be next to impossible." Just the sunlight reflecting off the docked configuration made it nearly impossible to see stars on the way to the Moon. They had to get the platform alignment data from the command module *now*, while it still had power.

During the days that followed, I kept shifts of astronauts working in the lunar module and command module simulators in Houston and at the Cape testing procedures for Jim's crew, as they looped around the Moon and headed back toward Earth. I took a turn, along with Gene Cernan, John Young, Dave Scott, Joe Engle, Ken Mattingly, and others. Thanks to their work, and that of hundreds of engineers and specialists in Houston and at industrial firms around the United States, we approached re-entry on the morning of Friday, April 17, with a good chance of bringing Jim, Jack, and Fred home safely.

First they had to power up their frozen, dead command module Odyssey, which would have enough battery power to fly through re-entry and splashdown. That went well: The guidance system showed no ill effects from having been cold-soaked for so long and the whole CM getting wet from melting condensation. Then they jettisoned the service module, and got their first look at the damage—one whole section had been blown cleanly away. Wires were dangling and the oxygen tanks were a mess of ripped metal.

This gave us a new worry. Had the violence of the explosion cracked Odyssey's heatshield? It hadn't, though Odyssey's longer-than-anticipated voyage through re-entry seemed endless. Apollo 13 splashed down safely, and I turned to Dr. Gilruth, who had been watching in mission control, and told him I thought this was our greatest day. After a stop at Eric's, a favorite of the astronaut group, for the splashdown party hosted by Grumman, builders of Aquarius, I went home to collapse. I calculated that I had slept about eighteen hours in the five days of crisis.

About 2 A.M. I was awakened by Faye, who handed me a phone. The caller was Jack Swigert aboard the carrier USS *Hornet*. "Tom," he said, "my new girlfriend is flying down to Houston from New York. Can you and Faye take care of her until I get there?" We were happy to do it. It was all part of being chief astronaut.

Some weeks later, during the investigation into the accident, I learned that the oxygen tank that failed had originally been installed in the service module for Apollo 10. My flight.

The realization that we'd had such a close call caused many NASA officials to do some soul-searching. Bob Gilruth was very concerned about additional lunar landings and, I believe, didn't want any more attempts. In any case, because of additional budget cuts in fiscal year 1971, something had to give. The Apollo 18 and 19 landing missions were officially canceled in September 1970, eliminating six flight crew opportunities.

Nine chances remained in the Skylab program. Deke and I weighed those assignments carefully, since we had many more astronauts than we had seats, and anyone who missed out was going to be waiting a long time for a chance to fly. As branch chief for Skylab, Pete Conrad would command the first mission and have a lot to say about who would fly the others. We settled on Al Bean and Jerry Carr as commanders of the second and third missions. Scientist-astronauts Joe Kerwin, Owen Garriott, and Ed Gibson would be science pilots. Pilots would be Paul Weitz, Jack Lousma, and Bill Pogue, all of whom had done tours in Apollo support teams. I could have assigned myself to the first mission, but chose not to: After flying to within ten miles of the Moon, going around the earth for twenty-eight days wasn't something I wanted to do at the time.

The Soviets were interested in sending cosmonauts around the earth for extended periods. On June 1, 1970, Soyuz 9 was launched, carrying Andrian Nikolayev and Vitaly Sevastyanov. They wound up spending almost nineteen days in orbit, though they were in such terrible physical shape when they landed that they spent several weeks in rehab.

Their condition was of great concern to Soviet space program managers because the cancellation of the circumlunar loop program left long-duration flights on space stations as their primary manned program.

Nikolayev and Sevastyanov recovered sufficiently to be sent on a world-wide publicity tour in the fall, including a visit to the United States. They were the first cosmonauts I met face-to-face.

Buzz Aldrin had gone through a tough time after the Apollo 11 mission. The sheer volume of public appearances had worn him down. He could have bowed out but chose not to. "My public demands it," he said.

At one point in 1970, I learned that Buzz and his father, Edwin, Sr., were prowling the halls of the Pentagon trying to get Buzz promoted to brigadier general. It wasn't doing Buzz any good, and it sure wasn't doing any good for the image of Air Force astronauts assigned to NASA. There was a war going on in Vietnam; to them, that's where the real heroes were.

I called Buzz in and told him to stay out of the Pentagon. "They want to hear about the program," he said. Nevertheless, I told him he wasn't going back. In spite of that disagreement, we remained good friends. Finally, however, Buzz showed up with the news that he was returning to the Air Force as commandant of the test pilot school at Edwards.

I could see trouble right away. "Look, Buzz," I told him. "You're a good fighter pilot. You shot down two and a half MiGs in Korea, and you've done a good technical and flying job on the program here. But, remember, you're still not a test pilot.

"There's a hell of an old boys club out at Edwards. There are two factions—the test pilot school, and flight test ops. Flight test ops has always looked down on the test pilot school as second-class. If you're going to go, go with some humility, and listen. Don't talk! Don't be in transmit mode."

Unfortunately, Buzz barely lasted six months in the job before he took medical retirement.

fourteen
Life and Death on Salyut

On Saturday morning, January 23, 1971, the prime and backup crews for Apollo 14 were at the Cape, preparing for launch on the thirty-first. I was still in Houston, fresh from a visit to a doctor's office (a checkup for a minor skin cancer), when I got a call from Deke Slayton that Gene Cernan had crashed a helicopter into the Indian River. He had been on a proficiency flight in his role as backup commander to Al Shepard. He was shaken up, singed around the edges, but otherwise unhurt. There would be an investigation, of course, but Gene had already admitted that he had simply flown the chopper into the water on a clear morning, an obvious case of pilot error. (He was "flat hatting," buzzing the water at a very low altitude.)

Assuming 14 went well, in a few weeks Deke would name the crew for Apollo 17, the last lunar landing mission now planned. As 14's backup commander, Gene rightly expected that assignment, along with his command module pilot, Ron Evans, and lunar module pilot, Joe Engle. The problem was, Gene's crew had competition. The Apollo 15 backup crew, commanded by Dick Gordon, with Vance Brand as command module pilot, had geologist Jack Schmitt as lunar module pilot. Jack had been one of the first scientists accepted into the astronaut program in June 1965. He had good scientific credentials, but no flying or operational background at all prior to joining NASA. He had gone on to provide great geology training and support to the first lunar orbit and landing missions, including Apollo 10.

Both commanders were capable; both crews were well-trained and ready for the assignment. Both crews had their own supporters. Deke, Al, and I leaned toward Cernan, who was fully qualified. For me, seeing the diminishing support for manned space flight, Gene would be a great spokesman for future manned flight, as the "last" man on the Moon. Dick Gordon's team had Pete Conrad (who had worked with Dick on two missions), Jim McDivitt, and Dave Scott pulling for them. They also had the National Academy of Sciences in their corner. The scientific community wanted Jack Schmitt to go to the Moon.

I got Gene on the phone. "You dumb son of a bitch," I told him. "Here I am, trying to help you fly on Apollo 17, and you go and pull some damn stupid trick like this."

I was afraid he had taken himself out of it. But he had been honest about the accident, and honesty carried a lot of weight with Deke. Two days after the helicopter crash, Deke put Gene back on flight status. And after Apollo 14, he submitted the crew of Cernan, Evans, and Engle for Apollo 17 to headquarters for approval.

In June, Al Shepard, fresh off the Apollo 14 lunar landing mission, said he wanted to return to his job as chief of the astronaut office. The Navy wanted Al back for active duty and had promoted him to rear admiral for that reason. But Al chose to stay in Houston, a decision that perturbed the Navy and put a stop to any future promotions past captain for future Navy personnel assigned to NASA.

I became Deke's deputy director of flight crew operations, moving up the NASA corporate ladder, expanding my own responsibilities beyond the astronaut office to the Manned Spacecraft Center's fleet of aircraft, the spacecraft simulators, and crew equipment. My new job gave me a chance to take Faye, Dionne and Karin on our first real family vacation in years. We left for Europe the first week in June.

While we were traveling, the manned space station era began. As had happened so many times in the early days, the Soviets got there first. Salyut ("Salute" in English) had been launched from Baikonur on April 19. Though the Soviet press had described it as a "multipurpose spacecraft for scientific research," the use of the huge Proton launch vehicle tipped us to the possibility that Salyut was actually something big and new.

Four days after the launch, on April 23, the Soyuz 10 manned spacecraft followed Salyut into orbit. Soyuz 10 carried Vladimir Shatalov, Aleksei Yeliseyev, and Nikolai Rukavishnikov, and now the Soviet press revealed that they were to visit Salyut. Which is all they wound up doing: A day after liftoff, as Shatalov piloted Soyuz to a rendezvous with the big station, he and his colleagues ran into problems. They managed to make a good soft docking, but the latches on the adaptor between the two vehicles didn't close, didn't give them a "hard" dock. They couldn't enter Salyut, and so, after only five and a half hours, they had to undock and come home.

The Soviet press said that Soyuz 10 had "fully accomplished" its goals, which was to "test" the rendezvous and docking systems, but we knew that was bull: You wouldn't send a crew to make that kind of test, then bring them home after forty-eight hours. Over the next month the Soviets decided that Shatalov's "soft" docking had been too hard for the system, and they beefed up the couplers on the next spacecraft, which would be Soyuz 11, commanded by Aleksei Leonov, with Valery Kubasov, and Pyotr Kolodin as flight engineers.

This prime crew and its backups flew to Baikonur on May 28, 1971. Five days later, everything got balled up as Kubasov's final medical checks showed a spot on his lung. The musical chairs that followed were a lot like what happened to the Apollo 13 crew, when Jack Swigert took over for Ken Mattingly at the last minute. Soviet training rules said that Leonov's whole crew had to be replaced. Leonov tried to convince his bosses to give him an engineer named Vadim Volkov from the backup crew. But Leonov and Volkov had an immediate disagreement, and the Soviets decided to swap out the whole crew. Aleksei was bitterly disappointed. Kolodin went even further, having a few shots of vodka and personally telling Vasily Mishin, head of the Korolyov Bureau and one of the most senior officials present, just how stupid the decision was. But the State Commission had spoken.

Soyuz 11 launched on June 6, 1971, with commander Georgy Dobrovolsky, and flight engineers Volkov and Viktor Patsayev. The next day Dobrovolsky guided the Soyuz to a docking with Salyut. The strengthened adaptor worked fine this time, and soon enough Patsayev floated through the open hatch into the other vehicle.

Physically, Salyut was about twenty-three meters in length, with a pressurized working volume of about a hundred cubic meters, quite an improvement over Soyuz and Apollo. Power came from two sets of solar panels, one mounted on the forward transfer section, the other on the propulsion module. (This basic Salyut design would go through several evolutions, ultimately becoming the Mir core module.)

What we heard in the West at this time was all good news. The crew moved right into Salyut and set up housekeeping, like three guys on a campout. They were on television almost every night and seemed to be having fun. For the Soviet audience, it was like the good old days of Sputnik and Vostok. Americans may have gotten to the Moon, but Soviet cosmonauts were the world's first space colonists.

The cosmonauts had to make the usual adjustments to life in space. Medical questions came up throughout the mission, which was scheduled to last twenty-four or twenty-five days. The longest flight to that time was nineteen days by Nikolayev and Sevastyanov on Soyuz 9, June 1970. That crew had been so worn down by the experience that they had to be carried from their spacecraft on stretchers. To avoid that, the Salyut cosmonauts were supposed to work on a treadmill for an hour each day.

The cosmonauts also had problems getting along. In the Soviet system then, and in the Russian system today, space crews consist of cosmonauts from different teams—a commander from the military with an engineer from the civilian Korolyov Bureau. In this case, various last-minute swaps in personnel had limited integrated crew training. Dobrovolsky hadn't teamed up with Volkov and Patsayev until mid-February 1971.

Eventually, however, the mission staggered to a finish. On June 26 the cosmonauts started mothballing Salyut for the next visitors, a process that took three days. On the evening of the twenty-ninth, they climbed into Soyuz and said good-bye to the world's first manned space station. They were supposed to thump down in Kazakhstan on the third orbit after undocking, just before local dawn.

The crew did a fly-around, then maneuvered to re-entry attitude. Two hours later, the retros fired, at which moment all voice communication between Soyuz 11 and the flight control center ceased. The propulsion and orbital modules separated automatically, separations confirmed by telemetry, and the descent module parachuted to earth as planned.

When the recovery teams reached the Soyuz and opened the hatch, however, they got the shock of their lives: Dobrovolsky, Volkov, and Patsayev were dead. They got the cosmonauts out of Soyuz and tried CPR, but it was clearly too late. The crew had died of hypoxia and air embolisms due to depressurization of the descent module.

What happened was this: Moments after retrofire, the orbit module separated from the command module. Twelve small pyro bolts were supposed to fire in sequence, but because of some screwup, all of them fired at the same time. The jolt of this stronger-than-designed separation caused a valve in the descent module to open prematurely. (It was supposed to open at low altitude, to allow fresh air into the spacecraft.) The cosmonauts noted the drop in pressure. Dobrovolsky, in the center seat, unbuckled and pulled himself up to the front hatch, thinking that was the source of the leak, while Volkov and Patsayev manually shut off the radios to aid hearing.

Seeing that the front hatch was still sealed, the crew realized that the leak was probably coming from that ventilation valve, which was located under Dobrovolsky's seat. They tried to crank it shut—there was a backup master valve, but this unit, like a basic steam valve, was mounted over the crew's shoulders and took nineteen turns to close. Bad design, like the hatch on Apollo 1.

By now the descent module had been venting air for at least twenty seconds. This rapid depressurization would have been horribly painful: The crew passed out. Fifty seconds after the initial jolt, they were dead. The crew was not wearing pressure suits, which would have saved them. That configuration of the Soyuz descent module simply did not have room for three suited cosmonauts and their equipment.

By June 30, 1971, my wife and daughters and I had visited England, France, Switzerland, and Italy, and were on our way to Germany to see old friends from service there, Hank and Hanny West. Hank West was now the USAF colonel in charge of the American section of the air corridor connecting West Germany and Berlin. I was scheduled to make a side trip to the International Aeronautical Federation Conference in Belgrade, Yugoslavia, so I sent Faye and the girls on to Berlin.

Before I reached Belgrade, I heard the news that the Soyuz 11 cosmonauts had died on their return to earth. My first worry was that the stress of a long-duration flight had killed them and wondered what that would mean to our Skylab crews. Clearly we needed to know more than what was in the news. Sure enough, when I reached Belgrade, aides from the American embassy took me right off to see the ambassador, Malcolm Toon, who wanted me to accompany him to the Soviet embassy, where we paid our respects and condolences.

The conference began as scheduled that night, minus cosmonaut Pavel Popovich, who had returned to Moscow. There was a big banquet and a bunch of toasts, and I didn't reach my hotel room until 11 P.M. Forty-five minutes later, the phone rang, and it was Ambassador Toon. "Pack your bags, Tom. You're going to represent President Nixon at the cosmonauts' state funeral tomorrow in Moscow." This was a surprise. When Vladimir Komarov was killed in 1967, State had asked to send an American representative to his funeral, only to be slapped down with the statement that the ceremony was "private."

Getting there was easier said than done. It would be impossible to get a USAF T-39 Saber Liner executive jet cleared into Russia on such short notice, but Toon got one to fly in from Wiesbaden, West Germany, to take me to Copenhagen, where I would catch a specially chartered SAS DC-9 direct to Moscow. Still feeling the effects of a few vodkas, not to mention hobbling from a knee injury in a recent motorcycle accident, I realized I was facing a very long night. I asked the embassy staff to get a message to Hank West in Berlin, telling Faye I would catch up with her and the girls for the flight home.

I think I got a little sleep in the T-39. When we arrived in Copenhagen, the sun was already up, even though it was still very early in the morning. The SAS plane had a pilot, a co-pilot, two stewardesses, and me, not one other passenger. I had the flight attendants spread out some blankets and pillows on the floor, so I could sleep on the flight to Moscow.

At Moscow Airport I walked off the plane, bleary-eyed and stiff, to be met by Boris Klausen, the chargé d'affaires of the American embassy, who wanted to brief me before the funeral. But a big Russian general appeared out of the crowd and hauled me away from Klausen. I recognized him from news pictures: It was Georgy Beregovoi, the cosmonaut who had first tested Soyuz in space after Komarov's accident, and he wanted me to come with him. All poor Klausen could do was strip off his own black tie and hand it to me: I was still wearing a red one from the conference.

I rode with Beregovoi to the Red Army Officers' Club, a huge palace on Spasskoye Street, where the urns of the three Soyuz 11 cosmonauts were lying in state. Their families were present, so I went up to them and paid respects on behalf of President Nixon, the American people, and the NASA astronauts. Many other cosmonauts were present: Shatalov and Yeliseyev, who had failed in the April attempt to reach Salyut, and Valentina Tereshkova, the first woman in space, and her husband, Andrian Nikolayev, whom I had met the year before when he visited Houston. Here I also first met Aleksei Leonov, who should have commanded the fatal flight—though I didn't know it at the time.

Time to carry the urns out to the three hearses. Each urn rested in a metal, rectangular cradle with large handles extending from the ends. As one of the pallbearers, it was my job to help with the lifting. A coffin would have been lighter. I realized that the handles and the cradle were filled with solid lead. Each hearse was an olive-drab vehicle much like a school bus, with fold-down gray velour seats for the family inside, who boarded last. The hearses took off for Red Square. I rode in Beregovoi's limo.

A huge crowd was waiting in Red Square, led by General Secretary Brezhnev, Prime Minister Kosygin, and President Podgorny, plus hundreds of other Communist Party officials. We formed up three abreast to march into the square. With Beregovoi behind me, I was positioned right up front behind Dobrovolsky's urn. Brezhnev, weeping openly, was in the same rank on the front of the left handle.

After marching in I stood with the cosmonauts in front of Lenin's Tomb, while on the reviewing platform, the chairman of the State Funeral Committee talked forever. Then Nikolayev said a few words. Then Shatalov made a long speech. Then Brezhnev himself got up. My heart sank: I had heard about his six-hour-long addresses to Party congresses. The day was hot and humid. I had a slight hangover and was sore from my biking accident. All around us, Soviet honor guards were fainting and falling to the pavement. Fortunately, years of living in Houston had given me some training in dealing with heat and humidity.

Finally, after what seemed like hours, another procession took the urns to the Kremlin Wall, behind Lenin's Tomb. Cannons fired a salute to the crew of Salyut, and the urns were placed in their niches in the wall. I expressed America's sympathies directly to Brezhnev and Kosygin. They thanked me, then walked away into Lenin's Tomb and back into the Kremlin.

I looked at my watch. I had been with people who spoke nothing but Russian for six hours. Thank God Klausen found me then and drove me back off to his apartment in the American embassy, where I could wash up and grab a bite to eat. Then Klausen and his wife drove me around to see a few sights of Moscow before returning to the apartment, where I spent the night. (Faye and the girls were in Berlin, hearing on the news that an American astronaut had been present at the funeral of the Soyuz 11 cosmonauts, but they had no idea it was me!)

The next morning I was off to the airport to catch a commercial flight to Vienna. Beregovoi was there waiting for me. "We need some vodka," he announced.

I protested. "The plane is supposed to leave in a few minutes . . ."

"The plane doesn't leave until I say it does." Then he said, "Do you like caviar?" I said I did. "Come here! You need a snack!" He told me and the interpreter to sit down then passed out caviar and onions and started to make a toast. I was in no mood to drink vodka that morning. I told General Beregovoi that I didn't drink during working hours. But he started with the usual toast of friendship to our countries, and on and on. I wound up eating caviar and trying to match Beregovoi toast-for-toast for at least half an hour, while a whole planeload of very pissed-off-looking passengers waited.

That was my introduction to dealing with the Soviets.

fifteen
Behind the Curtain

Apollo 15 returned to earth on August 7, 1971, with Dave Scott, Al Worden, and Jim Irwin flying our most scientifically ambitious lunar mission yet. Now it was time to announce the Apollo 17 crew. For months Deke had resisted pressure from the National Academy of Sciences and others to name geologist Jack Schmitt to the 17 crew. As far as he was concerned, 17 still belonged to Joe Engle. Joe was an outstanding aviator who had qualified for astronaut wings by flying the X-15 before ever joining NASA. He had labored hard in support and backup roles, and there was no reason other than politics to rank Jack Schmitt ahead of him.

Ultimately, though, the matter was taken out of Deke's hands. Dale Myers, the head of manned space flight at NASA HQ, and the new administrator, James Fletcher, rejected Deke's proposed crew of Cernan, Evans, and Engle. Well, not Cernan and Evans, just Engle. HQ wanted Jack Schmitt to fly. And Cernan, Evans, and Schmitt was the crew announced on August 13. Joe Engle took the news better than I would have. He went off to work on the Shuttle program, piloting several of the unpowered approach and landing tests at Edwards in 1977 then commanded the second orbital flight in 1981 and another in 1985.

Before he left NASA in October 1969, George Mueller directed the agency to develop a reusable winged spacecraft—a space shuttle—as the next logical step after Apollo for the American space program. For one thing, having a reusable vehicle that could return to a runway freed us from having to depend on the U.S. Navy for a large support effort every time we had a spacecraft in orbit. And we wouldn't be throwing away an expensive piece of equipment with each launch.

Our original plans called for a winged orbiter to be launched atop a winged, reusable booster. The booster would have its own two-man crew and would carry the orbiter to a staging velocity of about six thousand feet per second, roughly two-and-a-half minutes after launch, when it would separate. The orbiter would then fire up its engines and continue into space while the booster flew back to the launch site using conventional jet engines. Orbiter and booster would be capable of flying at least a hundred missions. Test flights would be in 1977; development costs and operations for the first twelve years were expected to be eleven billion dollars. That was the idea, anyway.

What emerged at the end of 1971, following severe budget cuts due to lack of political support, was a stage and a half, partly reusable Shuttle with a winged orbiter that would be launched by its own engines and two solid rocket motors. The liquid oxygen and hydrogen fuel for the orbiter's main engines would be in a giant external tank, which would be discarded.

My brief brush with a political career had given me a friend and personal political adviser in Clif White, who had a direct line to President Nixon. Every chance I had, I continued to sell Clif on the Shuttle's importance, knowing the information would be passed to the top. Many presidential advisors, including a lot of personnel at the Office of Management and Budget, didn't want to go ahead with the Shuttle. But Vice President Agnew was a strong supporter. President Nixon personally approved the so-called "stage and a half" version of the Shuttle in January 1972. NASA would have half the money it asked for two years earlier, five and a half billion dollars. First orbital flight was set for 1978. In June 1972, Rockwell International was named the prime contractor for the orbiter.

I hoped to fly the new vehicle, but I shuddered at the compromises we'd had to make, beginning with the use of solid rocket motors as the first stage. The most frightening compromise was the lack of any kind of escape system.

Every concept for getting a crew of six or eight out of the Shuttle orbiter (such as a detachable cockpit, like that of the early B-1 bomber) called for a horrific amount of added weight, fifteen to twenty thousand pounds. That was half the proposed payload capacity.

Vance Brand called from the Rockwell Downey plant, having heard that Milt Silvera, on Max Faget's direction, had ordered the removal of the ejection seats from the first orbiter. I blew my stack, went into Deke's office, and told him of Vance's call. No vehicle was one hundred percent reliable and certainly not the first one to fly. Deke's view was the same as mine, and we immediately went to Bob Gilruth's office and basically put it on the table: "No seats, no fly." I also called Rocco Petrone, the new director at Marshall Spaceflight Center, and he agreed.

Gilruth readily understood, and after a few weeks of heated discussion between the flight crew and engineering directorates, it was decided to put ejection seats back into the Shuttle for the test flights. Nevertheless, none of us was comfortable with the overall design. But there wasn't a damn thing any of us could do about it.

Following Apollo 11, NASA and the Soviets had begun talking about a possible joint Soviet-American manned mission. Over the next two years, various groups had traveled back and forth between the countries, discussing such matters as docking mechanisms, flight control and communications, and differences between spacecraft.

In early April 1972 a working group led on our side by George Low met with the Soviets in Moscow and finalized details for a docking between an Apollo and a Soyuz in Earth orbit in the summer of 1975. The agreement allowed President Nixon and Soviet president Aleksei Kosygin, during a summit meeting in Moscow on May 24, to sign a formal document authorizing the flight—the Apollo-Soyuz Test Project (ASTP)—as part of a five-year exchange on scientific and technical matters.

Hearing the news in Houston, I got excited about flying the American side of the mission. With my three previous flights, and having flown more rendezvous than any other astronaut or cosmonaut, I knew I would have a good chance at the assignment. But there was also a new, senior competitor in the field—my boss, Deke Slayton. Grounded since 1962, forbidden to fly solo in aircraft because of an irregular heartbeat, Deke had undergone medical tests at the Mayo Clinic in Rochester, Minnesota, at the end of 1971. He had noticed that a regime of vitamins had caused the irregular heartbeat to vanish. The tests confirmed that he was healthy, and in March 1972 he was officially promoted to a NASA Class I physical status—and eligible for assignment to a flight crew.

The problem was, in March 1972 there was no flight crew to be assigned to. The Apollo 16 and 17 crews were already deep in training, and we had just announced the nine astronauts on the three Skylab crews. It would have been unfair to simply bump one of them for Deke, and he never suggested it. But here, in May 1972, came Apollo-Soyuz. Deke recommended himself as commander of the flight, then relinquished his authority over crew assignments, turning the ASTP matter over to the MSC director. Robert Gilruth had retired as director in January 1972 and been succeeded by Chris Kraft. Chris had many strengths, and I admired him. But he always resented the power of the astronaut office and some of the antics of the first astronauts. When he took over the MSC he put another layer of management between the astronauts and the center director.

The only obstacle was Deke himself. Assigning Deke to ASTP would be a skillful way of moving him out of his powerful job. So I assumed that Deke was a sure bet for the crew. But there were going to be three seats. I let Chris and his deputy, Sig Sjoberg, and also George Abbey know that I was interested in the mission, specifically in commanding it. And I bought a book on Russian.

When the Soviet delegation arrived at MSC on July 8, 1972, I found myself in meetings with two of the three working groups. One of the issues still to be resolved was fairly basic: Who launches first? Our original idea was to have Apollo go first, and let the Soyuz be the active partner in the rendezvous. Apollo's ability to maneuver in orbit gave us greater flexibility when it came to a launch window.

The Soviets wanted Apollo to launch first. When we asked them why, we found ourselves in a discussion that went on for days. Finally, the reason for the Soviet position became clear: They couldn't torque their launch platform to launch early or late. They had a window of only a few seconds. "What happens if you miss the window?" I asked.

"Then we don't go." Did they go the next day, perhaps? They shrugged. "If we don't go, we don't go." Maybe something was lost in the translation.

In any case, from this session emerged a joint decision to have the Soyuz launch first. They had two pads; they would prepare two spacecraft and rockets, and two crews, in case the first one "missed the window."

The differences in leak rates between spacecraft were also discussed— Apollo might lose up to a tenth of a pound per hour during a mission, which was easily replaced by carrying a few dozen additional pounds. Soviet spacecraft carried no extra oxygen and nitrogen, so they were required to be virtually leakproof. (Leak rates would be a contentious issue to the beginning of the International Space Station twenty-five years later.)

We discussed communications, flight control, exterior spacecraft lighting, the docking module and docking system, dozens of matters, each exchange complicated by the language barrier, and by wildly different approaches to solving problems. I was glad we had three years to get ready to fly.

In the fall and winter of 1971–72, program managers at the Korolyov Bureau had redesigned Soyuz to correct the problem that killed cosmonauts Dobrovolsky, Volkov, and Patsayev. Among the bigger changes was a reduction in crew size from three to two, enabling the crew to launch and return wearing pressure suits. One of these improved Soyuz vehicles was launched unmanned on June 26, 1972, as Kosmos 496 and operated safely. It cleared the way for manned missions.

Ustinov and other ministers for the Soviet Union wanted to have a successful civilian or scientific manned space station before the American Skylab, which was scheduled for launch in the spring of 1973. So the next space station was the second built by the Korolyov Bureau. Four crews were training from September 1971, led by Aleksei Leonov and Valery Kubasov, who were to spend three to four weeks aboard Salyut 2 following launch on Soyuz 12 in late August. But during launch on July 29, 1972, the Proton carrying Salyut 2 suffered a failure in its second stage. Salyut 2 never reached orbit (and was not announced at all by the Soviet press), and Aleksei, Valery, and the other cosmonauts went back to training while a replacement booster was prepared.

During the last week of August 1972, my daughter Dionne, who had graduated from Clear Creek High School in League City in the spring, left home for the University of Texas in Austin. Faye and I drove her there, delivering her to her dormitory. It was a little difficult to see her go, but we had high hopes for her future.

Shortly after I got back to Houston, I received a telephone call from Gen. Sam Phillips, the former head of Apollo, now director of the National Security Agency. He had news for me: I was being promoted to the rank of brigadier general. I was as surprised as I was pleased. Jim McDivitt had made general, but only after leaving the astronaut office to become Apollo program manager. I walked into Deke's office and told him the news. He offered his congratulations and took me off to Chris Kraft to let him know.

The timing of the announcement was especially gratifying, because a few weeks later I attended the twentieth reunion of the Annapolis Class of 1952, as the first member to reach flag rank. I remembered the conduct and attitude grading I had received my last year at the academy. It was very satisfying to be back as a brigadier general-nominee. Jim Lovell was there, too, and Donn Eisele, then assigned to NASA Langley. It was great to catch up with former roommates, such as Stan Storper, now working for Loral; Victor Vine, still flying P-3s for the Navy; and Ron Hattin, now in private business after time in the Air Force. Bruce Brown, who had been in the company next to mine, was still in the Air Force (and eventually to retire as a three-star).

From Annapolis I continued on to Moscow, as a member of Working Group 2, arriving in the Soviet capital on October 7. Unlike my emergency trip to the funeral the previous summer, this visit allowed me a chance to look around Moscow and do some sightseeing with Glynn Lunney and his translator, Alex Tatistcheff. We stayed at the cavernous Rossia Hotel, right near the Kremlin. Thanks to my status as an Apollo astronaut and chief of the astronaut office, the Soviets had given me a huge suite on the top floor. All of our group would relax there after the days' negotiations.

Nevertheless, I didn't think much of the Rossia, and I was unimpressed by Soviet construction. Some of the buildings I saw were practically falling apart, with netting to keep bricks from falling on pedestrians. The city was colorless, too; no advertising. But the Soviets themselves seemed friendly, if careful. After all, we were still enemies, with thousands of nuclear weapons aimed at each other. Another thing that struck me was the number of military officers in uniform. The only place in the United States where you would see a comparable percentage would be right outside the Pentagon.

Shortly after our team returned from Moscow, Chris Kraft called me into his office and told me I was being assigned as commander of ASTP. The only other crew member who was set was Deke Slayton. I suggested Jack Swigert as the CMP, and Chris promised to think that over.

It wasn't too long, however, before Swigert was removed from consideration. The Apollo 15 crew, Dave Scott, Al Worden, and Jim Irwin, had caused a recent flap when it turned out that some stamps they had carried on the 1971 lunar mission were being sold, with a good chunk of the money going to the crew. NASA investigated, and the whole thing got messy because some of the stamps had been approved as part of the crew's personal kits and some hadn't. This incident caused NASA to re-evaluate all personal items carried on all flights up to that time. Had all the materials been authorized? If not, had they been sold? If sold, what had happened to the money? (I had signed a few unflown postal covers and had allowed them to be sold—but I had donated all of the small proceeds to charity.) We even got quizzed about such activities as hunting trips we had taken with individuals from Rockwell.

It wasn't strictly a legal issue: No laws were broken. But NASA policies were another matter, and Deke's ability to trust his astronauts still another. Dave Scott, Al Worden, and Jim Irwin left the astronaut office. Scott lost his shot at commanding ASTP, an assignment he really wanted. When first asked about these items, Jack Swigert had denied having any involvement. Then, some months later, with Apollo-Soyuz looming, he changed his story. That was all Chris needed to take him out of the crew.

While the CMP assignment was still up in the air, several unflown astronauts dropped by to let me know of their interest, notably Bruce McCandless, Don Lind, and Vance Brand. They were all assigned to dead-end jobs in the Skylab program, and ASTP looked to be the last flight available for at least five years. Some, like Vance, had even been paying for private Russian language lessons. Since Vance was an experienced test pilot who had served on two support crews and a backup crew, I told Chris that he was my choice. And so Chris selected Vance. The crew of Stafford, Brand, and Slayton was announced on January 30, 1973.

There was never a moment's tension between Deke and me over the fact that I had been named commander over him. I told him I knew we had a good crew and a good mission to fly, and that was as close as we got to talking about the issue.

In the early discussions about ASTP, the Soviets said they preferred to announce the Soyuz crew in January 1975, giving us only six months of joint training time. During the working group meetings, I told the Soviets this was unacceptable. We had too many challenges, such as simply being able to communicate. Learning to be fluent in Russian required at least two years of full-time language training. That was how long you studied at the Defense Language Institute in Monterey, California, for example. We weren't required to be conversational or fluent, just functional. But even that would require two years, given the other demands of training and travel. So by announcing in January 1973, we forced them to respond with a crew announcement of their own.

It was rumored that Shatalov and Yeliseyev would be assigned as our crew, or possibly Nikolayev and Sevastyanov. All were veterans of previous missions. In the spring of 1973, Aleksei Leonov and Valery Kubasov were deep in training for a twenty-eight-day stay in orbit aboard the third civilian Salyut, scheduled for launch later that year.

Under pressure from the Politburo to beat Skylab, the Soviets launched another Salyut 2 on April 3, 1973. This was not Leonov and Kubasov's Salyut, but a different model—the first all-military "Almaz" station built by the Vladimir Chelomei organization. Teams of military cosmonauts were to visit Almaz for periods of up to two weeks at a time, performing reconnaissance duties. On April 14, after accomplishing its 177th orbit of the earth, for reasons unknown, the station suffered a loss of pressure as it passed out of range of the Soviet tracking network. The manned launches were cancelled. Salyut 2 re-entered in late April, with a vague announcement by the Soviets that it had "fulfilled its mission."

But the Soviets still had one chance to upstage Skylab: An improved civilian Salyut was already at Baikonur. (Imagine if the United States had had both a Skylab and an Air Force Manned Orbiting Laboratory ready at the same time.) Launch day was set for May 11, with the crew of Leonov-Kubasov to follow on May 14—the same day we were scheduled to put the unmanned Skylab into orbit. But the new Salyut suffered a bizarre failure in its propulsion unit shortly after reaching orbit. It was written off so quickly, the public announcement of its launch identified it only as "Kosmos 557." For the second time in a year, Aleksei and Valery were stood down.

A few days later, back at Star City, Aleksei was called into Shatalov's office and told of his new assignment as Soviet commander of Apollo-Soyuz. Kubasov would be his flight engineer. Aleksei told Shatalov, "But I don't even speak English!"

"No problem," Shatalov said. "You have two years and two months to learn it."

We launched Skylab on May 14, 1973, and immediately ran into problems. The micrometeoroid shield around the station tore off during ascent, taking one of Skylab's two vital solar-power panels with it. Once Skylab was in orbit, the second panel failed to deploy. Pete Conrad's crew was supposed to launch the next day, but given the problems, we had to postpone. Meanwhile Skylab was up there, underpowered and overheating. It was up to the flight control team to nurse the station along, orienting it to minimize heating while still generating enough power to keep systems functioning, long enough for us to develop some solutions.

Engineers at MSC and Marshall went into overdrive, inventing an umbrella-like device that could be pushed out of the Skylab experiments airlock, deployed, then retracted back against the exterior to create a sun shield. They also added cable cutters to an extendable pole that could be used to deploy the failed solar array. On May 23, a Saturn 1B carried Pete Conrad, Joe Kerwin, and Paul "PJ" Weitz into orbit. They made rendezvous with Skylab and visually confirmed what telemetry had shown: the missing shield and solar panel, with the surviving panel caught up in tangled metal. Pete flew the command module in close while PJ stood up in the open hatch and tried to muscle the panel free. It didn't work.

When they tried to dock with Skylab, the command module's drogue and probe wouldn't engage, so they had to depressurize the cabin while Pete and Joe disassembled the mechanism, allowing the CM to dock without it. The crew was so exhausted by this work that they pretty much collapsed for the night without trying to enter Skylab. When they did, the next day, they found temperatures so high they couldn't remain for long. Nevertheless, they were able to erect the parasol, which started temperatures dropping. Then Pete and Joe did a spectacular EVA, cutting the solar panel free. Pretty soon they had power, too, and their twenty-eight-day mission—which had almost ended before it got started—began to shape up.

Here was one major difference between our system and that of the Soviets: When their stations had problems, they had to give up on them. Soyuz wasn't capable of carrying much in the way of tools; it couldn't maneuver sufficiently or even stay on orbit more than a couple of days. With Apollo hardware, designed for flights to the Moon, we had the tools and flexibility to make repairs. And since Skylab was our only station (they had Salyuts rolling off an assembly line), we *had* to fix it.

Because of the situation with Skylab, Deke Slayton and Vance Brand remained in the United States, so I was the only representative from the American half of the Apollo-Soyuz crew to attend the Paris Air Show on May 24, the same day Pete's crew was entering Skylab for the first time. The Apollo 17 team—Gene Cernan, Ron Evans, and Jack Schmitt—also came along. Charles "Chuck" Biggs, one of the NASA public affairs officers, had arranged a full-scale Apollo-Soyuz display for the show, locating it right at the entrance of the main exhibit. It consisted of a full-sized Apollo and Soyuz linked together and was the only major display at the air show promoting a cooperative project; all the others were selling military hardware or the latest commercial air product.

I arrived in Paris on the morning of the twenty-fourth after flying all night and checked into the George V Hotel, one of the most luxurious in Paris. It turned out I had a suite with three bedrooms, complete with bottles of champagne. It had been arranged by Art Brundt, a friend who formerly ran the Miami Springs Villas in Miami, where a lot of astronauts went for relaxation. The Villas were now part of the Trust House Forte, which also owned the George V.

Jet-lagged or not, I had to leave the suite and drive with Gene Marionetti, my NASA escort, to Le Bourget Airport to meet the Soviet delegation. (The Soviets had said they would announce their ASTP crew members at the Paris Air Show.) First to debark was Aleksei Yeliseyev, whom I still expected to be on the Soyuz crew. We had gotten to know each other during the ASTP discussions, and I liked him. Then came Aleksei Leonov, whom I had met at the funeral for the Soyuz 11 crew two years earlier, and Valery Kubasov, whom I didn't know at all. We posed for photos and answered questions from reporters but got no private time.

It wasn't until that evening, at a small reception in Leonov's tiny hotel room on the Left Bank, that I learned, over a feast of Russian black bread, vodka, cognac, caviar, and crab, that Leonov and Kubasov would be the Soyuz team. The crew for the second, standby Soyuz would be veterans Anatoly Filipchenko and Nikolai Rukavishnikov. The two backup crews were all rookies: Vladimir Dzhanibekov and Boris Andreyev in one crew, Yury Romanenko and Aleksandr Ivanchenkov in the other. (This was the first time the Soviets had revealed the names of cosmonauts before they flew.) Yeliseyev was to serve as ASTP mission director, counterpart to NASA's Pete Frank.

We made the public announcement the next day, May 25, 1973, followed by a real party that night in my "little hotel room" at the George V, toasting our future.

sixteen
"ASTP Is Dead!"

Aleksei Leonov and his team first visited Houston on July 8, 1973. It was time for the eight cosmonauts to get familiar with Apollo, to sit in our simulators and see a mockup of the docking module, while their flight support people coordinated with ours. Maj. Gen. Vladimir Shatalov, the former cosmonaut, was with Aleksei—as director of cosmonaut training for the Soviet Air Force, he always accompanied the crews on their visits to the United States.

We had hoped to get to know Aleksei and his group a lot better. Thanks to Nina de la Cruz, our side was ahead of the Soviets in the language department. Deke had logged 140 hours, I had 115. But almost every minute of this session was programmed. We knew we'd have to do better.

On July 11, we all flew to Los Angeles, to see CSM-111 in the factory and the docking module at Rockwell. The docking module was the major piece of hardware to be developed for ASTP. It looked like an overgrown beer keg with ears on it but actually consisted of two parts: an airlock module, and an "androgynous" docking adaptor. The adaptor would use a set of fins that looked like the petals of a flower to line up with a similar adaptor on the nose of the Soyuz. Once we had a soft dock, the adaptors would be pulled together, sealing the two spacecraft in a perfectly aligned hard dock.

We needed the airlock to equalize pressure as the crews moved from

Apollo to Soyuz and back. The Soviets had always operated their spacecraft with a mixture of normal air at sea-level pressure of 14.7 psi, while in flight we still used pure oxygen at 5.0 psi. For ASTP, the Soyuz was modified to operate with a pressure of 10 psi (after a day on orbit), which saved us from having to prebreathe every time we crossed over.

The crews had dinner at the Queen Mary in Long Beach and saw a few other attractions in the L.A. area. Then it was back to Houston. The cosmonauts went by a NASA Gulfstream I—we asked the pilot to fly over the Grand Canyon—while the American astronauts flew T-38s. The Soviets had originally planned to stay for three weeks, but they went home a few days early, probably to avoid a discussion of whether to attend the launch of Al Bean's Skylab crew on July 28. If they accepted our invitation, it would obligate them to invite us to a launch at Baikonur.

In spite of our slight lead in the language department, Aleksei was the champion when it came to humor. At one of our press conferences, he used his halting English to announce, "In visiting United States, I vant to go to Hollywood . . . because I vant to be a movie star." Everybody laughed. Then he corrected himself. "No, I don't vant. . . . *Tom Stafford* vants to be a movie star."

In addition to the prime crew of Vance, Deke, and me, ASTP had a backup crew of Al Bean, Ron Evans, and Jack Lousma, who came aboard full time in fall 1973. There were four support crew members: Bo Bobko, Bob Crippen, Dick Truly, and Bob Overmyer. Overmyer was going to represent us at Soviet mission control, which we hadn't yet seen. Gene Cernan was special assistant to Chris Kraft for ASTP, so he was on our trips, too.

The Soviet delegations to the United States always included a few of the usual KGB types. We assumed that the cosmonauts did their own recon. So did we. After all, our four support astronauts had all spent several years training to spy on the Soviet Union from orbit in the MOL program. They held clearances above mine, which was "secret." Glynn Lunney and Gene Cernan also stopped by CIA headquarters in Langley, Virginia, on their return from Moscow, to be debriefed.

I had no idea about this at the time. Given my prominence, I knew any contact between me and the CIA would eventually become public. So I made it clear to NASA management that I wanted no contact with the agency and didn't want to know of any. If ever asked by a reporter, I had plausible deniability. Of course, my good friend and mentor, Gen. Sam Phillips, was now head of the National Security Agency, and when I was in the Washington, D.C., area, I would make a social call at his home in Maryland, to see him and his wife, Betty Ann. We would discuss various matters of interest.

The Soviets were playing their games, too, at a far greater level. First of all, the whole idea that the Soviet Academy of Sciences ran their manned space program was complete fiction. Yes, Academy President Keldysh had been a key figure in their space programs for twenty-five years but in the business of calculating trajectories for ICBMs and spacecraft. Management was split among various ministries and organizations. The Soviet Air Force, which ran the Star City, was under the Ministry of Defense, for example. So was the Strategic Rocket Force, which launched the Soyuz, handled flight control at its center in Yevpatoria, Crimea, and ran the Baikonur Cosmodrome. Then there was the Korolyov Design Bureau, which reported to the Ministry of General Machine Building. The bureau, then headed by Vasily Mishin, designed and built the Soyuz spacecraft, and was teamed with yet another organization (TsNIIMash, an analytical institute somewhat like our Aerospace Corporation) in the construction of a new "civilian" mission control center.

We had a general idea of the nature of the different organizations but very little specific information. It was amusing, though, to see the Soviet technical director, Konstantin Bushuyev, a spacecraft engineer and program manager much like George Low, being passed off as "Professor Bushuyev" of the Academy of Sciences. Bushuyev was actually a senior official at the Korolyov Bureau. We learned years later that whenever the Americans came to town, or tried to get in touch with him, Bushuyev would have to rush off to Moscow, to the Academy's Institute of Space Science, which was supposed to be his office. Even in meetings with his American counterparts, such as Glynn Lunney, Chet Lee, or Pete Frank, Professor Bushuyev would say, "I have to excuse myself," and he would go consult with his KGB handlers—and with his colleagues at the Korolyov Bureau—on whether it was permissible to answer a certain question.

They were pretty basic questions, too. "Where do you build your spacecraft?" I asked.

"In one of our factories." That was the entire answer.

"I want to see the mission control."

"After a while. We're still completing it." Which raised the question: What had they been using for a control center until now?

Finally, they relented and took us to the new facility, which was built on the grounds of TsNIIMash in the Moscow suburb of Kaliningrad, right across the street from a massive industrial complex that turned out to be the Korolyov Bureau. Throughout ASTP, I would continually feel sorry for "Professor" Konstantin Bushuyev. He was a superb gentleman, a solid engineer, and obviously a man under a lot of pressure.

In November 1973, during the first training visit to Russia, the American delegation lived in the Intourist Hotel in downtown Moscow. My specific complaints about the Rossia had encouraged the Soviets to relocate us. Every morning we would be bussed the forty kilometers out to work at Star City in a convoy with a police escort, one car in front and one trailing. At Star City we would take classes and work in the simulators. We really got to know Soyuz and its flight control and environmental systems during this time. When our working day was over, we sometimes gathered in the Marine Bar in the American Embassy for relaxation. We even had time for a snowball fight along the road from Star City to Moscow.

One thing that was clear was that the cosmonauts had caught up and passed us in the language race. We learned that each of the Soyuz crew members had an English instructor with him day and night. I used a telephone in the American Embassy to call Chris Kraft, and told him we were not going to be successful in this mission without more Russian instructors. "I don't need a separate one for each crew member," I said, "but I need four at a minimum to teach us." That meant no union rules, either: If we needed instructors on weekends, or 6 A.M. or midnight, they had to be available.

Chris promised to support me, and when we returned from the trip, we started to hire four new instructors: Jim Flannery, a former U.S. Army linguist; Nina Horner and Vasil Kiostun, recent émigrés from the USSR who were studying at the University of Wisconsin; and Anatole Forostenko, a professor of Russian language and literature from the University of California, Riverside, who was born in Belorussia but grew up in the United States.

Anatole became the primary instructor for Vance and me. I had a good ear for the language and seemed to pick it up fairly quickly. Of course, Russian has more consonants than English, and my tendency to mumble them, combined with my regional accent, caused Aleksei Leonov to claim that I was speaking not *Anglisky* (English) or *Russky*, but *Oklahomsky!*

As training for Apollo-Soyuz ramped up in the winter of 1973–74, there were management changes on both sides of the program—small ones for us, much larger ones for the Soviets. In Houston (where the Manned Spacecraft Center had now been renamed the Johnson Space Center, in honor of the late president), the Skylab program ended and the long-awaited reorganization of center management took place, with flight crew operations (Deke's and my former directorate) being moved under flight operations (formerly headed by Chris Kraft). Kenny Kleinknecht, a former manager in the Skylab program, was put in charge of both flight controllers and astronauts. Under him, Al Shepard remained chief of the astronaut office, which now shrank to twenty-six pilots, ten assigned to ASTP, the rest to Shuttle development. All of the scientist-astronauts were dispersed to "astronaut offices" within the Life Sciences and Science and Applications directorates.

Aleksei and his team returned to Houston in April 1974, for their second working and training visit. This time they brought veteran Vostok 5 cosmonaut Valery Bykovsky, who was training manager for the Soyuz crews. We devoted these two weeks to simulating docking between Apollo and Soyuz. It reminded us of the value of joint training sessions: The second time we did an exercise we usually improved our speed and efficiency by fifty percent or more, just because we were that much more familiar with the other side's procedures. We laid out a schedule of the work still to be accomplished in the fourteen months remaining before launch and in doing so validated my original insistence on two years of training was correct.

Then the Soviets returned home to a bombshell: On May 15, 1974, Vasily Mishin, head of the Korolyov Bureau since 1966, was fired. The Kremlin and the Ministry of General Machine Building had gotten tired of continued failures with space stations (even though many of the problems were due to launch vehicles built by a different organization) and Mishin's insistence on a manned lunar program (which was still in the works).

Not only did Mishin get removed, but the ministry replaced him with Valentin Glushko, one of the pioneers of the Soviet missile and space programs. His bureau designed and built most of the rocket engines used by Soviet launch vehicles. The ministry merged Glushko's bureau with the Korolyov/Mishin bureau to form a gigantic new entity, the Energia Scientific-Production Enterprise. We had no inkling of the change, not one bit. Konstantin Bushuyev, one of Mishin's primary deputies, remained in his job as head of ASTP, and the joint program was unaffected.

We returned to Moscow in June 1974 for another training session. This time instead of heading from the airport to a downtown hotel, our convoy went directly to Star City. The Soviets had built a three-story hotel there called the Hotel Kosmonavt. It was roomy; the astronauts and support people of the American ASTP team were the only residents at the time. It was also bugged, a situation we assumed everywhere we lived in the USSR. (I had always reminded the team that surveillance on rooms and telephones was standard Soviet operating procedure.)

Our first day in the Hotel Kosmonavt was hot, and my room was full of flies. To test the surveillance system, I started complaining, loudly. "The Russians are very wonderful and hospitable people, but it's too bad they decided to be so cheap about this hotel. There's not even a fly swatter." We went out training for four hours, and when we returned, every room had a fly swatter. Better yet, every fly in my room had been killed and dumped in the unflushed toilet.

I didn't want to become the team's designated complainer, so a few days later, when we had all gotten tired of the poor quality Russian beer, I asked Bob Overmyer to "talk to the walls" about it. The next day, when we went off for training, I encouraged Jack Riley, our public affairs rep, to hang around and see what happened. Sure enough, about three in the afternoon, a big truck with "Pivo" written on the side (Russian for "beer") pulled up, and its crew started unloaded cases of Czech, East German, and Egyptian beer for us. "Talking to the walls," worked better than room service.

We were free to travel to Moscow, provided we used our assigned driver and car. When we did, of course, we were followed, partly for surveillance, but also for our own protection. Anatole Forostenko, who had made several trips to the Soviet Union as a university professor prior to joining ASTP, had a number of acquaintances in the "dissident" community, including some artists he wanted to support. So one evening, we went into Moscow for dinner then stopped by the embassy to see some friends. As we started around the Garden Ring Road, we noticed that a car behind us only had one headlight. I told Anatole to tell our driver to speed up, and sure enough, the one-eyed car stayed with us.

We got onto some of Moscow's broader streets, where we had our driver pull several sharp right and left turns then a U-turn. Our one-eyed tail hung in there. But with the traffic, we got boxed in, and our tail came right up next to us—two men in the front, a man and woman in the back. They all wore trenchcoats and hats, like old plainclothes policemen. I reached over and knocked on their window, and told them, in Russian, to go screw themselves. Of course, even then we realized that for every obvious tail, there was at least one we would never see.

On June 27, President Richard Nixon arrived in Moscow, too. In spite of his growing problems with impeachment due to the Watergate scandal, he was in the middle of a world tour. The President was originally scheduled to visit Star City along with Prime Minister Leonid Brezhnev. I noticed that the little antique cottages along the road from Moscow had all been painted, and the potholes in that road had been filled in. But plans changed. Instead, we were invited to the reception in the great Hall of St. George at the Kremlin. The band played "Ruffles and Flourishes," and then Nixon and Brezhnev marched in, followed by Henry Kissinger, Andrei Gromyko, and Anatoly Dobrynin. Lined up along the hall were admirals, generals, and senior political leaders. Our group of astronauts and cosmonauts waited at the far end, where the group of leaders eventually stopped, with many handshakes.

Champagne was passed around, and Nixon made several toasts to progress in arms control and to the success of Apollo-Soyuz. Shortly thereafter, he said to me, "Tom, we have accomplished so much here. When you talk about twelve thousand nuclear weapons, just how many villages in India do you want to destroy?" I wasn't about to get into a geopolitical discussion on the subject, so I replied, "That is a very difficult question to answer, Mr. President." It was obvious to me, having arrived only a couple of days before from the States, where all hell was breaking loose on Watergate, that Mr. Nixon wasn't facing reality.

The major goal of the summer 1974 training session was communications. All crew members had sufficient language skill to read and understand basic commands, so we spent hours literally following scripts for a variety of situations we expected to encounter. The original ASTP agreement called for each crew to speak its own language, and we were finding that to be insufficient to carry out the required procedures.

One night at a party, I found myself talking with Anatoly Filipchenko, commander of the second ASTP craft. It was almost as if we had ESP—the first thing we did was try to speak the other's language. When you do that, you naturally speak more slowly and distinctly. The next day, we presented this arrangement to the other crew members and flight planners. Since nobody thought what we had was working especially well, we all agreed to give this a try. It became our standard method.

There were occasional mix-ups. To Russians, the English word "maneuver" sounds just like "manure." So we had shared a few laughs over upcoming Apollo "manure." On our side, the Russian word for "separate" sounds like the word for "strangulate." And so when I, in my Oklahomsky, would say, in Russian, "We are separating," the cosmonauts thought I said, "We are strangulating."

On the evening of the Fourth of July, after returning to Star City from a magnificemt reception at the American ambassador's residence, Dom Spasso, we decided to have our own patriotic celebration. Ron Evans had somehow managed to smuggle half a suitcase worth of fireworks into the Soviet Union, and we proceeded to set off a string of firecrackers on the front patio of the Hotel Kosnonavt.

General Beregovoi's police arrived swiftly, ready to investigate those who would dare disturb the peace and quiet of Star City. When they hesitated to approach us from the other side of the fishing pond, I ordered Evans to fire a bottle rocket in their general direction. It exploded about a hundred feet over their heads, and they all jumped. We continued out barrage until one of them, the head policeman, slowly crossed the fifty yards to our group. As the other astronauts gathered around, I explained, in Oklahomsky, "Good evening, Comrade. We are celebrating the birthday of our revolution. Would you join us in a drink to celebrate our holiday?" The policeman smiled, politely refused, and went off with his men.

On June 26, 1974, the Soviets launched a new space station named Salyut 3, announcing the event only after it was safely in orbit. Pavel Popovich and

Yury Artyukhin reached it in Soyuz 14 and spent two weeks aboard, returning safely on July 19. On August 25, another crew was launched, aboard Soyuz 15. Gennady Sarafanov and Lev Demin's mission only lasted two days, however. The automatic Igla guidance system failed during the final approach to Salyut 3 and mission control aborted the docking attempt. With life support aboard Soyuz limited to two days, Sarafanov and Demin had to return at the first opportunity, thumping down in darkness.

The official explanation in the Soviet press was that Soyuz 15 was completely successful. The cosmonauts had tested automatic flight systems while "inspecting" the station. No docking was planned, they said. This explanation didn't make sense to George Low, who asked me to come to his office at headquarters ahead of the Soviet delegation, which included General Shatalov, scheduled to arrive in Washington, D.C. on Friday, September 8, 1974.

It was ridiculous, George said, to believe that the Soviets had sent a crew to fly around and inspect a station they had previously occupied. If the Soviets stuck to that story and the United States held intelligence data contradicting it, that information was sure to leak through congressional committees to the press. And if Congress and the press could claim that the Soviets were liars, ASTP was dead. Senator William Proxmire, who liked to kick NASA at every opportunity and who was very critical of ASTP, would be against us; so would many politicians who were on the fence. We would even lose some of our supporters. "Tom," he said, "you have to find out the truth. If the Soviets had a problem, they have to come clean by midweek." I knew George, like a few senior NASA leaders, held several top-level security clearances, so I took his warning seriously and promised to learn what I could. He said to call him at home, regardless of the hour.

I went to Washington National Airport to meet Aleksei, Valery Shatalov, and the other members of the Soyuz team. While waiting, I chatted with several staffers from the Soviet embassy, who were also there to meet the cosmonauts. One official raised the subject of technology transfer, pointing out the benefits for world peace, prosperity, and friendship with the Soviet Union if the United States would send them the technology for heavy interstate trucks, heavy forging presses, and electronics.

Evel Knievel had just tried and failed to jump the Snake River aboard his rocketcycle. I said to the Soviet official, "Maybe we could have Evel Knievel work on transferring his technology, since the Soviet Union has so many great rivers and canyons." The official got my joke and stopped pressing me.

The next evening there was a small dinner and reception for the crews at the Washington Hilton coordinated by Gene Marionetti, chief of astronaut appearances, who did his usual outstanding job. During the evening I went directly to Shatalov and said I needed to talk with him on a very serious matter concerning Apollo-Soyuz. I added that I only wanted to talk to him—not his interpreter, Konstantin Samofal, who went with him everywhere outside the Soviet Union.[2] I also said that I would need Anatole Forostenko with me because I still could not pronounce some Russian words, and I wanted to make sure he understood the problems.

As the last toasts were offered, Shatalov, Forostenko, and I went to my suite, which had a large sitting room, bar, and bedroom. I poured us each a drink of Scotch then told Shatalov, "We have a problem. We have to know the truth about Soyuz 15 because you just don't go to a space station that's already been occupied, fly around, and come home."

Shatalov wasn't ready to give in. "We didn't have a problem."

I was pretty blunt and made sure Anatole told him exactly what I wanted. "Let me explain this to you," I said. "Washington isn't Moscow. Everything leaks to the press. What's 'secret' today winds up on the front page of the *Washington Post* tomorrow; 'top secret' will be in the *New York Times* in a week. If you say you didn't have a problem, and somebody from an intelligence agency knows differently, and Congress leaks that you really did have a problem, ASTP is dead."

Shatalov, who had a slightly ruddy face, got very pale.

I continued: "The Congress is going to ask me if the cosmonauts have been honest with me, and if you have had a problem with Soyuz 15, I'm going to have to say no, not entirely."

I could tell he was angry about being lectured. It wasn't a general-to-general conversation, but rather general-to-young lieutenant. I felt I had to do it, though. I wasn't especially worried about the Soyuz 15 docking failure. The Soviet automatic docking system had failed before, on Soyuz 3 and Soyuz 8. On ASTP we would be using a completely different system, with Apollo doing the maneuvering. It was the political danger that worried me. "Please go see Ambassador Dobrynin and tell him the situation. Call Moscow, if you need to." Shatalov agreed to go to the Soviet embassy the next morning.

We all had another drink. Shatalov said he wanted the mission to work because it was good for both countries. I thanked him for his effort. After he and Forostenko left about 11 P.M., I called George Low at home and briefed him on the situation. He was pleased and hoped we would soon have some word out of Moscow and the Academy of Sciences.

The next morning was Sunday the tenth, and the group was scheduled to visit the Smithsonian. Aleksei said Shatalov told him he had to go to the embassy first but would join us later. About 11:30 A.M. Shatalov rejoined the group, took me aside, and said he had talked to Dobrynin, who understood the situation, and that they both had called Moscow. I thanked him again for his help.

On Monday, from Moscow, Professor Bushuyev made the announcement that a malfunction on Soyuz 15 during the docking phase of this mission had precluded a successful docking. Not until years later would we fully understand how difficult it had been for Shatalov and, especially, Bushuyev, to comment on Soyuz 15. Both men knew that Salyut 3 had been built by the Chelomei Bureau, an organization dedicated entirely to military reconnaissance.

After the announcement George Low called and thanked me. He said it was a close call that could have cancelled the mission. We were learning to work together. But we still found it difficult to be completely open with each other.

My father, Dr. Thomas Sabert Stafford, on graduation from Vanderbilt University Dental School, 1912.

My mother, Mary Ellen Patten, on her wedding
day, 1921.

The Stafford family, 1936.

Working for the forest service in the
Sierra Nevadas, summer 1946.

Annapolis graduate, class of 1952.

With my daughters, Karin and Dionne, at Hahn
Air Base, Germany, 1958.

Test pilot instructor, Edwards Air Force Base, 1961. (Courtesy of U.S. Air Force)

With Faye, the girls, and a T-38 at Edwards, just prior to our departure for Harvard Business School, July 1962.

The second group of NASA astronauts after our introduction at Rice University, September 17, 1962. *Back row standing, from left to right:* Elliot See, Jim McDivitt, Jim Lovell, Ed White, me. *Front row, kneeling, from left to right:* Pete Conrad, Frank Borman, Neil Armstrong, John Young. "One of us is going to be first to the Moon!" (Courtesy of NASA)

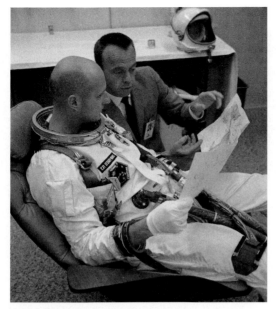

Tom Stafford and Alan Shepard, the original first Gemini crew. Shepard is briefing me on weather conditions prior to the Gemini 6 launch. (Courtesy of NASA)

Gemini 6, Wally Schirra and me, 1965. (Courtesy of NASA)

Me and Snoopy. (Courtesy of NASA)

The real Snoopy, LM-4 ascent stage, in lunar orbit, April 1969.(Courtesy of NASA)

My mentor in the space program and
the Air Force, Gen. Sam Phillips.
(Courtesy of NASA)

The Soyuz 11 funeral, Red Square, July 1971.

Chris Kraft and Faye help with my promotion to brigadier general, 1972. (Courtesy of NASA)

The ASTP crew, 1974: *Front,* Deke Slayton, the Mercury astronaut who was my boss for ten years; Vance Brand; and Valery Kubasov. I'm in the back with Aleksei Leonov, who became one of my closest friends. (Courtesy of NASA)

Snowball fight in Russia near Star City, 1973. Vance Brand is on the left; Ron Evans is third from left. I'm being hugged in the middle, with snowballers Gene Cernan and Jack Lousma to the right.

In Kazakh robes during the first visit to Baikonur, 1975. *From left:* Anatoly Filipchenko, Aleksei Leonov. I am fourth from left, with Vance Brand peering over my shoulder. Deke Slayton, Gene Cernan, and Konstantin Bushuyev are on the right.

Soyuz seen from Apollo, July 1975.
(Courtesy of NASA)

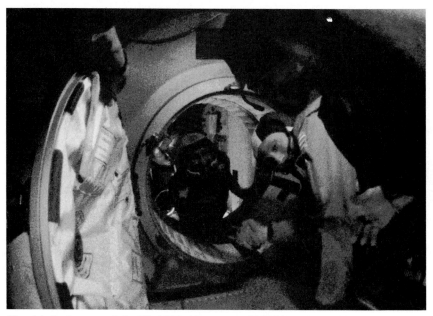

Handshake in space, July 17, 1975. (Courtesy of NASA)

With Deke Slayton *(far left)*, Aleksei Leonov, and Anatoly Filipchenko at the tenth anniversary of Apollo-Soyuz, Star City, 1985.

Rollout of the B-2 bomber, originally the Advanced Technology Bomber, at Palmdale, 1989. I started this program by drafting its specifications on a piece of hotel stationery in Chicago in early 1979.

Linda and I on the Orient Express, 1996.

George Abbey *(far left)* with members of the Stafford-Utkin Commission at a Houston rodeo, 1997. Joe Engle is third from left, and Academician Utkin is next to him.

seventeen
Handshake in Space

Though we had some struggles getting the Soviets to communicate to our standards and stick to agreed-upon schedules, it was obvious that they had committed a lot of resources to Apollo-Soyuz. They actually modified six Soyuz launchers and spacecraft for the program, flying three unmanned test flights. They had said all along that they would also launch a manned test in the autumn of 1974, which would not only verify communication systems in both countries but would also allow NASA's network to track Soyuz. The trouble was, the Soviets wanted NASA to agree to keep the launch secret until Soyuz was in flight. We couldn't agree to that, so we wouldn't let them tell us the launch date in advance.

At 6:35 in the morning of Monday, December 2, 1974, a security guard in the halls of JSC picked up a ringing telephone at a desk belonging to Glynn Lunney's secretary. Vladimir Timchenko, one of the Energia managers for Apollo-Soyuz, was trying to reach Lunney. The guard told Timchenko that Lunney wasn't in yet, then relayed a message to Lunney's home that the Soviets would call back at 8:15.

The news was that Soyuz 16 had been launched earlier that day from Baikonur with Filipchenko and Rukavishnikov flying a spacecraft modified for ASTP. Once we had the data from Timchenko, we were able to track Soyuz 16. Filipchenko and Rukavishnikov spent six days in space simulating the Soyuz ASTP trajectory. They landed safely in Kazakhstan on December 8.

Aleksei, Valery, and the other cosmonauts and support people, including Shatalov, returned to the States on Friday, February 7, 1975. We met in Washington, then flew to the Cape. Vance, Deke, and the rest of the Apollo team joined us there. The next day we showed them the firing room for Pad 39B, the Saturn 1B in the Vehicle Assembly Building, and our Apollo command module, CSM-111, which was undergoing checkout. Ernst Vaskevich, one of the KGB interpreters and handlers for the cosmonauts, couldn't hide his amazement. "This is the *real* spacecraft?" he kept asking. The Soviets were also amazed that we allowed tourists to wander all over the Cape.

On Sunday, the ninth, we all paid a visit to Disney World in Orlando. Aleksei and Valery had a ball going on rides like Space Mountain. They told me they were impressed by how clean Disney World was, and by the fact that everything was artificial. That evening, on our hotel balcony, we happened to see some ducks swimming near the edge of a pond. "The ducks," Valery announced, "are not real."

As Aleksei and I grew more fluent in each other's language, we began to speak more freely. For example, one evening in an American hotel I happened to find Aleksei watching the evening news on television. "Tom," he said, "you have such a beautiful country. People drive nice cars and wear nice clothes. You have good health care and the stores are full. Why does it say only bad things on television? You have nothing but shooting and death on television." It was difficult to reply, because I agreed with him. It has always been a mystery to me why Americans preferred to watch murder and mayhem all the time.

After one additional day at the Cape, it was back to Houston for three weeks of work in the simulators and procedures trainers.

Once we returned to Houston, I made my move. I had always wanted to visit the secret Soviet launch center known as Baikonur, and back in 1973 George Low had gotten the Soviets to agree that such a visit was possible. But nothing firm had been set, and time was running out. There was a solid, operational reason: I couldn't imagine flying in a spacecraft my crew and I hadn't checked out personally. To check out the Soyuz, we had to go to Baikonur.

I felt that if I made my desire known too early, the Soviets would find some way to keep stalling. But once they had visited the Cape and seen our spacecraft, they would be in a poor position to say no.

I first mentioned it to Aleksei who simply said it was impossible, the whole place was secret. But over the next few days I repeated the request, raising it with Shatalov, then Viktor Legostayev, one of Bushuyev's deputies. Then Bushuyev himself. Academician Boris Petrov and one of his deputies were also in Houston at the same time, and I leaned heavily on them with the same argument. I got turned down everywhere but kept raising the ante until it got to this: "If I don't get to see inside that Soyuz," I said, "I'm not flying this mission."

Now I had their attention. Bushuyev and Shatalov wondered aloud if it was possible to fly my backup crew. But Al Bean, my backup commander, was in total agreement with me. He wouldn't fly the mission, either. Chris Kraft, Glynn Lunney, and George Low supported me, too. To close the deal, I told the Soviets, "Look, I've seen many detailed satellite photos. I know what the place looks like. Fly us in and out at night, if that's all you're worried about." They finally agreed to let us visit on our final training trip to the USSR, in April.

During these intense conversations I relied on Anatole Forostenko, who did a tremendous job as my translator.

Things seemed to be marching smoothly toward Apollo-Soyuz until the morning of April 5, 1975, when the Soviets launched Soyuz 18 and cosmonauts Vasily Lazarev and Oleg Makarov, for a sixty-day mission to Salyut 4. During launch, the central, sustainer stage of the Soyuz launch vehicle failed to separate after shutdown. The upper stage, which was designed to put Soyuz 18 in orbit, began firing with this hundred-foot-long dead weight still attached.

The crew immediately knew something was wrong. They were going sideways. Lazarev reported, "We've shut down, we've shut down!" That was the only option at that altitude—shut down, separate from the upper stage, and fly an aborted suborbital ballistic mission. Their launch escape tower had already been jettisoned.

But the only response from mission control was "Vyo normalno." Everything is normal.[3]

Lazarev again: "Hey, we've shut down and we're aborting!"

Same thing from mission control: "Everything is normal." Obviously there was a delay in their tracking data.

Then one of the cosmonauts started asking, "Are we going to come down in China?" The Soyuz launch trajectory skirted the Chinese border at this point. "Don't you dumb bastards know what's happened to us?"

Finally there was a real-time response from mission control. "You're going to come down in the Motherland." And they did, on a mountainside, after withstanding eighteen to twenty Gs. It took rescue parties a day to find them. Only then was there a public announcement of the aborted launch, which the Soviet press called "the April 5 Anomaly."

Coming after the Soyuz 15 docking failure, this meant more trouble for Apollo-Soyuz. Senator William Proxmire had another example to add to his list of Soviet failures going back to the Soyuz 1 tragedy in 1967. He wrote to the CIA, he wrote to James Fletcher, he complained to anyone who would listen.

I certainly was concerned about the abort. This time, however, unlike Soyuz 15, the Soviets spoke right up about the problem. Bushuyev called Lunney directly on April 8 to discuss the matter, saying that the preliminary investigation showed that one of the pyrotechnic charges intended to separate the sustainer from the upper stage had fired prematurely, inhibiting the other pyros from firing and causing the booster to deviate from its trajectory. Bushuyev also said that the booster used on the April 5 Anomaly was from a batch older than the one programmed for ASTP, and that those used for the three of the four ASTP test flights (including Soyuz 16) had improved pyrotechnic systems.

Our side was satisfied. As far as the reliability of Soviet systems, I thought they were fine for operating in low Earth orbit and said so publicly.

In addition to technical and political matters, the protocols for Apollo-Soyuz called for both sides to engage in "cultural" exchanges. For example, we had invited the cosmonauts to choose places in the USA they would like to visit, emphasizing that it was all open to them. They had been cautious, however, asking to see museums in Washington, for example, and Disney World.

I had always felt that the American team needed to break out of the cozy cocoon the Soviets wrapped us in and get out of Moscow. The two crews visited Zagorsk, seat of the Russian Orthodox Church, and Kaluga, home of Konstantin Tsaikovsky. I also wanted to see some of the other republics and gave Anatole Forostenko the job of coming up with some possibilities.

He suggested the cities of Tashkent, Bukhara, and Samarkand in the Uzbek SSR, not far from Kazakhstan. They were ancient, truly Asian cities that would provide a nice contrast to European Russia. To help sell the idea to the Soviets, Anatole also pointed out that the conqueror Tamerlane, who was buried in Samarkand, had been a supporter of astronomy and mathematics.

While we awaited approval for travel, we began our final training session at Star City on April 14. The crews spent their time in the Soyuz simulators, rehearsing all phases of the mission. During the first week, on the nineteenth, we finally got our first look at the new mission control center in Kaliningrad—"TsUP" was what the Russians called it: Tsentr Upravleniya Polyotov, or, logically enough, the flight control center.

It wasn't until the middle of the next week that we got a definitive date for the Baikonur trip—Monday, April 28—piggybacked onto our trip to Tashkent, Bukhara, and Samarkand the weekend prior. On Friday afternoon, the twenty-fifth, we were driven off to Vnukovo Airport on the other side of Moscow, where we boarded a Tu-134. Bushuyev, Shatalov, and Bykovsky came with us. Before long we were flying in darkness over what seemed to be a trackless wasteland.

We landed in Tashkent late at night, then we were up and on our way to Bukhara the next morning. To get around we had our own fleet of three Yak-40 executive jets—assigned to us on Brezhnev's personal order, we were told. Each plane could carry about thirty passengers. Prime crews went in one, backup crews in another, and support crew members in a third.

The Soviets had been reluctant to let us loose in Asia because we would be exposed to the poverty and would see just how little impact the Communist Party had in these place. Yes, we saw the hammer and sickle on certain buildings, and there was always a facility named after Lenin, but once you got away from the airport and the main square, you were in a culture that, in places, seemed to have changed little in hundreds of years, with people who had seen other "conquerors" come and go.

We returned to Tashkent from Samarkand Saturday night, then spent Sunday seeing the sights of that city, including a reception from the local party secretary. (He made a special welcome to Vladimir Dzhanibekov, one of the

Soviet backup commanders, who had attended grade and high school in the city.) From Tashkent on Sunday night it was a short hop to Baikonur, specifically to Leninsk, a city of fifty thousand people based on the Syr Darya River. The Baikonur Cosmodrome lay to the north of the river.

As expected, it was dark by the time our plane touched down. After a night in the same hotel used by Soviet cosmonauts in Leninsk—and run, at least for our stay, by the same woman who ran the Hotel Kosmonavt in Star City—we were loaded onto a pair of very plush buses and driven thirty kilometers north to the heart of the Cosmodrome. Along the way a television in our bus played a Soviet cartoon called *Napu Guidi,* much like the Roadrunner cartoons. It was a favorite of the cosmonauts.

We were taken to the assembly building, which served the two Soyuz pads. The work crews at Baikonur had spruced up the place. They had even painted the sides of the train rails leading from the assembly building to the launch pad. We didn't see any military uniforms—just a lot of men in crew cuts and ill-fitting civilian clothes. Two Soyuz spacecraft were sitting upright in the assembly building, with Aleksei and Valery's open for inspection. I immediately crawled inside with Aleksei and started taking pictures of the console and switch positions. I made sure every one of the prime, backup, and support crew members got inside in ones and twos.

Having accomplished our mission—and become the first Westerners other than Charles de Gaulle to visit the secret center—we did a bit of sightseeing, and each of us planted a tree on cosmonaut lane, as previous Vostok, Voskhod, and Soyuz crews had. Then it was back to Leninsk, to a public reception in the main boulevard and square. The whole town seemed to have turned out to see the Americans. It was great fun to see the children and shake hands with them and their families.

Our next event was a relatively informal party held on the banks of the Syr Darya, in a traditional tent surrounded by Kazakh cowboys and their small ponies. We sat cross-legged on carpets and made toasts to friendship. Aleksei and I even wound up donning Kazakh robes. There were snacks, including what appeared to be a round pastry, slightly larger than a donut hole. Deke Slayton and Anatole Forostenko each took one and bit in—only to find that the snack wasn't pastry, but congealed sheep fat. Our hosts were also passing around a drink that was liquid sheep fat, and fortunately I managed to avoid it.

Then it was time for the main reception, hosted by the local secretary of the Communist Party. Here I faced one of my greatest challenges of the Apollo-Soyuz program: A boiled, skinned ram's head sat on a platter right in front of me, and across from Aleksei, the party secretary, and Professor Bushuyev. Aleksei picked up the platter and announced that it was "tradition" that the main host and guest each had to eat one eyeball out of the ram's head. I thought he was joking, right up to the moment when he handed me a fork. I'd had a few vodkas by then, so I dug the eyeball out of the head, plopped it in my mouth and chewed it. Seeing this from the next table, Bo Bobko threw up. Deke and Anatole had to leave our table shortly thereafter, too, but that may have been due to the Kazakh fat treats.

The Soviets presented our team with gifts—albums containing all the space stamps issued in the USSR. They were really quite nice, and we spent a good deal of the dinner passing them back and forth for autographs. In return, we passed out Polaroids of Miss *Apollona Soyuzovna*. One of our more adventurous team members had convinced a pretty young female employee of a Houston gentleman's club to pose wearing only three strategically-placed Apollo-Soyuz emblems. Apollona's portraits were very popular: I saw Professor Bushuyev slipping one into his pocket.

It was a fun evening.

As we flew away later that night, in darkness, we could see the lights of the Baikonur facilities for at least fifteen minutes. That place was far bigger than the Cape.

There was one more curveball from the Soviets. On May 24, 1975, they launched a new manned Soyuz mission, Soyuz 18, with cosmonauts Pyotr Klimuk and Vitaly Sevastyanov. (The fixes to the Soyuz launch vehicle had obviously worked.) Two days later the cosmonauts successfully docked with Salyut 4 and moved aboard, planning to stay sixty days. But that was a problem: If Klimuk and Sevastyanov remained in orbit for that long their mission would overlap Apollo-Soyuz. Would the Soviets be able to control two missions simultaneously from the same facility? The answer was, probably not.

Fortunately, the new center we had seen in Kaliningrad—TsUP—wasn't the only one the Soviets had. Since 1966, their previous manned missions had been controlled out of a military facility at Yevpatoria in the Crimea. Bushuyev assured Lunney that while Apollo-Soyuz was in flight, Salyut 4 would be controlled from the Yevpatoria center.

Why did the Soviets choose to launch Soyuz 18? Well, they had an investment in Salyut 4. And every day brought it closer to the end of its lifetime. It was a matter of sending Klimuk and Sevastyanov now, in May, or losing the station altogether. It also showed that their program wasn't just Apollo-Soyuz. In their situation, I would probably have made the same decision.

While Apollo-Soyuz training proceeded relatively smoothly, I was facing family problems in Houston. Faye had been very supportive all during my time on Gemini and Apollo, tolerating the travel and the separations. But she had had periods of depression. And now, it seemed, after years of struggling with a weight problem, she had developed anorexia. Fortunately, Dr. Terry McGuire, a psychiatrist I had recommended to other astronauts and their families, came to the rescue, and by the summer of the flight, she had turned the corner on her problems.

Dionne hadn't fared so well, either. She had had to drop out of the University of Texas during her first year there, and took a job at a Howard Johnson's, then at Texas Instruments, while doing a little growing up. She was headed back to college now and seemed more prepared to concentrate on her studies.

Karin was in her senior year in high school. Faye and I didn't know what she had planned yet. Her main interest seemed to be her boyfriend, Ken Johansen.

We had our flight readiness review on June 12. There were no outstanding items and launch was confirmed for July 15. It had been an interesting three years. I had made six trips to the Soviet Union, one with the working groups, five as commander of Apollo. I had learned a new language. I had turned former enemies into friends. I had been able to look behind the curtain, so to speak, at Soviet technology and management. I looked forward to shaking Aleksei Leonov's hand in Earth orbit.

After a last preflight day, which I spent relaxing and then putting on an air show for family and friends in a T-38, I retired to the crew quarters. Deke, Vance, and I were sound asleep at 6:20 the morning of July 15, 1975, when Aleksei Leonov and Valery Kubasov launched aboard Soyuz 19 at 3:20 P.M., Baikonur time Our launch was scheduled for 3:50 P.M. eastern daylight time:

Both Soyuz and Apollo needed to be launched with similar sun angles—that is, at the same time of day. The thirty-minute difference was due to the fact that the Cape was twenty-four degrees further south than Baikonur.

Soyuz 19 was the first Soviet space launch ever carried live on television, and it went just fine, with the spacecraft entering an orbit of 186 by 222 kilometers. The only problem was the failure of an onboard television camera that would have showed Aleksei and Valery during ascent.

We were awakened at 10:30 by John Young, who was now the chief of the astronaut office. After a quick medical checkup, we sat down to breakfast with John, Ron Evans, Jack Lousma, and Dave Bauer, our training officer. Al Bean had flown back to Houston the night before, to serve as my representative in mission control.

Our weather briefing predicted a sunny afternoon with scattered clouds, visibility of ten miles, temperature about eighty-five degrees at launch time, winds from the southeast at ten to fifteen miles per hour. It was better weather than we'd had at the Cape in a few days—better than you usually got this time of year—and I was ready to go.

Three hours prior to launch, we got suited up and headed out to Pad 39B in the van accompanied by Charlie Buckley, chief of security at KSC. I felt confident, eager. I wondered what was going through Deke's head, since he had expected to be in this situation thirteen years ago and had watched sixty other men fly in his place. Even before we reached Pad 39B, Aleksei and Valery had opened the hatches between their Soyuz descent module and orbit modules, shedding their Sokol ascent pressure suits.

The elevator delivered us to the white room at the hundred meter level, where Bob Crippen and the pad team were finishing their checks on CSM-111. As I walked out on the swingarm, I thought about the hundreds of thousands of people lining the roads and beaches, ready to see the launch of the last Apollo. Many of my high school classmates and their wives were present for the launch. (The night before I had telephoned the group at their dinner near Orlando.)

I looked down at the pad and said to myself, "It'll be five years before anything launches from here again." At that time, NASA was projecting its first manned Shuttle launch for 1978, three years away. As it turned out, we were both wrong: It was nearly *six* years, and the next Americans to fly would be John Young and Bob Crippen.)

I was the first to enter, sliding into the left seat and hooking up my comm, checking in with Skip Chauvin, the test conductor, and Bo Bobko, our blockhouse capcom. I could also hear Aleksei and Valery's communications with TsUP. I joked with Bo, asking him if our countdown today would be in English or Russian. Deke climbed in, then slid to the right seat. Finally, Vance took his place in the center.

The final phase of the count went smoothly; there were no problems. Right on time at 3:50 P.M. EDT, July 15, 1975, 10:50 P.M. in Moscow, our Saturn 1B ignited—three seconds later, we rose from the pedestal at 39B. I reported "tower clear" as we thundered into the sky. The smaller, lighter Saturn 1B gave a smoother ride than the Saturn 5. The maximum G load was only four, compared to four-plus for the Moon rocket and even more for Gemini. The staging was noticeable but not nearly as violent.

Ten minutes later, we were in orbit, eighteen hundred kilometers northeast of Florida. (Aleksei and Valery, in Soyuz 19, were over Belgrade, Yugoslavia.) Even though I had made three orbital flights before this, I was seeing new sights. To be able to rendezvous and dock with Soyuz, Apollo had to be launched on a more northerly azimuth, 51.8 degrees rather than the usual 28.5. Our trajectory took us as far north as England. Also, given the limitations of Soyuz (which was not able to reach higher orbits), we were *low*. Our initial orbit was 155 by 173 kilometers. Of course, during that first revolution we were all too busy getting the spacecraft squared away to do any sightseeing. Since we quickly flew into night over Europe, we wouldn't have seen much, anyway.

Forty minutes into the mission, we blew the SLA panels open on the S-4B, exposing the docking module (DM). I flew Apollo out to a distance of a few dozen meters, turned around, and approached the DM. That's when I had problems. The sunlight reflecting off the Pacific Ocean was so bright, it effectively wiped out the cross reference of my crew optical-alignment system, a docking aid mounted in the window in front of me. I sat there, a few meters from the DM, and began to sweat. Finally I decided the only choice was to use the Mark I eyeball—lining up on the cross-shaped target mounted atop the truss behind the DM, and, once the DM had drifted toward a darker background, thrusting closer. *Capture*—only a hundredth of a degree off alignment, the best mark in the Apollo program. And I wouldn't have been able to do it without years of practice going back to 1968.

Vance, Deke, and I noticed that we had picked up a stowaway from Florida—a mosquito buzzed around the cockpit for the first few hours. Unfortunately, the pure oxygen atmosphere eventually did him in.

By the time we awoke at seven on the morning of the sixteenth, Aleksei and Valery had been up for five hours. (They would try to shift their sleep periods over the two days prior to rendezvous.) The cosmonauts had already performed an eighteen-second burn of their propulsion system, circularizing their orbit at 229 kilometers. We weren't able to communicate with them directly yet: From our vantage point, they were still halfway around the world.

With a fresh start, Vance was able to disassemble a balky docking probe, to allow Deke to float into the docking module for checkout. We sent our first color TV transmissions to Houston. Our highly inclined orbit meant that we were unable to use the usual ground stations in NASA's space tracking network. For ASTP, NASA had arranged to relay some of our downlink through the ATS-6 satellite in geosynchronous orbit, a forerunner of the future Tracking and Data Relay Satellite System used for the Shuttle and International Space Station.

We did another phasing burn the afternoon of the sixteenth. When it was over, Soyuz 19 was just thirty-one hundred kilometers away, with Aleksei and Valery bedding down for their second night in orbit. With the added room of the docking module, Vance, Deke, and I spread out for our second night, with Deke taking up residence in the DM and Vance bunking in the transfer tunnel. I slept under the crew couches. While we slept, we moved 255 kilometers closer to Soyuz with each revolution.

The next morning, Soyuz 19 was only 903 kilometers away, in a higher orbit, when I fired the SPS on the first rendezvous burn shortly before 8 A.M. This burn lowered our apogee, allowing Apollo to "catch up" with the Soyuz. Vance made visual contact with Soyuz—just a bright speck in the darkness—and soon thereafter we were able to talk via VHF for the first time. Deke said hello to Valery and Aleksei in Russian, and they replied in English.

Around 8:30, with the two spacecraft 222 kilometers apart, Soyuz switched on its rendezvous radar transponder. I fired the SPS one more time thirty-seven minutes later, our co-elliptic maneuver. We were crossing from the Pacific and over South America, closing in on Soyuz 19 from below and behind. It took one more rev for the final distance to narrow.

"Soyuz and Apollo are shaking hands now," Aleksei said.

The contact had been very smooth. "Tell Professor Bushuyev the docking was soft," I radioed. We retracted the system to a rigid configuration. Docking completed, I wanted to thank the Soviet engineers and technicians, so I hit my tape recorder and played them a rendition of "Hello, Darlin'" by Oklahoma's very own Conway Twitty, with lyrics that Conway had phoneticized in Russian.

We got ready to open the hatches between the two spacecraft, a process that would take three hours as both crews did pressure integrity checks. Aleksei and Valery had already received a congratulatory message from Brezhnev via TsUP when Deke and I entered the DM. We had to close the hatch leading to Apollo, then raise the pressure inside the DM by adding nitrogen to what had been a one hundred percent oxygen atmosphere. Aleksei and Valery had lowered the pressure inside Soyuz over the previous two days.

Since we were actually running ahead of the timeline, I decided to have a little fun. I rapped on the hatch leading to the Soyuz orbital module. Aleksei rapped back, so I called out, "Kto Budet tam?" ("Who's there?")

Eventually we were squared away. On worldwide live television, I opened hatch number three into Soyuz and saw a smiling Aleksei Leonov swimming toward me from a tangle of cables. "Ah, good to see you!" he said.

I took his hand. "Ochen rad." ("Very good.")

I moved into Soyuz, where I got a hug from Valery. Deke followed me, and there we were—two Americans and two Russians inside the orbital module of a Russian spacecraft, 130 miles above Europe. We had come a long way from flights along the Iron Curtain, secret missile tests, and the moon race. There were no big speeches; we left that to the teams of dignitaries in Houston and elsewhere. (Those on hand in mission control included NASA administrator James Fletcher and Soviet ambassador Anatoly Dobrynin.) We received a call from President Gerald Ford in the White House. Then we exchanged flags and signed certificates from the Fédération Aéronautique Internationale, officially validating this first international docking.

My first Russian-style space dinner consisted of reconstituted strawberries (dried, with water added) followed by *borshch*. Before the mission, we had had some fun with Aleksei and Valery joking about whether or not we would be able to make a true Russian toast in space, with real alcohol. Sure enough, as Deke and I were eating, the cosmonauts handed us each a tube labeled "Vodka." To our great disappointment, both tubes actually contained *borshch*—Russian soup.

Deke and I returned to Apollo after a three and a half hour visit, closing the hatches behind us and lowering the pressure inside the docking module to 5 psi. We also vented the space between the forward hatch and the Soyuz, in case we had to rapidly undock. One anomaly showed up at this point: The pressure detectors on Soyuz showed a small leak. We couldn't find one, and the leak was apparently tiny, so we simply went to sleep. It had been a busy day but a great one. When we awoke the next morning, our environmental control teams had figured out the "leak": It turned out that the air in the DM expanded as it heated up, and the sensors on Soyuz had mistaken the expansion for a leak.

On day two, Aleksei came aboard Apollo while Vance moved over to Soyuz. It was during his time there that Valery gave the world a televised tour of Soyuz in English, something American and European audiences had never seen before. Then it was time for Aleksei, Deke, and me to do the same with Apollo—in Russian.

After lunch, everybody swapped places again, and we had an orbital press conference from Soyuz, where we fielded questions from reporters in both control centers about the benefits of the joint project. Finally, one of the Soviet journalists asked Aleksei how comfortable he was in Apollo and how well he liked American food. "As an old philosopher says, the best part of a good dinner is not what you eat but with whom." I agreed.

As our second work day ended, I presented Aleksei with a packet of spruce tree seeds to be planted in the USSR, a gift from the American people to create a living memorial to the project. Then we performed a final ceremony, joining two halves of an Apollo-Soyuz medal to symbolize the link-up and handshake in orbit. By 4 P.M., after a final "do svidania" to Aleksei and Valery, we were back in Apollo and had closed the hatch to the docking module.

Our last day of joint activity was the nineteenth. The highlight was undocking from Soyuz after forty-four linked hours and backing off so that we sat

directly between it and the Sun, creating an "artificial" eclipse to be pho-
tographed by the cosmonauts as part of an astronomical experiment. Once
that was accomplished, Deke flew the redocking and faced the same problem I had two days earlier: He was unable to see the cross line reference of
the COAS because of the light reflecting off the daylight background of the
earth. He proceeded with the docking, which appeared to go smoothly. But
the moment after contact and capture, both vehicles oscillated. It only happened for a few seconds, and was probably due to a slight misalignment in
the spacecrafts' X-axis. In any case, the second docking was well within limits, so I didn't sweat it. The two spacecraft remained linked for three hours,
then, at 1:42 that afternoon, we undocked and made a separation burn.

Here was our chance to get revenge for the "vodka" toast: Vance Brand
had brought along a cassette tape of girls giggling in a shower. So, as we
drifted to a distance of thirty miles from Soyuz—out of range of our ground
stations—I radioed Aleksei and asked him what he was doing now.

"Tom, we are resting because we have worked so hard."

I told him we were still working. He wanted to know why. "Listen," I said.
Vance hit play on the recorder while Deke held down the microphone button. The sound of giggling girls and running water could be heard quite
clearly.

"Tom!" Aleksei said, quite seriously, "what are you doing over there?"

"Working hard," I told him.

He was still unsure. "You are kidding, aren't you?" Finally I had to tell
him we were.

And we said good-bye to Soyuz 19 for the last time.

Aleksei and Valery remained in orbit for two more days, conducting a series
of experiments for Soviet scientists. They landed successfully in Kazakhstan
on the twenty-first, the first "thumpdown" carried live on global television.

Vance, Deke, and I remained in orbit three days longer, until the twenty-
fourth, running through our own package of twenty-seven experiments—the
last man-tended experiments American scientists expected to fly in space until
1980 or so. On the twenty-third we jettisoned the docking module; it would
remain in orbit until November, when it would re-enter and burn up. On July
24 Vance, Deke, and I fired our propulsion system then separated from the

service module. The command module sailed through re-entry, headed toward splashdown near the carrier USS *New Orleans,* 285 miles northwest of Hawaii.

Vance was in the left-hand seat, I was in the center, and Deke was on the right. At eighty thousand feet, I was supposed to throw a switch that would electrically kill the reaction control thrusters. But during our re-entry, we had noticed a loud squeal in our headsets, an irritating noise like feedback in an auditorium, the result, we found out later, of a short in the communications loop. The noise made it impossible for us to hear each other or Houston after we emerged from the blackout caused by the plasma of re-entry. In order to be heard in the cockpit, we had to shout. Either the noise kept Vance and Deke from hearing me, or I was too distracted to give the command. But that switch didn't get thrown at eighty thousand feet.

We fell to twenty-four thousand, the drogue parachute deployed to stabilize the spacecraft, and the vent valve opened to let in fresh air. The guidance system, reacting to the rolling of the command module under the drogue parachute, began firing to stabilize the craft. The vent valve was located right below the roll thrusters, and it sucked some of the nitrogen tetroxide into the cabin. I recognized the smell of that yellow-brown mist and knew instantly what it was.

On the instrument panel in front of me were two switches that would close the propellant gate valves and shut off the fuel supply to those thrusters. I reached up and activated them, but some residual fuel was still in the lines. Our eyes started to water, and we all started coughing as the fumes burned our faces, mouths, and throats.

The main parachutes were scheduled to deploy automatically at ten thousand feet. I hit the manual switch to back up the automatic. The deployment was perfect and we descended, still coughing, until *wham!*—we hit the water in a real bone cruncher, nearly ten positive Gs. Then we flipped over, nose down, with six negative Gs, in what NASA calls the Stable 2 position. We were hanging by our shoulder harnesses and seatbelts, facing downward.

There I sat, thinking, Damn, nine days and three million miles, everything's gone so good, and now here we are, locked upside down with this toxic gas in the spacecraft.

I knew we had to get oxygen. The masks were stored behind my seat—

above and behind me in that position. The control panel was in front of my face, and below that was the tunnel. I told myself, Release the straps, get the masks, but don't fall down the tunnel.

I unbuckled, and fell straight down into the tunnel, slamming my right shoulder and elbow, but I came up fighting like hell, grabbing onto switches, whatever I could to pull myself back up and over to the couches. I reached the masks, ripped the cover off them, gave one to Vance, one to Deke, and put one on myself. I turned the valve to start the oxygen flow. "Wow," Deke said, "good idea." He had been coughing a lot.

Things started to settle down. I got the compressor going to inflate the airbags on the command module's nose and raise us back to the Stable 1 position. I lay on my back on the instrument panel and started going through the postsplashdown checklist. Since I was facing Vance and Deke, I noticed that while Deke was still coughing, Vance didn't answer me.

I saw that the oxygen mask had slipped off his face. He was comatose, his hands clenched. I put down my checklist and reached over to get the mask on his face, pushed the high-flow valve on it to give him more oxygen. In a few seconds, Vance came to, and started thrashing his arms around. One of his hands hit me right on the face and knocked me back onto the instrument panel. With all the thrashing, the mask fell off his face, and he passed out again. So I moved back to him, and got the mask back on his face. This time I made sure to do a bear hug around his neck and his shoulders as I hit the high-flow valve. He revived, and started doing the same struggling, but I was locked on to him and wouldn't let go. Then he settled down and we got the mask tight.

We were back in Stable 1 now, and the oxygen supply for the masks was running out. I reached for the side hatch, but Deke said, "Goddamn, don't open the hatch! We might sink like Gus!" He still had the shade of Gus Grissom coming at him.

"There's frogmen out there," I said. "I'll just crack the hatch a little and we'll get some fresh air in here. We can close it instantly."

The frogmen were there, of course. Normally when you come out of the plasma of re-entry, you can talk to the ground. But because of the problem with our communications, we had not talked to anybody since going into the plasma. So I told the frogmen we wanted to be hauled aboard the carrier inside the spacecraft. It was the last Apollo, and that's how I wanted the program to end.

Even though we were less than a mile away, getting the *New Orleans* to us and winching us aboard took an hour. By that time we had recovered enough to face a welcome, though we were still coughing and our eyes were watering. It was a rough finish to what had been a very successful three-year journey.

eighteen
Edwards and Red Hats

Onboard the carrier deck we had festive ceremonies and talked to the president. I told our chief flight surgeon, Dr. Arnauld Nicogossian, that we had breathed in rocket fuel from twenty-four thousand feet down and it had burned our noses, throats, and lungs. Our postflight medical examinations in the sick bay of *New Orleans* showed that we had come very close to serious injury. Dr. Nicogossian eliminated all extra ceremonial activities. Instead of being guests in the admiral's quarters, we spent our first night back on Earth in sick bay, a few decks below the hangar deck. Flying us to Hawaii was out of the question, so *New Orleans* steamed toward Honolulu all night, the whole ship shaking as they put the power to it.

The next morning, X rays showed that our lungs were filled with edema, as though we were suffering from chemical-induced pneumonia. When I started up the ladder toward the admiral's quarters and breakfast, I found I could only take a few steps at a time before I had to stop and rest. Deke passed out briefly.

In Honolulu, we were taken in ambulances to Trippler Army Hospital for more extensive examinations. That was when a precancerous lesion was discovered on one of Deke's lungs, requiring surgery when he returned to Houston—a lucky break, when you think about it. The lesion had actually appeared in preflight X rays, but nobody had caught it; you had to be a very good radiologist to see it. If the doctors at Trippler hadn't found it, God knows how long it would have been before the lesion got discovered. With cortisone treatment therapy, we started to improve, and by the thirtieth our chest X rays had returned to normal. We then moved to a resort at the Marine Corps Air Station, Kaneohe Bay, on the east end of Oahu. Faye, Dionne, and Karin joined me there, and so did the other families. Faye had a little bombshell waiting: Karin and her boyfriend, Ken Johansen, wanted to get married. She was eighteen and had just finished high school. I told her she was too young. She listened, to some extent. At least we didn't start planning a wedding right away.

After a week in Kaneohe Bay, we flew to Washington, D.C., for a meeting with President Ford, where in addition to receiving the NASA Distinguished Service Medal, I was officially promoted to the rank of major general. President Ford personally pinned on my second star at a postlaunch ceremony on the south balcony of the White House.

Deke had surgery to remove the lesion in his lung and had recovered by mid-September. Later that month the Apollo crew and families boarded an Air Force KC-135 and flew to Moscow for the first leg of a two-part ceremonial tour. I had insisted that the families be included: They had had to put up with our frequent absences over the past two years, and they deserved the chance to see where we'd been. Gene Marionetti (protocol), Anatole Forostenko (translation), and Chuck Biggs (gifts and protocol) came too.

Aleksei and Valery and their families greeted us. We had last seen the cosmonauts when we closed the hatch in orbit. We received awards from Brezhnev at the Kremlin then hit the road, from Moscow to Leningrad, then to Kiev, and after that, to Novosibirsk in Siberia. We took a break at the resort town of Sochi, on the Black Sea, then made one more stop in Tbilisi.

We returned to the United States in early October, and soon after, Aleksei and Valery and their wives, Svetlana and Ludmila, joined us for the American leg of the tour, along with Vladimir Shatalov and his wife, Muza. We began with a visit to the White House. Afterward, President Ford took us all to Old Town Alexandria, where he had lived as a congressman, for a barbecue with the local fire department. From Washington, we and the cosmonauts flew to Omaha, then Salt Lake City, for a meeting with the head of

the Mormon Church. Las Vegas was to have been next on the agenda, but
the Soviets ultimately decided it might be bad for their image, so we went
to Lake Tahoe instead.

Our next stop was San Francisco, including a visit to the NASA Ames Research Center, then down the coast to Los Angeles and Orange County. We
stayed at the Newporter Inn in Newport Beach, where we met the actor John
Wayne. After some initial grumbling about meeting "commies," the Duke
had a few drinks and warmed up to Aleksei and Valery. "These are pretty
good guys after all!" We finished up with San Diego and Houston, then back
to Washington. That was the last Aleksei and I saw of each other for almost
ten years.

Even before the launch of Apollo-Soyuz, I knew I would be leaving NASA
and the space program. My old friend Jim McDivitt used to say there are
four ways to leave the astronaut office: You get killed, you get grounded, you
get fired, or you pick the time to go. In the spring of 1975, I knew it would
soon be time to go. There was no chance of another flight until the 1980s.
With the reorganization of the Johnson Space Center under Chris Kraft, I
had less power and input to the Space Shuttle Program. And, having had a
good look at the Soviet Union and its technical capabilities, I knew I had
skills and knowledge useful to the Air Force.

In the spring of 1975, I spoke with Gen. Sam Phillips, then head of the Air
Force Systems Command, about my options. He promised to look around
on my behalf, and in June, three weeks before the ASTP launch, General Sam
called me at the Cape to say he had a new assignment for me. "You'll love
it," he promised, and he was right: He wanted me to become commanding
general of the Air Force Flight Test Center at Edwards Air Force Base. I
would be going back to where I'd served as a captain and instructor, only
now, thirteen years later, I'd be the commander.

I immediately called Faye to tell her the good news, though I was a little
tentative because I knew how much she loved Houston. She was willing to
go back to Edwards, though. Once the post-ASTP goodwill tours were concluded, I flew out to Edwards to meet the leadership and look things over.

By then I knew the transition might be bumpy. Two recent commanders
of the flight test center—famed test pilots Robert White and Robert Rushworth—had had problems. Both were outstanding officers and good friends

of mine. White's tenure had been marred by several aircraft accidents, as well as Buzz Aldrin's disastrous tour as commandant of the test pilot school. Rushworth had the bad luck to be commander when some of his officers threw a stag party at the officers' club, complete with several scantily clad dancers, that later drew a written protest in the pages of the *Los Angeles Times*. This was years before the Tailhook problem with the Navy, and the Edwards event wasn't even a fraction as rowdy and only lasted a few hours. Nevertheless, it perturbed Gen. David Jones, Air Force chief of staff, and was enough to end Rushworth's tenure.

General Jones advised me to get Maj. Gen. Howard "Mac" Lane's perspective on Edwards before taking over. Lane had been commander of the flight test center between White and Rushworth and was now head of the Air Armaments Center at Eglin AFB. (He had been in flight test when I was an instructor at the test pilot school.) Lane suggested that I come up with four or five goals, make them known throughout the command, and concentrate all my energy on getting them accomplished.

I spent a few hours coming up with a credible list. *Number one,* make sure Edwards was accomplishing its primary mission—successful, safe flight testing of experimental and high-performance aircraft. *Two,* make sure base facilities were at a high state of readiness. *Three,* take care of enlisted men and their families, which would certainly help the first two objectives. And *four,* build a spirit of pride and cohesion.

Before I took over, I got another important tip from Col. Phil Conley, Annapolis '50, now General Sam's chief of staff in Systems Command and former flight test center vice commander. "Don't start flying airplanes around," Phil told me. "Everybody likes to fly airplanes. Stay on the ground a while and get to know the people." He warned me that some blue suits were waiting for another ex-astronaut to fall on his face. Phil, who had been in engineering at Edwards when I was at the test pilot school, was a longtime friend. He would prove to be a constant source of sage advice. We continued to talk an average of once a week—often more. He was always looking out for my six o'clock position.

I would have additional strong support from my vice commander, Col. Stan Burklund; test wing commander Col. Joe Guthrie (a classmate from test pilot school); and base commander Russ Turpenting.

The formal change of command was on November 15, 1975. Faye re-

mained behind in Houston to sell the house. By now, Karin was in her first
year at Steven Austin University in Nacogdoches, Texas—still unmarried—
and Dionne was back at the University of Texas.

I stayed out of the cockpit for six weeks, the longest time I'd gone without
flying since 1952. What I did was get to know Edwards, rising at five every
morning to do my own inspection. It was quite a challenge: Edwards was
one of the largest bases in the Air Force, covering 550 square miles, and serving as the workplace or home to fifteen thousand contractors and military
personnel and their families.

It was my goal to meet every one of the people who worked on the base,
military or civilian. I went to the firehouse and met all the firemen. I went
down into the basement of the photo lab, where repairmen were working on
circulation pumps, and introduced myself to a plumber who had been working at Edwards for twenty-three years without meeting a single commander.
Getting to know the team made it easier when I needed money for a project
or volunteers for grunt labor.

And a lot of sheer labor was needed. Even as I assumed command, I was
struck by the poor physical conditions on the base. Fences were leaning over.
Paint on the barracks and other buildings was garish—faded pink, orange,
and green, what I called "early Juarez" colors. (From this point on, the
dominant color for buildings at Edwards would be earth tones.) I noticed a
lot of dilapidated buildings on the center and had them torn down—fifty-
four of them.

You couldn't separate the physical improvements from operational ones.
Those falling-down fences, for example, were a sign of a larger problem with
base security. I realized that with the exception of the flight line itself, the
whole base was accessible to anybody with a truck, car, or motorcycle. I tried
to close the base, but Kern County officials put up a tremendous fuss. We
finally reached a compromise in which I agreed to keep open Avenue 121, a
small east-west road that ran from the south gate and through the far bound-
ary of the rocket test site.

Even the issue of security guards was a problem. Not only did we have
Air Police, but every contractor on the base had its own staff. They ranged
in style and price from Rockwell's spiffy B-1 security team (who looked like

Marines), down to Republic Aviation's lone gunman in his blue jeans, faded T-shirt, tennis shoes, and six-shooter. I worked to consolidate security with a single contractor at a lower cost to the Air Force.

The mission control for our B-1 test force was in an old office building. It literally consisted of people sitting around tables on folding metal chairs. Coming from NASA, I was used to having the best, most advanced technical systems—I saw no reason why the United States Air Force's cutting edge test center shouldn't have the same. I claimed two Control Data Cyber-74 computers from a canceled program in the Air Force Logistics Command and installed them here, while I went to work planning the construction of a dedicated mission control center.

My willingness to go out and meet people, and to improve their environment and situation, paid off. By the end of my first eighteen months as commander of the flight test center, Edwards had doubled its first-term re-enlistment rate and reduced absent-without-leaves by 85 percent. The work was completely different from what I'd been doing at NASA, but satisfying in its own way.

I left the space program after Apollo-Soyuz, but Aleksei Leonov remained at Star City. He had been promoted to major general immediately after the end of our mission, while retaining his job as deputy director of the Gagarin Center for air-space training. The center was going through another reorganization in the winter of 1975–76, partly to accommodate the new Buran Space Shuttle Program, and also to allow for flight opportunities on Soyuz-Salyut by citizens of "brother" socialist countries like Czechoslovakia and Poland.

The center's cosmonaut groups were brought back into a single unit on March 30, 1976, and Aleksei was named commander or chief cosmonaut. He was now responsible for the selection of the first new candidates to be chosen since 1970, as well as the daily activities of forty military cosmonauts, half a dozen Interkosmos pilots, and the floating number—anywhere from six to a dozen—civilian cosmonauts who used the center's facilities.

Aleksei was as busy in Star City as I was at Edwards. And we had no direct contact. Once or twice a year I would write him a letter, but each one took months to reach him. Phone calls were out of the question. I noted Aleksei's appearances in the news, however. As chief cosmonaut, he usually accompanied Soyuz and Salyut crews to Baikonur.

Many of those crews included cosmonauts I knew from ASTP: Valery
Kubasov and Nikolai Rukavishnikov became the only two civilian Soviet
mission commanders, on Soyuz 36 and Soyuz 33. Vladimir Dzhanibekov and
Yury Romanenko commanded flights to Salyut 6 between 1977 and 1981.
Aleksandr Ivanchenkov made a flight in that time, too. It was good to see old
ASTP friends and colleagues doing so well.

Karin and Ken got married in March 1976. Faye and I flew back to Texas
for the ceremony, which took place at this lodge at Elkins Lake, near the
town of Huntsville, about an hour north of Houston. We had taken Karin
fishing there several times when she was younger. The Elkins facility was
named for Judge James A. Elkins, Sr., who founded the 1st City National
Bank and the prestigious law firm of Vinson and Elkins in Houston. We had
planned a beautiful outdoors ceremony for a hundred-plus guests. I was am-
bivalent about it, of course. I wanted Karin to be happy, but I still thought
she was too young.

As I prepared to walk her up to the gazebo, where the Methodist minister Rev. Connie Winborn waited, I happened to spot a gift deposited on the
sidewalk by a passing canine. So my last parental advice to Karin as a single
woman was, "Don't step in the dog do." After they were married, Karin and
Ken both transferred to Southwestern Texas University in San Marcos, the
same town where I'd gone through flight training in 1953.

In addition to the Flight Test Center at Edwards, I was also responsible for
the Parachute Test Range at El Centro, California, for a portion of the Hill-
Wendover-Dugway Range in Utah, and for the secret test area commonly
known as Area 51 or Groom Lake. During my time at Edwards, the range
was highly classified and referred to—when it was mentioned at all—as
Dreamland.

For years I had assumed the United States had a secret test center in
Nevada because the U-2 and SR-71 aircraft hadn't been tested at Edwards.
But I had no idea of the facility's exact location until just prior to the Apollo-
Soyuz launch, when an Air Force colonel came to NASA and gave our crew
a special briefing, complete with satellite photographs of a barren landscape
dominated by a huge runway going into a dry lakebed. He said to us, "Do
you see this area? This is the Groom Dry Lake Facility. Do not talk about

this, do not take any pictures of it from orbit." Today you can view satellite photos of the base on the Internet.

The physical state of Dreamland, then over twenty years old, wasn't much better than Edwards when I found it. So I pushed for improvements there, too. There were no alien bodies stashed at Dreamland, only vehicles we wished to fly and test in relative privacy, much as we had from the North Base at Edwards back in the early 1950s.

One class of secret aircraft can now be discussed: We had a veritable fleet of purchased Soviet military aircraft based at Dreamland and flown by pilots from the 4477th Test and Evaluation Squadron, a handpicked team of su-pertalented NCOs and test pilots also known as the Red Hats. Maj. Dave Fer-guson was the squadron commander. Some of the flying was basic test work, getting to know the performance capabilities of MiG-17s and MiG-21s, as well as Soviet radars and surface-to-air missiles. The NCOs did a tremen-dous job of keeping the Soviet aircraft in top flight condition. The Red Hats also flew mock aerial combat against operational Air Force test units out of Nellis Air Force Base, near Las Vegas. Occasionally B-52s would make planned penetration bomb runs against the facility and would evaluate the abilities of the Soviet radar, missile, and fighters to intercept them.

I loved flying with the Red Hats and even had my own MiG-17 with "General Tom Stafford" painted on it in the Russian Cyrillic alphabet, along with a red flag and two yellow stars. (A Navy exchange pilot later spun the aircraft into the ground in a simulated air combat maneuver and, un-fortunately, was killed.) Along with my MiG-17, I flew a number of other for-eign aircraft. I would be one of the first American pilots to make a ski-jump takeoff in the British Harrier, and I was the first American to fly the British-German-Italian Tornado fighter. The Air Force wanted the head of research, development, and acquisitions to stay current, and I was happy to oblige.

How did we obtain the Soviet aircraft? I didn't know the operational de-tails. But in September 1976, a defecting Soviet Air Force pilot named Vik-tor Belenko flew a late model MiG-25 Foxbat across the Sea of Japan and landed at Hakodate Airport. The Soviets demanded the immediate return of the aircraft and pilot.

I had heard about the MiG landing on the evening TV news, and at three the next morning I received a telephone call from Dave Ferguson asking to come to my quarters immediately. Twenty minutes later I was signing special travel orders for him and several senior Red Hat NCOs to fly to Japan to examine Belenko's MiG. Eventually Belenko wound up in the Washington D.C. area being debriefed by the CIA. Given my responsibilities, my background as a pilot, test pilot, and astronaut, and my ability to speak Russian, Dave Ferguson asked me to have a chat with him. I flew commercial to Dulles Airport, where Dave and a driver—both in civilian clothes—met me. As we drove to Washington, Dave explained that I could ask any questions I wanted but should not reveal my identity.

I said hello to Belenko in Russian, but used the interpreter for the majority of the interview. I questioned him about Soviet pilot selection and training practices and whether or not he knew of cosmonaut selection and training. I also asked him if he had any knowledge of Yury Gagarin's 1968 crash in the MiG-15. All Belenko knew was what had been passed around in the Soviet Air Force on the accident.

Belenko kept saying, "I think I know you." I replied, in Russian, "No, we have never met before." About six hours after I left, he suddenly told his handlers, "I know who that man is! It is General Stafford who commanded Apollo from the Apollo-Soyuz Test Program! I have seen him on Russian TV!" He asked them for an autographed picture, if I would give him one. I sent one via Dave Ferguson a few weeks later. Over the past twenty years I have met Belenko twice, and we both laugh about that interview.

The NASA Dryden Flight Center was a tenant on Edwards, using the same runways, air traffic control system, and many support systems. Former astronaut Dave Scott was Dryden's director at the time, and one of his major projects was the approach and landing tests (ALT) for an unpowered Shuttle. Deke Slayton was the Johnson Space Center's program manager for ALT.

The first vehicle, named Enterprise, had been trucked thirty-five miles up the highway from Rockwell's facility at Plant 42 in Palmdale, on January 31, 1977. Within two weeks, Enterprise had been hoisted atop a converted Boeing 747 for its first captive flight tests. It also underwent weight and balance tests in the large Air Force hangar. Veteran Air Force and NASA test pilot Fitz Fulton, who commanded the 747, called the combined vehicle "the biggest biplane in the world."

I took the position that the military and the Air Force supported the Shuttle program and allowed the public into the base to watch the drop tests, which began on August 12, 1977. Astronauts Fred Haise and Gordon Fullerton separated Enterprise from the 747, and glided down to a landing on the lakebed, verifying the orbiter's basic aerodynamics. Over the next few months, Fred and Gordo, and their alternates, Joe Engle and Dick Truly, made four more free flights. The ALT flights were successful, as far as they went. But it was a long way from drop tests to orbital flight.

One of the most exciting aspects of the Edwards job was being involved in the newest technology. The Shuttle was just one new program. We also had the B-1A, YF-16, A-10, F-15, and others. The military world was also making the transition to a new aircraft technology: stealth aircraft.

The first application of stealth technology was the SR-71 Blackbird. But in 1973 the Air Force began to study the issue further, looking for ways to reduce the radar cross section or signature of their aircraft. The studies led to a DARPA/Air Force Lockheed skunk works program called HAVE BLUE, which resulted in the construction of a pair of experimental tactical aircraft—XSTs.

In November 1977 the first XST was shipped from the skunk works in Burbank, California, to Dreamland, in the belly of a giant C-5A transport. The skunk works technicians came along, too, though they were ferried into the facility in the morning and again out each night. Secrecy for the XST tests was extremely high. The entire base was ringed with electronic detectors, and security teams on the ground and in helicopters patrolled the perimeter, responding rapidly to any intrusions. Pilots were forbidden to overfly the area.

Lockheed's Bill Parks was at the controls on the morning of December 1, as I parked my jeep in the sagebrush near the runway and watched the strange-looking black wedge roll out and take to the sky for its first flight. I knew then it was the beginning of a new era in combat aircraft.

I was attending a conference at the Pentagon in February 1978 when Chief of Staff David Jones took me aside to say he wanted me to replace Al Slay as deputy chief of staff for research, development, and acquisition. Slay was going to take over the Systems Command, succeeding Gen. Bill Evans. Evans was to become commander, U.S. Air Forces, in Europe. I was delighted. For one thing, that particular job fit well with my interests in high technology. For another, it meant a promotion to lieutenant general. And it would also allow me to keep flying.

The research, development, and acquisition job, of course, required me to move to Washington. I was eager, but Faye wasn't. She had gamely given up her life in Houston to move to the desert and had found a new home in the relaxed, informal Edwards community. She didn't like the idea of Washington, with all its glitter and receptions. For the first time Faye started to talk about my retiring from the Air Force.

We had a wonderful going-away party in early March 1978 then started driving east. Faye cried nearly all the way to Arizona. In two days we reached San Marcos, Texas, where Karin and Ken lived. Rather than continue on to Washington, where, owing to a lack of general officers' quarters, we would have to rent temporary housing, Faye decided to stay on with Karin and Ken.

I got back on the road to Washington.

As deputy chief of staff for research and development I was fortunate to have several old friends on my team, including Maj. Gen. Charlie Kuyk, my classmate from test pilot school, and Mj. Gens. Jim Brickel and Bill Maxon, classmates from Annapolis

March 1978 was a bad time to take up a high-tech weapons development position in the American military. President Jimmy Carter had made wholesale cuts in defense spending, dropping it to 4.8 percent of the Gross Domestic Product and projecting an even lower percentage. This was far less than the 8.0 to 8.5 percent we had under Eisenhower and Kennedy, and the 7.0 percent under Nixon. Carter was riding high in popularity, too. It appeared he would be president for two terms.

Along with putting the Pentagon on a starvation diet, Carter's defense advisers struck me as a group of lightweights chosen more for their liberal political credentials than for their technical or military expertise. There were exceptions: Harold Brown was a knowledgeable secretary of defense, and William J. Perry was an excellent under secretary for research and engineering. But most of the Carter team seemed to have been chosen by Vice President Walter Mondale, who didn't like or trust the Pentagon. These advisers had encouraged Carter to cancel the B-1 bomber and to stretch out the MX missile and the Navy's Trident sub and missile programs.

That was bad enough, but shortly after I arrived at my new office in the Pentagon, the CIA and DIA informed me that the Soviet Union was accelerating its military buildup even as we were slacking off. If they kept up, projections showed they would pass us within eight to ten years. At the same time, according to Brig. Gen. Jasper Welch, head of Air Force Studies and Analyses, all the United States had to do was raise defense spending back to 6.5 percent of the gross national product, a little below where it had been in the years after the Korean War, hold it for a few years, and sooner or later the Soviets would have to cry uncle. We could then have meaningful arms reduction negotiations.

It was obvious to me that we needed to maintain our strength and especially to preserve the MX. That became my first mission. The MX was the first new strategic missile developed by the United States since the Minuteman III in the 1960s. The MX was our first "mobile-based" missile, designed to be launched from a silo or from a platform that could be moved around a circuit many miles in diameter. Arms control advocates wanted us to give up on the program because it would antagonize the Russians. Environmentalists hated the basing scheme.

But the Soviet Union kept right on adding to its "missile shield," with new modifications of their SS-11s and SS-13s, plus new vehicles like SS-17, SS-18, SS-19, and their own mobile missile, the SS-25. I knew just how capable the Soviet missile builders were; those birds wouldn't be as sophisticated or reliable as ours, but they were adequate for the job, and they were rolling out of the factories "like sausages," as Nikita Khrushchev had promised twenty years earlier.

So I felt strongly that the MX had to stay on track. My deputy for requirements was Maj. Gen. Kelly Burke, a former operations and planning officer in the Strategic Air Command. He was tall and serious, an excellent writer and lecturer. I told Kelly I needed a deputy specifically for the MX program. "I'd like to have a fighter pilot who's had some SAC experience. And I want a country boy who's a politician." I knew the technology, but I wanted someone who could spend lots of time presenting the details of the MX to Congress.

Kelly had just the guy—Brigadier General–select Guy Hecker, Jr., then commander of the 45th Air Division at Pease AFB, New Hampshire. He turned out to be a short, stocky individual with a ready laugh and a constant smile. He was just what I needed, and I assigned him to lobby the Hill to keep and save the MX. Secretary John Stetson and Undersecretary Dr. Hans Mark also did a good job of helping me to keep Air Force technology moving forward.

Having seen the XSTs from the Lockheed HAVE BLUE program at Groom Lake, I knew the Air Force had to develop stealth aircraft. I called a team into the "black vault" in the Pentagon and asked them to start formulating design specs for a stealth fighter based on HAVE BLUE. We wanted an attack aircraft that would be able to hit high-value targets like command and control centers, political headquarters, power plants and weapons storage bunkers, flying at night, mostly undetectable by the enemy. The aircraft had to be able to carry at least two two-thousand-pound bombs while flying subsonic. This new project became known as SENIOR TREND.

By November 1978, Lockheed was hard at work on SENIOR TREND, which eventually became the F-117A, a black, arrowlike vehicle whose surface was composed entirely of many flat facets coated with radar-absorbing materials. I thought that a bomber using stealth technology might win President Carter's approval and support. So I asked Lockheed to see if they could stretch the SENIOR TREND design to bomber size.

They responded with HAVE PEG, a bomber concept based on the faceted-surface technology, which was so draggy it would need three or four aerial refuelings to reach its final target in the Soviet Union. You could stand higher drag on a short range attack aircraft but not on a long range bomber. I started calling the Lockheed bomber HAVE PIG.

Meanwhile, the Northrop Corporation had been working on a prototype slow battlefield recon stealth aircraft using smooth surfaces. At an appearance before the Air Force Association in Chicago in July 1979, I encountered Thomas V. Jones, head of Northrop, who asked me what his company should be looking at for future programs. Frustrated with Lockheed's HAVE PIG, I got out a sheet of paper and wrote down figures for the range, payload, and gross takeoff weight of a new bomber comparable to the Soviet Backfire. I added the desired radar cross section and handed it to Jones with the warning that I couldn't pay him for the studies.

A week later, on a blank piece of paper, I wrote the same specifications and gave them to Ben Rich, head of the Lockheed skunk works and told him to see what he could do with it. It was a set of goals that greatly exceeded the performance outlined in their HAVE PEG design. Lockheed eventually returned with drawings that incorporated a modified faceted and smooth-surface design but that would've still had too much drag for a long-range bomber.

In three weeks Jones was at the Pentagon carrying not one but two designs. One was a highly swept delta-wing vehicle, the other was a radical flying wing that bore an eerie resemblance to the famous one Jack Northrop, the founder of the company, had tried to perfect thirty-five years earlier, with such disastrous results. Test pilot Capt. Glen Edwards was killed on June 5, 1948, when flying wing YB-49 crashed. Muroc Air Base was later renamed Edwards Air Force Base in his honor.

The new Northrop flying wing design had been developed independently, its shape driven by the requirements. The bird looked like an L-shaped ruler from above, with a raised hump for a cockpit and two smoothly blended pods for the engines. The trailing edge had a sawtooth design intended to mask the infrared signature of the engines. Any instability due to the lack of a vertical tail would be handled by a computer-driven, fly-by-wire system using split ailerons.

I took the Lockheed and Northrop drawings to Gen. Lew Allen, Air Force chief of staff, and to Hans Mark, the new secretary of the Air Force. They gave me the go-ahead to present them to William Perry, the under secretary of defense, and he approved the concept of an advanced technology bomber (ATB), later to be known as the B-2. A final selection was made to go with Northrop and its modified flying wing design.

For every concept that made it safely through to development, there was another that got tripped up. I devoted a lot of time to developing remotely piloted vehicles (RPVs) called TACIT RAINBOW and SEEK SPINNER. Both were ahead of their time. But the failure of the RPV programs wasn't my only frustration. Hans Mark and I both tried to encourage the Air Force to support manned space flight using the Shuttle without much success.

Nevertheless, as I reached the end of my first year in the Pentagon, I felt I had created a solid record of accomplishment with the F-117A program rapidly being developed, the ATB (B-2) poised for approval, and several unmanned stealth recon programs and a stealth cruise missile in the works. General Allen said that down the road a fourth star was a good possibility.

Good as things were at the office, they were bad at home. Faye had never been comfortable with the public appearances required of an astronaut's wife during our time in Houston and had enjoyed the relative privacy we had at Edwards. Washington was a whole different deal. My job required me to attend receptions and events at embassies and on Capitol Hill. Faye became more and more reluctant to go with me. At one embassy reception, she even told me she was going to pass out if we stayed. We had known she was mildly agoraphobic. Faye agreed to see a psychiatrist, but her condition eventually worsened so much that she wouldn't leave the house at all.

In April 1979 Faye told me she couldn't take it any more. She hated Washington so much, she wanted to go back to Oklahoma—without me, if necessary. I spent several weeks agonizing over the situation. Eventually, however, I went to see General Allen and told him I was going to request retirement in the fall. Allen knew that Faye had been having problems, though not the total extent of them. He suggested that I might take a leave of absence and then return to the Air Force. But I couldn't. Then I had a similar meeting with Gen. David Jones, chairman of the Joint Chiefs of Staff, who had promoted me to the research and development post. He was also understanding.

I returned home and told Faye we would be moving back to Oklahoma in September. My retirement was officially set for November 1, 1979, thirty-one years and two months after my arrival at Annapolis, over seventy-five hundred hours of flying since my solo at Greenville, Mississippi.

nineteen
Opening the Door Again

Faye and I built a home in Norman, seventeen miles south of the state capital, home of the University of Oklahoma and a small group of technology companies. Our transition to civilian life was rocky. Faye thought at first she would take classes at the university, but it was obvious that she wasn't ready to deal with crowds of students. I had my challenges, too. Here I was, just forty-nine years old, too young to retire. My health was superb, and I was used to living at full intensity. I had a tremendous amount of unique experience in aviation, space technology, and management. I was sure I would find a position on some corporate boards and possibly have a chance to become an executive in a Fortune 500 company some day.

But I was, in many ways, restricted to Oklahoma, where there were few aerospace companies of any size. James "Mr. Mac" McDonnell, knowing my situation, graciously offered me the job of president of McDonnell's Tulsa Division, but after consideration, I had to turn it down.

I did accept executive positions or seats on the board of American Farmlines, a transportation company; Omega, the Swiss-based watch manufacturer; Gibraltar Exploration, an oil exploration and production firm; KMS Industries, an energy research and development firm; NL Industries; Gulfstream Aerospace; and Bendix (later AlliedSignal), the technology conglomerate. I got the business education I'd missed at Harvard back in 1962. Plus.

The Soviets invited the Apollo crew for a five-year ASTP reunion timed to coincide with the 1980 Summer Olympics being held in Moscow, but because the Soviets had invaded Afghanistan in 1979, President Carter made the decision to boycott the Olympics, and the reunion was off. Each year at Christmas I would send Aleksei and Valery a card and note. I would also send them an occasional message via our ASTP instructor, Jim Flannery, who went back and forth to Moscow for NL Industries in its oil field support office.

After nearly three years of work on corporate boards, and with a growing list of technology consulting contracts, I realized I needed a central office that could help me focus my energies. My two associates from the Pentagon research and development office, Lt. Gen. Kelly Burke and Maj. Gen. Guy Hecker, were scheduled to retire within a couple of months of each other in the fall of 1982. Beginning that spring, the three of us discussed forming a consulting firm, Stafford, Burke, and Hecker, which opened for business in November.

Our headquarters was a three-story Victorian house in Old Town Alexandria, Virginia, complete with a loft. It was anything but corporate, which we all liked. The firm never got too big, either, usually numbering about six full-time employees. We'd review programs for our clients, helping them answer that all-important question: What did the customer, that is, the government, *really* want?

We were busy. The Reagan administration was putting a lot of resources toward neglected military programs and later started on the Strategic Defense Initiative. Kelly Burke had been on the SDI technical advisory council to the White House, and I knew many of the players, such as Dr. Edward Teller and James Abrahamson. We did relatively little work in that area, however. In January 1984 the president also took the long overdue step of committing the United States to the construction of a manned orbiting space station within the next ten years. At first glance, the station design seemed admirably simple, and the price—eight billion dollars to build it—was right. I certainly approved. It was about time.

In July 1984 I attended a White House reception given by President Reagan for the fifteenth anniversary of Apollo 11. Jim Fletcher and Hans Mark were present, too, and they chose the occasion to ask me to join the National Research Council's Aeronautics and Space Engineering Board (ASEB). The National Research Council is the operational arm of the National Academy of Sciences and the National Academy of Engineering. The ASEB was an independent committee that reviewed NASA and other government research programs. Apparently it was dominated by Dr. James van Allen and other unmanned space flight advocates; manned space was getting short shrift. I agreed to join up.

In the spring of 1985, I received a telephone call from Dr. John McLucas, former secretary of the Air Force and FAA administrator, now president of the American Institute of Aeronautics and Astronautics. The AIAA and the Planetary Society were planning a celebration at the National Academy of Sciences and the National Air and Space Museum to commemorate the tenth anniversary of Apollo-Soyuz. (The other theme was Mars exploration.) McLucas wanted Aleksei and Valery to be present, but so far the only response he had been able to get from the Soviet embassy was vague.

McLucas asked me if I knew Ambassador Dobrynin. We had met many times during ASTP, of course. I also knew that Dobrynin and his wife had been aeronautical engineers at the Yakovlev Bureau during World War II and retained their interest in space flight. At Dobrynin's request, I had presented him with two copies of the famous Earth picture taken from Apollo 10, one for his Washington residence and another for his apartment in Moscow. I arranged a "nonpolitical" meeting with him.

Over tea at the Soviet embassy, I told Dobrynin how important it was for the cosmonauts to attend this celebration. Dobrynin agreed completely and promised to send a telex to Moscow immediately recommending the meeting and to follow up with a personal appeal on his trip home the next week. But weeks passed with no word. July 15 was approaching, and McLucas and I were getting nervous.

Finally, I had to call one of Dobrynin's deputies at the embassy; after an initial bit of stalling, the deputy called back to inform me that according to the ambassador, the cosmonauts would arrive. I asked when. All the deputy would say was, "They will be here." So we went ahead with our preparations. I made another call two days before the event, just to confirm. "They will be here!"

Aleksei and Valery arrived via Aeroflot at three on the morning of the fifteenth, just five hours before the celebration was to begin. (They had a couple of KGB "babysitters" with them, too.) It was great to see them face-to-face again at the National Academy of Sciences celebration after nearly ten years. The dinner that evening was cohosted by Carl Sagan, Lou Friedman, and the leadership of the Planetary Society. The next day we had a serious discussion on the potential for U.S. and Soviet joint partnership in a manned Mars exploration program.

The next night Omega Watch and Paul Fisher of the Fisher Pen Co. hosted a dinner, and I invited the cosmonauts to stay over for a few days as my guests. Nothing doing: The KGB whisked them out of Washington early the next morning. But not before they had invited the Apollo crew to come to Moscow for a Soviet celebration in honor of ASTP in October.

The door was open again.

Our delegation to the Moscow event numbered thirty-nine people, including Deke Slayton and me (Vance was still in active astronaut training); Thomas Paine, the former NASA administrator; and several members of the Science and Technology Committee of the U.S. House of Representatives—Manuel Lujan of New Mexico, Peter Toricelli of New Jersey, Bob Walker of Pennsylvania, and the ranking member of the committee, Bill Nelson of Florida. We flew out of Andrews Air Force Base in Washington on an Air Force VIP KC-135. When we arrived in Moscow, it was back to the Rossia, that huge, dilapidated place I had so disliked back in 1972. What made it even worse this time was that we were sharing the hotel with Libya's Mu'ammar Gadhafi and his entourage.

Aleksei was our host at Star City, which had grown enormously in ten years. There were new training facilities for the new programs, though we weren't told what they were. Our former Hotel Kosmonavt had been converted into a hostel of sorts called the Profilaktorium, where crews from long-duration Salyut missions would live for weeks under medical observation before launch and after return from orbit.

Congressman Nelson, who had just been invited by NASA Administrator James Beggs to fly aboard the Shuttle as a payload specialist, was hoping to raise his public profile by meeting with Mikhail Gorbachev, the new Soviet president.[4] But the Soviets wouldn't accommodate the congressman until the last day of the trip, when we were told we could meet with Andrei Gromyko, the Soviet foreign minister. Gromyko was a familiar figure in world politics: He had been Soviet ambassador to the United States during World War II, the first Soviet representative to the United Nations, and had been in his current post since 1957. Now seventy-six years old, Gromyko was still tall, slim, expensively dressed. And just as smooth and obstinate as ever.

We had met on several previous occasions, so when I reached him in the receiving line, I greeted him in Russian and received a friendly reply. We chatted for several minutes. Then I took my place on the American side of the table next to Nelson, who noted the "wonderful cooperation" our two countries had had in the past on Apollo-Soyuz and suggested that we might now discuss future joint projects timed to the International Space Year (1992), possibly including unmanned and manned missions to Mars.

That was as far as he got. "How can you tell my people of the Soviet Union that you want to cooperate in space?" Gromyko said. "Today the United States is taking the arms race into space!" He was talking about the Strategic Defense Initiative. He went on in that vein, leaving Nelson little room for reply. "We cannot cooperate if the USA does not stop the arms race."

I think Nelson was surprised by Gromyko's vehemence. Nelson was a nice guy, and his heart was in the right place. But he had been torn apart by an old pro. I returned to the United States thinking we had little chance for future joint space programs with the Soviet Union for a considerable period of time.

I made a fast trip back to Moscow that December, as representative of NL Industries and its chairman, Ted Rogers, to the US-USSR Trade Council meeting. I got to see Aleksei, Valery, and their families again at the large reception in the Kremlin. Soviet president Gorbachev went down the receiving line and shook hands with the American delegates. When he came to me, I spoke Russian to him, and he stopped for a lengthy period of time and discussed the program and the friendship it brought between the two countries. I was glad he could understand my Oklahomsky Russian.

The winter of 1985–86 was a time of change for me personally, too. Faye and I had returned to Oklahoma and originally settled in Norman in search of a lifestyle that wouldn't trigger her agoraphobia. This soon proved to be *too* quiet, and Faye decided she would rather be in Oklahoma City itself, where she had more friends. So in 1984 we bought a large condo in the new, elegant Waterford Complex, and for a while our relationship improved.

We were also grandparents by now. After transferring to the University of Oklahoma, in May 1981 Dionne had married Medhi Mohammadi Maraj, a student from Iran. On August 23, 1983, they had a son, Siad Thomas Maraj. Unfortunately, though, Dionne and Mohammadi's marriage didn't last: They broke up in November 1986, and Dionne continued at OU. She graduated in 1989 and went on to obtain her master's degree in 1991 in human relations.

The strain of my travel and Faye's uneasiness eventually brought our marriage to a breaking point. In late 1985 we mutually decided to separate, then divorce. I moved out the week between Christmas and New Year's 1985 and rented an apartment in the northwest section of the city.

Dick Scobee and El Onizuka were two of the seven crew members assigned to Shuttle mission 51-L, scheduled for launch on January 22, 1986. Both men had worked for me at Edwards and were close friends. I had personally written letters to recommend them as astronauts, and they invited me to attend the launch.

Even before I left for Florida, however, 51-L was delayed to the twenty-sixth—Super Bowl Sunday. The mission prior to theirs, 61-C (with Congressman Bill Nelson in the crew) had suffered through a series of launch delays. Columbia reached orbit safely on its seventh try, but there had been an error in tanking the vehicle that could have resulted in an abort.

It was a warning sign for anyone who paid attention. NASA was ramping up its Shuttle schedule, planning a dozen launches in 1986, up from eight in 1985. At the same time, the administrator, Jim Beggs, was on a leave of absence due to a frivolous lawsuit brought against him by the government for his work at General Dynamics; the acting administrator, William Graham, had only been at NASA for a couple of months. And the director of the Johnson Space Center, Gerry Griffin, had resigned a few weeks before. There was a vacuum at the very top posts of the agency. It was obvious to me that the great era of the management team of Webb, Seamans, Mueller, Phillips, Gilruth, von Braun, Debus, and Low had been replaced by second string players or walk-ons.

And down at the operational level, things weren't going too well, either. I was sitting in a hotel in Cocoa Beach on a beautiful sunny Sunday after launch managers had canceled the day's attempt—because of weather. The next try, on Monday the twenty-seventh, turned into a fiasco when a bolt got stuck in the hatch of the Challenger. One of the pad crew tried to remove it, but the battery on his drill died. It was amateur hour!

I had waited two days and was needed back in Washington on Tuesday. So, with great regret, I phoned Dick and El in their crew quarters that night and made my apologies—I would have to miss the launch. They understood, of course.

After an unseasonably cold night, I flew back to Washington the next morning. I was in a cab around noon when I heard, on the taxi's radio, that Challenger had exploded during launch, killing the whole crew, including Dick and El, and Christa McAuliffe, the schoolteacher who was aboard. I was shocked. I always knew an accident like that could happen—anyone who knew the Shuttle did. But you never expect it. I went looking for a telephone and called my good friend, Buz Hello, who was then head of Rockwell's office in Washington. I joined him, and we sat in his office watching the endless replays of the accident, horrified at seeing the pieces plummeting into the water.

Back in the early 1970s, I had pushed hard to put ejection seats in the orbiter, at least for the flight tests. As for the rest of the crew on operational missions, we considered a system that had worked in Vietnam. Called the Yankee system, it used a harness with a small rocket to pull each crew member free of the cabin. I don't know whether it would have worked on Challenger, but the cabin appeared to come out of the fireball intact, and later analysis showed that three of the seven personal emergency egress packs (PEEPs, small containers of compressed air designed to allow crew members to breathe during emergency egress on the pad) had been activated. So at least three of the crew members were conscious during that horrible two minutes and thirty-some seconds it took to fall to the ocean. Better to have *something* you could try.

An investigating committee was formed, chaired by former attorney general William Rogers. Neil Armstrong, Chuck Yeager, Dr. Eugene Covert, Dr. Richard Feynman, Gen. Donald Kutyna, and other experienced space and engineering professionals were also involved. The technical cause of the accident—an O-ring failure in one of the Shuttle's solid rocket boosters caused by exposure to low temperatures—was an issue, as were the appalling series of managerial lapses. Rocco Petrone of Rockwell had recommended against launch the morning of the twenty-eighth. So had George Abbey and a number of other people in the chain of command. Yet the Challenger had taken off in weather so cold there were icicles hanging off the pad. It turned out that a whole number of critical issues were not addressed.

I did not participate directly but talked to some of the commission members and later was asked to testify before the U.S. House of Representatives Science Committee. One factor contributing to the decision to keep the Shuttle flying despite its obvious problems was that the astronaut office's complaints didn't get heard because of the NASA bureaucracy. John Young, for example, had written a lot of memos that had no effect. I told Don Kutyna, Bud Wheelon, and Gene Covert that the flight crew operations directorate *had* to report directly to the director of JSC as it had during the Mercury, Gemini, and Apollo programs.

And I decided I should take a more active role in my dealings with NASA. If I saw something going wrong, I was going to speak out and try to help ensure that mistakes were corrected—quickly.

I was back in Moscow again that summer, for a whole week, for the 1986 Goodwill Games sponsored by Ted Turner and CNN. Apollo-Soyuz had been selected as the symbol for the event, and I found myself standing in an open-air convertible at one end of the gigantic Lenin Stadium, in front of 120,000 people, heading for a "rendezvous" with Aleksei and Valery in another convertible approaching from the other end. It was great fun but strictly ceremonial. The Soviets had launched the Mir Space Station and had just begun operations with its first crew. The Shuttle, meanwhile, was grounded for repairs. It was good, however, to see Aleksei, Valery, and many of my cosmonaut friends and Soviet space leaders from Apollo-Soyuz days. I had a good chat with Gorbachev during the event, too.

My mother had always been nervous about my going into aviation. Then she got even more worried about my being a fighter pilot, a test pilot. Being an astronaut—oh, jeez! Nevertheless, she was happy and proud, especially of the way the whole city of Weatherford took part in my flights. The whole town would put flags on Main Street. My mother would fly flags at our house and appear on Oklahoma television. I had been able to buy her her first color television in 1965, in time for her to see my flight on Gemini 6. She had lived in Weatherford since 1921. I would visit her whenever I could and made sure to spend every Christmas with her. In August 1987, she died.

At the end of the year, my personal situation improved. I happened to be at a New Year's Eve party when I was introduced to Linda Dishman, a petite blonde with a great sense of humor, who had come to the party with her brother, Neil. She asked me to dance. Like me, Linda was recently divorced and had two grown children, Mark and Kassie. She worked as a marketing and sales coordinator for Scrivner, a large food distributing company. Then she asked what I did. I laughed and told her I had been an Air Force test pilot. She didn't like that. "I've just gotten rid of one Air Force man and I don't care to know another!" And she turned and walked off the floor.

Well, I'm nothing if not persistent. I gave her some time to cool off, then about fifteen minutes later, scooped up a pair of champagne glasses and approached her. We toasted the New Year and then had a more productive conversation. As the party broke up, we went out to the local Denny's for breakfast. As we were leaving, a couple of friends happened to say good night and Happy New Year to "General Stafford."

Linda turned and asked, "Did they call you 'General Stafford'?"

"Yes." She burst out laughing, so I asked her what was wrong with that?

"You'll never know."

Well, I found out later that Linda's ex-husband had been an Air Force master sergeant. Now she was with a general and a former astronaut. Over the next few months we grew closer, and soon we were seeing each other frequently.

On December 27, 1988, we were married at a private home in Las Vegas at a small ceremony. An old friend, Ernie Baer, had arranged the event and acted as best man. Paul Fisher also attended, as did Gen. Bill Creech and his wife.

Slowly but surely, I found myself being drawn back into the world of manned space. Dick Truly was named NASA administrator in 1989 by President George Bush. I knew Dick well, of course, having overseen his selection as a NASA astronaut in 1969. He had worked for me on Apollo-Soyuz then gone on to make two Shuttle flights before being reassigned to active duty as the head of the Navy Space Command.

In 1986, after the Challenger disaster, Don Fuqua, the former congressman who was then president of the Aerospace Industries Association, asked me if Truly could handle the job of running the Shuttle program at HQ. "Yes," I said, "if he has help." And at that time, everybody in the world wanted to help him.

In December 1988, outgoing administrator Jim Fletcher called to see if I would like to be considered as a candidate to succeed him as head of NASA. I told him that personal commitments made that impossible, but I would be happy to serve on NASA advisory panels. (I had been asked the same question twice during the Reagan administration and had turned them down both times for the same reason.) Fletcher then asked what I thought about Truly as a potential administrator. Much as I liked Dick and respected his intelligence, technical expertise, and determination, I doubted that his management background qualified him to manage NASA at that level and said so. No matter; he was appointed.

I saw Dick frequently at various events that spring, and in mid-July 1989, he phoned me at my office in Old Town and told me I should be sure to listen to what President Bush was going to announce in a few days' time. On July 20, the twentieth anniversary of the Apollo 11 landing, Linda and I sat with other former astronauts on the mall north of the Air and Space Museum, hearing President Bush announce that he wanted to "re-establish the United States as the pre-eminent space-faring nation." He was proposing a "long-range, continuing commitment: back to the Moon, back to stay. And then, a journey into tomorrow, a journey to another planet, a manned mission to Mars." The President went on to order Vice President Dan Quayle to lead the National Space Council in determining how, and on what schedule the new "Space Exploration Initiative" (SEI) could be accomplished.

These were words I'd waited twenty years to hear from a president. But even as I listened, I asked myself, Where in the heck is the money coming from?

Money wasn't the first barrier. Within a few months, the Berlin Wall came tumbling down and the Soviet bloc in Eastern Europe began to break up. It was obvious that the reduction in America's military expenditures was going to free up many times what was needed for a vigorous, peaceful space exploration program. No, the first problem with the Space Exploration Initiative was NASA itself.

The space agency launched a ninety-day in-house study headed by Aaron Cohen, director of JSC, a smart, experienced veteran of Apollo and a good friend. But what he and his team delivered in December 1989 made the vice president and the Space Council very unhappy. The unofficial price tag for the NASA version of SEI—five hundred billion dollars—made *everyone* unhappy.

I was asked to be one of fifteen members of a National Research Council special committee to review NASA's response. Other members included Gen. Sam Phillips, who was unable to take part unfortunately because he was battling cancer and died shortly after our first meeting; Dr. Guy Stever, former presidential science adviser; and Joe Gavin, former lunar module manager for Grumman. We convened at the National Academy of Science Building in Washington on Monday, January 15, 1990, and worked straight through to Friday, eating breakfast, lunch, and dinner there, frequently staying until 11 P.M. while we reviewed reports from private industry, universities, the Department of Defense, the Department of Energy, from NASA and the national laboratories, trying to make sense of the study.

The best thing to be said about NASA's 90-Day Study was that it had some good basic data but overall was more of the same. Every proposed mission was based on the Shuttle and Space Station Freedom, as though SEI existed to justify those two programs. For example, to return to the Moon, NASA proposed to use four Shuttle missions to carry pieces of a lunar return vehicle (as well as hundreds of thousands of pounds of fuel) to Space Station Freedom, where all would be assembled and launched on a lunar trajectory. Cohen and his team seemed to have forgotten that in Apollo, in 1969, NASA had performed the same mission with one vehicle and one launch.

The 90-Day Study team barely looked at nuclear propulsion. Our review committee got briefings from the Strategic Defense Initiative Organization (SDIO) on a classified test program called Timberwind. This program could have led to a nuclear thermal rocket capable of propelling a spacecraft to Mars. When I asked Cohen about it, he replied that they had briefly studied that form of propulsion and thought it had promise, but they didn't think it was politically acceptable. I replied that they should make technical recommendations, not politically acceptable ones.

By early February our critique was ready, and it was largely negative. In response, Vice President Quayle asked how SEI could be accomplished faster, better, safer, and cheaper. The National Space Council suggested that NASA immediately conduct an outreach program to gather ideas from universities, industrial firms, professional organizations, and government agencies. Unfortunately, NASA was slow getting *this* effort started. Not only did the vice president and the space council grow frustrated with NASA's foot-dragging, but so did President Bush and his son, George W., who was working at the White House at the time. Both men would remember how NASA wasted this opportunity to articulate a vision for the country's future in space.

During this time I returned to my corporate work. But in late May 1990 Dick Truly called; he wanted to see me as soon as possible.

twenty
Charting the Future

On May 30, 1990, I met with Dick Truly and J. R. Thompson, NASA's deputy administrator. They asked me to volunteer to head up a team called the Synthesis Group that would examine the data and ideas collected by NASA, RAND, AIAA, government institutes, and industry, and then produce two or more "architectures" and the technical priorities to accomplish SEI.

After a moment's thought I decided to take the job, but I had conditions. First, I did not want to receive any compensation. Second, I wanted to be able to preserve my memberships on a number of corporate boards as well as the consulting services I had through Stafford, Burke, and Hecker. I proposed to give NASA a "No Conflict of Interest" letter describing those relationships and promising not to take part in any consulting work concerning SEI matters during the time I headed the Synthesis Group. Both men thought that would work, so I gave them a list of the boards and clients; they were surprised by its length. The next step was a meeting with Vice President Quayle the following day, Thursday, May 31, 1990.

A US-USSR Summit happened to be opening that day, with President Bush hosting President Gorbachev. I had already been invited to a special luncheon for "American intellectuals" hosted by Gorbachev at the Soviet Embassy. Other invitees included economist John Kenneth Galbraith, actor Charlton

Heston, civil rights activist Jesse Jackson, former secretary of state Henry Kissinger, Ted Turner, and Jane Fonda. The luncheon was my third chance to meet Gorbachev, who was bubbling over with energy and enthusiasm for all the changes taking place in the Soviet Union. He was even proposing to open a stock market in Moscow.

He was just finishing his long talk when I had to excuse myself to get to the White House, where Dick Truly met me and took me into the west wing. There we sat down with the vice president, and with Mark Albrecht, secretary of the National Space Council. The vice president approved my conditions and thanked me for volunteering. I did a lot of thinking on my taxi ride back to the office in Old Town Alexandria. It was gratifying to meet both a Soviet president and an American vice president on the same day. But I had to be realistic about the mission I had just accepted. Yes, I had the chance to help shape America's future in space for the next thirty years.

I could also fall flat on my face.

My experience with the NRC/ASEB review panel, not to mention ten years in the corporate world, had made it clear to me that NASA needed a coherent strategic plan. We could have the funds and resources required, and we could have the right architecture and technology, but if we didn't have the right management structure, the SEI would not succeed.

Dick suggested that I base the Synthesis Group somewhere isolated, like Sandia Labs or Los Alamos in New Mexico, where we would be undisturbed. I disagreed: The various groups working with us could travel to Washington easier than to New Mexico, and a lot of them would have Washington offices. I also wanted to remain near my office. We finally decided to have NASA rent a floor in Crystal Gateway number 2, an office complex on Jefferson Davis Highway in Crystal City, Virginia, near the Pentagon and National Airport. The site was home to a number of military program offices and government contractors.

At Dick Truly's suggestion, the first person I hired was my old friend George Abbey. George had come to HQ in 1987 in the wake of the Challenger disaster as Truly's deputy for manned flight. When Dick became administrator, however, he brought in Bill Lenoir as head of manned flight over George, and there were problems. Lenoir was a former astronaut, a veteran of the

STS-5 mission. He had left NASA in the first place because George had informed him it would be "a long time" before he would ever fly a second time. In other words, never. I knew that George was very capable and was familiar with the inner workings of NASA and its centers. I made him my deputy.

At George's suggestion, I also hired Spence "Sam" Armstrong. Sam was an Annapolis grad (1956) who had gone into the Air Force and had served as my one-star deputy for space at the Pentagon prior to becoming vice commander of Systems Command. He had just retired that spring as a lieutenant general and when I tracked him down he was painting his house in South Carolina.

George and I spent the Fourth of July weekend in our new, empty Crystal City offices, laying out a course of action for the Synthesis Group.

To begin with, we had 1,697 ideas collected by the RAND Corporation, which we soon boiled down to 215 we wanted to consider further. The AIAA submissions numbered 542. We also had ideas of our own, but the mission of the Synthesis Group was to cast a wide net. So we went looking for people with background, imagination, and vision to evaluate these concepts and build them into architectures.

Among the people we found was Lt. Col. David Lee, USMC, the son of Chet Lee, the former NASA HQ program manager for Apollo-Soyuz. David had worked in Navy space and was soon to retire from the Marines, so his assignment to the group was not a problem. Not so with Lt. Col. Mike "Mini" Mott, USMC. George Abbey had met Mike when he applied for the 1984 astronaut group and had stayed in touch. Mike was commander of the Marine air group at Andrews AFB when we asked him to join us. The Marines balked, but eventually I convinced the assistant commandant, Gen. Jack Dailey, to let me have him. "General," I told him, "all I need is a few good men."

Within a few weeks, we had assembled a team of 42 full-time and 150 part-time or volunteer helpers. To encourage team unity, George Abbey came up with "Vespers," a Friday afternoon happy hour that would be hosted by one of the teams in the group. Whoever happened to be briefing us that day would also be invited. (Aleksei Leonov was one of our guests.) I enjoyed these events so much that I often flew back early from other engagements to be present. The wives would prepare food dishes and join us, too.

Through the rest of 1990 and into the new year, we developed four major architectures for returning to the Moon around 2004, and going on to Mars in 2012–14. All architectures shared those goals, but the purpose and technology of each mission differed. Architecture I was titled "Mars Exploration," and treated a return to the Moon as preparation or rehearsal for a voyage to Mars. Architecture II was "Science Emphasis for the Moon and Mars" and expanded the first architecture to give equal emphasis to science and exploration on the Moon and on Mars. The most ambitious scenario, Architecture III, was titled "Moon to Stay and Mars Exploration" and called for the long-term human habitation of the Moon combined with a few trips to Mars. The wild card in the deck was Architecture IV. It dealt with human flights to the Moon and Mars but concentrated on treating those planets as storehouses of resources that could someday be transformed into useful products. (For example, the Apollo missions had shown that the Moon has an abundance of helium-3, which is relatively rare on Earth. Helium-3 would make a terrific fuel source for fusion power plants.) The technical means to achieving any of these architectures included a heavy-lift launch vehicle and advanced propulsion systems, especially a nuclear thermal rocket for the orbital transfer and Mars missions.

The report, titled *America at the Threshold,* was delivered to Vice President Quayle on May 3, 1991. We delivered the results to the press at a joint press conference at the old Executive Office Building on June 10. It had been a busy eleven months, and Linda and I left the next day for the Paris Air Show.

NASA seemed to respond. JSC Director Aaron Cohen strongly supported our suggestion for a strategic plan. Michael Griffin came from the Strategic Defense Initiative Organization to head up the SEI Office at NASA Headquarters. But NASA was not a unified organization. The support at HQ was lukewarm, at best. Dick Truly and Bill Lenoir seemed completely focused on flying the Shuttle and developing Space Station Freedom. Some of NASA's senior managers privately told congressional staffers that SEI was a low priority and not to fund it. They encouraged the staffers instead to concentrate on robotic space exploration. Some of these managers even slammed funding for Space Shuttle and Space Station programs.

The Fiscal Year 1992 budget cycle didn't help us, either. Liberals in Congress chewed up the SEI budget that President Bush had proposed, effectively strangling our chance to return to the Moon and go to Mars.

For the moment, that is. The architectures remain as valid today as they were in 1991.[5]

In August 1991 Communist Party hardliners attempted to overthrow President Mikhail Gorbachev. They failed, and the attempt was the last official death spasm of the brutal, corrupt Soviet system, which began to unravel. Boris Yeltsin replaced Gorbachev, and a number of top ministers retired. Gen. Yevgeny Shaposhnikov became the new Minister of Defense. Shaposhnikov was a career officer in the Soviet Air Force, a former fighter pilot, and he ordered the automatic retirement of any officer over the age of fifty-five. Among those swept away was sixty-two-year-old Lt. Gen. Vladimir Shatalov, director of the Gagarin Center at Star City. Also ticketed for retirement—Maj. Gen. Aleksei Leonov, now fifty-seven. He was relieved of his job on September 12, 1991.

This was a bitter blow for Aleksei. He had served faithfully and well as deputy director and was the logical successor to Shatalov as head of Star City. Instead, Shaposhnikov appointed Maj. Gen. Pyotr Klimuk, forty-nine, as the new commander. Klimuk had flown three missions between 1973 and 1978. Since then, however, he had served as Star City's political officer and commissar, a post that was now being abolished. Nevertheless, Klimuk survived, no doubt helped by the fact that he and Shaposhnikov had been students together at the Chernigov Higher Air Force School in the early 1960s.

Dick Truly had angered the Bush team by failing to control the NASA bureaucracy or to get an adequate response from the space agency to the original Space Exploration Initiative. They realized he had to go. And, after a series of awkward meetings, culminating in a face-to-face meeting with President Bush himself, Dick was out. This unfortunate episode would have consequences years later. NASA was simply not a priority when George W. Bush became president in January 2001.

Truly's replacement was Daniel Goldin, a program manager from TRW. I had never met him. But on April 3, 1992, his third day on the job, I went to see him at the urging of Vice President Quayle and Mark Albrecht. Dan Goldin and I sat down at 6:30 A.M. for breakfast, and there I gave him my perspective on NASA's problems. I discussed the conclusions of the Synthesis Group, as well as the possibilities for Russian-American joint missions. It was our first meeting ever, and I believe we hit it off.

As the new administrator of a vast agency, Goldin was under tremendous pressure to take command and get results. Neither goal was easy. Dan had worked at NASA Lewis in Cleveland for five years back in the 1960s, but since then he had been on the contractor side of the business at TRW, for many years in classified programs. When it came to NASA, he didn't know who to count on and who to watch out for. I suggested that he rely on George Abbey; I also gave him a list of suggested actions that would enhance the agency's effectiveness. We chatted frequently after that, and he would tell me how many of my policy and personnel suggestions he had implemented.

George and the Space Council helped Goldin prepare for the Bush-Yeltsin summit in July 1992, which produced agreements for a number of joint space projects, including the flight of a Russian cosmonaut aboard the Shuttle, the flight of an American astronaut for ninety days aboard Mir, and a rendezvous and docking between a Shuttle and Mir in 1994–95. The details were left to Dan Goldin, and to Yury Koptev, head of the new Russian Space Agency. Koptev was a former Energia engineer, part of the ASTP team at one time, who had been in his job only since that February. Because Dan had other pressing engagements, he asked me to look after Yury when the ceremonies with Yeltsin at the Air and Space Museum were finished. I presented him with an Omega watch, invited him to my office in Old Town Alexandria for a few quick toasts, then took him to dinner at Genario's, a nearby favorite Italian restaurant. We got along very well, which was a good thing: We had some tough negotiations ahead of us.

Goldin was ordered to head for Russia in late July to negotiate and sign the final Memorandum of Agreement for the new programs. He asked me to come along, the only member of the team who wasn't a government employee. I realized I was becoming NASA's unofficial messenger to Russia, which was fine: It was a logical move, given my familiarity with the country, its language, and the leaders of its space enterprises.

The group that flew to Moscow in a NASA Gulfstream III also included Brian Dailey, the new executive secretary of the National Space Council; Martin Faga, former assistant secretary of the Air Force for space; and George Abbey. An advance team that included Samuel Keller, the veteran NASA associate administrator for international programs, and former astronaut Bryan O'Connor, was already in Moscow.

As soon as we arrived at Sheremetyevo Airport Saturday afternoon, July 11, 1992, we received a warning from James F. Collins, the American chargé d'affaires in Moscow. He alerted us to Russian concerns that America was going to use the pretext of cooperation to "suck up" their technology at bargain rates, and that we weren't serious about a true economic partnership. We had to avoid raising their expectations to an unrealistic level, and we also had to be careful about weakening the existing agreements on missile control technology. Then Sam Keller weighed in with another issue. It seemed that Yury Semyonov, director of the Energia organization, was insisting that *he* and his organization be signatories to any agreements.

It was a far different Russia than the one I'd worked with between 1972 and 1975. In those days, once the government approved a program, the various design bureaus and other organizations lined up in support. No dissent was allowed. Not any more, though. The Russian government was new, underfunded, and weak. The big organizations saw no reason to simply follow orders.

Goldin asked me what I thought about the Semyonov situation, and, frankly, I didn't know what to tell him. I promised, however, to find out as much as I could within the next forty-eight hours. So I opted out of Sunday's ceremonial visit to Zagorsk (site of the Energia rocket engine test facility) to do some recon. First I called Aleksei Leonov and Valery Kubasov and asked if we could get together on Sunday; Aleksei invited us to his *dacha*. Then I called Jim Flannery, one of my former Russian language instructors on ASTP, still working for NL Industries in Moscow and a frequent translator for me during my visits. I asked Jim to pick me up at the hotel early Sunday morning.

We drove first to a residential compound known as Khovanskaya. It was a collection of townhouses for civilian cosmonauts from the Energia organization—including Valery Kubasov. As we drove out of Moscow, headed toward Aleksei's dacha on a tributary of the Volga River, I turned to Valery, who was in the backseat with his wife, Ludmila, and asked him who owned the Mir Space Station—the Russian Space Agency (Koptev) or Energia (Semyonov)?

"Oh, Semyonov owns Mir," Valery said.

I couldn't quite believe this, and asked again. And Valery gave the same answer. "Well, what about TsUP?"

"The mission control center? That's owned by Koptev, the Russian Space Agency."

"And what about the people working there?"

"They belong to Semyonov."

I turned to the front, trying to analyze what I had just heard. It sounded like a bureaucratic and political nightmare. But I had worked with the Russians long enough to know I needed a second opinion. You need two data points to define a straight line.

After an hour's drive, we reached Aleksei's dacha—which, coincidentally, was right next to a dacha owned by Yury Semyonov—and after I delivered several presents, we had a ceremonial toast. I then talked to Aleksei as he was fixing a barbecue in the yard. It was great to see my old friend, even though I knew he was unhappy about leaving his job at Star City. These days he was making a foray into the wild world of Russian banking and investments.

I asked him the same questions I had asked Valery: "Aleksei, who owns Mir, Semyonov or Koptev?"

"Semyonov owns it."

"Who owns the control center?"

"Koptev."

"What about the people working there?"

"Oh, those belong to Semyonov."

As soon as I returned to the hotel that evening, I went directly to Dan. "It's unbelievable, from our point of view. It's as if Houston mission control belonged to NASA, but the Shuttle and all the controllers working in the center belonged to Rockwell."

Dan wanted my advice. I noted that the Apollo-Soyuz agreements had been signed by James Fletcher, the NASA administrator, and by Mstislav Keldysh of the Soviet Academy of Sciences—that is, from government to government. The Soviet aerospace industry or contractors, such as Energia, had not been part of it—at least, not openly. Since the 1992 summit document had been signed by Koptev, I felt we were justified in sticking with the precedent—treating the agreements as taking place between two government agencies.

Dan agreed. It didn't matter that the Russian Space Agency had a tiny staff: It was a government body. And even though the Russian government owned most of its stock and assets, Energia was a commercial organization.

A number of operational questions also needed to be resolved, the kind of issues that had been hashed out by Soviet and American working groups for three years prior to the launch of ASTP. We were trying to resolve them in much less time. Bryan O'Connor was head of these working groups, and he had run into a brick wall by the name of Valery Ryumin. Ryumin was one of the deputy directors of the Energia organization, a former engineer on the Salyut program, a former cosmonaut with a year in space on three different missions, and, most recently, the head of flight control for Salyut-7 and Mir. Physically he was one of the bigger Russians I knew: six feet, four inches tall, dark-haired, heavy, and imposing.

And completely uninterested in joint programs with NASA. He questioned the whole idea of having a Russian cosmonaut fly on the Shuttle. He clashed with O'Connor, who had flown two Shuttle missions, because he didn't believe that O'Connor's 16 total days in space compared to Ryumin's 362. Further, he insisted that the Shuttle was unsafe.

The Russian Space Agency wasn't much help in these meetings. Koptev's representative to the groups was Boris Ostroumov, a veteran *apparatchik* from the Ministry of General Machine Building, and while he was generally supportive and later a friend, he was a bit too fond of his vodka and sometimes fell asleep during the sessions.

None of Ryumin's points struck me as genuine issues. I told O'Connor, "Unfortunately, these people are broke and they need us. The Golden Rule is in effect here. We've got the gold, so we can sure help make the rules." I advised him to "be polite, smile, and say, 'This is what was agreed, and this is what we're going to do.'"

The Golden Rule made dealings easier. Semyonov had announced that since Energia was now a "private company," its products and services were for sale. He wanted us to rent his engine test stands in Zagorsk, for example, or lease space for experiments aboard Mir. Semyonov even offered to provide Progress logistics vehicles for Space Station Freedom. They also offered us a "universal" docking mechanism that turned out to be a slight modification of the ASTP docking adaptor. The original Soviet designer, Vladimir Syromyatnikov, was still in charge of it. Vladimir was a dear friend and one of the most brilliant engineers I have ever known. We'd had many interesting dinners and technical discussions during Apollo-Soyuz.

One new proposal was to use a Soyuz as an "assured crew return vehicle" for Freedom. Shuttles would not be able to remain docked to the station for more than a week at a time, while a Soyuz could remain on orbit for up to six months. In 1987 I had insisted on a crew return vehicle during a space station study for the National Research Council, never dreaming of using a Soyuz to fill the role. We promised to give that idea some serious thought.

On the afternoon of Thursday, July 16, following a visit by our delegation to the Khrunichev Enterprise in Fili, we gathered at the Foreign Press Center for the formal signing of the Memorandum of Agreement. Koptev signed for Russia. Semyonov and several of his associates were present but wisely didn't make a scene. The United States and Russia were back working in the manned space business, seventeen years after Apollo-Soyuz.

twenty-one

ISS Is Born

NASA was catching a lot of flak in the summer of 1992. You couldn't pick up a newspaper without reading a complaint about cost overruns and hardware problems in its programs. The prime example of a public NASA screw-up was the multibillion-dollar Hubble Space Telescope. Deployed in earth orbit from the STS-31 mission in April 1990, the Hubble turned out to have a flawed secondary mirror that blurred its vision. The agency spent two years developing plans to repair the telescope on a servicing mission.

Earlier that summer, the STS-49 crew had conducted a spectacular rescue of a wayward Intelsat satellite, culminating, on a Herculean third try, with an improvised game of "catch," in which astronauts Rick Hieb, Pierre Thuot, and Tom Akers literally grabbed the vehicle with their hands. Dan Goldin was pleased with the results of STS-49 but very unhappy with the need for improvisation. He asked Dr. Gene Covert to convene an independent panel to review that mission.

What we found was a mess. The Intelsat retrieval had not been properly simulated, and the documentation on the satellite didn't match the hardware. The biggest problem, however, was the lack of a single authority over the mission. I recommended that NASA return to the style of the Apollo era and appoint a mission director specifically for the Hubble servicing repair mission. Mike Mott, who had gone from the Synthesis Group to the corporate world, suggested a former Marine test pilot named Randy Brinkley for the job. Brinkley was then working at the McDonnell Douglas facility in St. Louis.

Goldin then asked me to become chairman of a special independent oversight committee for the Hubble Telescope Repair and Servicing Mission. I chose talented people with great experience, including retired major generals Ralph Jacobson and Joe Engle, retired colonel Brad Parkinson, and Dr. Joe Rothenberg, the Hubble program manager at NASA's Goddard Space Flight Center, and Mike Mott.

The bureaucrats at JSC and Marshall fought Brinkley tooth and toenail. They fought me, too, when I insisted that NASA start training a crew eighteen months before the launch. Aaron Cohen and his deputy, PJ Weitz, complained that they usually assigned crews at six months. I knew both men and liked them, but I raised hell. If NASA blew the Hubble repair, there would be little support in Congress for a space station. And if the space station went down, how much longer would there be support for flying Shuttles to orbit? Eventually that program would subside and die and then so would NASA, with its pieces parceled off to DOD, FAA, and the National Science Foundation. The stakes were that high.

I insisted that they needed a mission commander and a whole EVA crew *now*. Further, they had to increase the number of scheduled EVAs from three to five. They also needed to start using nitrox to allow the astronauts longer stays in the big underwater tank. (Astronaut Bill Shepherd helped on this issue, based on his experience as a Navy SEAL, and got a group of JSC people angry at him.) Finally, by late August 1992, astronauts Story Musgrave, Tom Akers, Kathy Thornton, and Jeff Hoffman, all veteran spacewalkers, had been named to the repair mission, STS-61. But Cohen and Weitz wouldn't give us the rest of the crew for months.

That was my first review assignment for Dan Goldin.

On January 19, 1993, the last day of the Bush administration, Vice President Dan Quayle presented me with the Congressional Space Medal of Honor at a ceremony in Washington, D.C. President Bush had signed the award in November 1992 and planned to present it to me, but had been called away that day to deal with a flap regarding Iraq. It was an unexpected honor, but one I treasured. I received the medal as my life reached a crossroads: By the early 1990s I had, through my consultant work, my memberships on corporate boards, and my own investments, reached the point where I was financially comfortable. This solid financial base allowed me to devote a lot of time to unpaid review work, such as the ASEB board and the Synthesis Group.

But now I had the opportunity to give something back, specifically to my hometown of Weatherford, Oklahoma. In 1948 my mother had borrowed $175 to buy the train ticket than carried me to the Naval Academy. Surely other young people in town had the intellectual ability to succeed in college but lacked the resources. I put up several thousand dollars of my own money, then used the matching charitable grants for the senior officers and directors of three different corporations, Wheelabrator Technology, Fischer Scientific, and AlliedSignal, for matching funds. (I was on the board of directors of all three companies.) I received grants ranging from one-to-one to three-to-one. That scholarship fund is now over a million dollars, and has put twelve different students with financial need from Weatherford through Southwestern Oklahoma State University. As of fall 2001, there were twenty-eight enrolled at the university under the scholarship.

I wasn't happy that Bill Clinton had defeated George Bush, but I wasn't surprised as the final weeks of the campaign unfolded. I knew that the work of our Synthesis Group was likely to be discarded; Clinton wasn't as antitechnology as Carter had been, but his party, which still controlled both houses of Congress, wouldn't spend money on major new space initiatives. We didn't have a Jack Kennedy or Ronald Reagan in the White House, or an LBJ and Sam Rayburn in the Congress. And we didn't have the Soviet Union continuing to press ahead with new firsts in space.

Space Station Freedom was in serious trouble even though candidate Clinton had pledged to support it during the campaign. By that time, Freedom had been in existence for nine years. Eight billion dollars had been spent, and a lot of good design work had been done on portions of the various modules. But there was still no hardware, and the launch of Freedom's first elements was still years off.

From my vantage point, Freedom was a managerial nightmare. After the Challenger accident, NASA had located the program's managers in the Washington suburb of Reston, Virginia, adding another layer of bureaucracy to a program that was already collapsing under its own weight. Dan Goldin had started to take steps to correct this problem, but he had a long way to go.

In fact, to help him out, I asked to see Al Gore, the new vice president, in early February. There were rumors that the Clinton administration—specifically, the President's wife, Hillary—was pushing former astronaut Sally Ride as the new administrator. Ride was very accomplished and smart, but I personally felt she lacked the experience to get results from NASA's stubborn bureaucracy at that time, especially with the problems regarding Space Station Freedom. I urged Gore to keep Dan Goldin on the job: "He's probably the best administrator the agency's had since Jim Webb," I told him. I also mentioned that Dan was a Democrat.

Ultimately, Clinton and Gore kept Dan in the job.

Almost immediately, in February 1993, Goldin commenced a review of Freedom aimed at not only cutting costs, but reimagining the whole concept. The options to be considered were called A, B, and C, and their prices ranged from five to seven billion dollars. Former Apollo program manager Joe Shea was asked to head the review, and he had until June 7 to come up with a space station that the Clinton administration would support.

The redesign was a struggle. Each of the option teams seemed to spend as much time at war with each other, through leaks, as it did on the business at hand. One day you would read that Dan was pushing hard for Option C (launching a large station module called a Can with a Shuttle-derived heavy lift vehicle), the next day he was supposedly tilting the studies toward Option A. From my own observation, Dan was keeping an open mind on the issues.

In March, Yury Koptev added to the festivities by offering the services of Russian firms in the construction of the station. We all took note of that, including an outside review panel chaired by Thomas Vest of MIT. Bud Wheelon was a member of this panel, and he got them to support the idea of using the Russians in the station, too. Dr. Mary Good, the senior vice president for technology of Allied-Signal, was another friend on the committee.

Late one Friday night in early April, Linda and I were in Ocean Reef, in the Florida Keys, at a Phillips Magnavox Electronics voting trust meeting, when I got call from George Abbey. He and Goldin had reached the breaking point with leaks over the various space station options. They wanted a secure, out-of-the-way place where they could work in private, and the third-floor conference room in our office in Old Town Alexandria seemed ideal. They wanted to start work at nine the next morning.

I was happy to offer up the conference room, of course, but there was no way I could get from Ocean Reef to Washington, D.C., by 9 A.M. So I phoned Tracy Pate, the Stafford, Burke, and Hecker secretary, waking her up, then explained the situation to her, adding, "This is a semi–national emergency." Tracy and her husband, an Alexandria police officer, lived an hour west of the city, but she agreed to be at the office on Saturday morning at 0900 to deliver the key to George Abbey and Dan Goldin.

The team gathered: Dan, George, Joe Shea, Max Faget, and Mike Mott. John Young flew up from Houston in a T-38. They worked all Saturday and all Sunday. When I arrived at midday on Monday, they were still at it. Finally, late Monday, there was a new concept: NASA would scale back the American elements in the space station and fill in with Russian modules, specifically the core command and habitation module (Mir-2). We would also use a "functional control module" (FGB was the Russian acronym) for initial propulsion and propellant storage. These modules would be vastly cheaper than American equivalents and would be available much more quickly.

We would, in essence, be transforming Space Station Freedom into an International Space Station (ISS), sharing the costs by bringing in outside hardware, especially from the Russians. I knew they had been rolling modules off an assembly line since 1970—why couldn't we use one or more of them, and save ourselves time and money? The Russian option didn't come free, of course. Using the Russian modules meant moving the station from an orbit inclined 28.5 degrees to the equator up to 51.6 degrees—with loss of payload capability in every Shuttle cargo mission. Nevertheless, I agreed that it was the only option that had a prayer of surviving politically.

Goldin briefed the president and his staff on the idea, and they saw the possibilities—not just to build a space station more quickly and cheaply but also to use the program to engage Russian space and missile workers in peaceful pursuits and keep them off the lucrative international arms market.

There was also a ticking clock on all of this. Vice President Gore and Russian prime minister Viktor Chernomyrdin were scheduled to meet in Washington in June. If we wanted to have the Russians involved, that was the time to make it happen.

A team of Russian engineers from Energia came to D.C. in late July. Their leader was Viktor Legostayev, who had been Professor Bushuyev's deputy for guidance and control and a great technical engineer on ASTP. There to meet them was a NASA team led by David Mobley, with Chuck Daniels as his deputy. They had some real head-knockings, but in two weeks they managed to agree on a configuration that both sides could approve. Goldin selected the Boeing Company as prime contractor for the American side of the project. And in late August 1993 Vice President Gore and Prime Minister Chernomyrdin signed the first protocol for the International Space Station.

With the intergovernmental agreements signed, the real work began. The most immediate challenge for NASA was the organizing phase I of the ISS program—the seven Shuttle-Mir missions. Some preparation had been going ahead at the Johnson Space Center for the two joint flights agreed to in the summer of 1992: Russian cosmonauts Sergei Krikalyov and Vladimir Titov were training to fly aboard the Shuttle, and astronaut Norm Thagard was in Monterey at the Defense Language Institute, learning Russian in anticipation of his training at Star City and flight to Mir in 1995.

But now we had five more Shuttle-Mir dockings to plan and review.[6] David Leestma, the head of flight crew operations at JSC, and Hoot Gibson, his chief astronaut, went looking for astronauts to fly those missions. They weren't stampeded: Veterans Shannon Lucid and John Blaha had been among the original volunteers back in 1992. A new astronaut, Jerry Linenger, a Navy flight surgeon, was willing to go. But since the Russians required all Shuttle-Mir crew members to have had at least one previous mission, Linenger had to be added to a Shuttle crew (STS-64) to get the experience.

There were also changes at a higher level. Aaron Cohen had left the post of director, JSC, in April 1993. P J Weitz had been acting director since then, but a permanent director was needed. Goldin chose Carolyn Huntoon, head of the life sciences directorate, as Cohen's replacement. To support Huntoon, who was a fine individual but lacked real experience with program management and operations, Goldin wanted George Abbey.

It was January, and Linda and I were in New Zealand on a vacation stop, when Mike Mott called at 3:30 A.M. to tell me that George didn't want to return to JSC, particularly as the number two, because he saw the move as a demotion. Mike then put Dan Goldin on the phone. Dan said that he had originally wanted George to be JSC director, but the White House personnel office had objected, primarily because congressional staff members blamed George for helping clean out some nonproductive people in NASA HQ. He told me I had to talk George into the deputy position.

I reached George within twenty minutes and did my best, invoking God and country, citing the examples of George Low and Joe Shea, who had taken "demotions" to help the Apollo program, and reminding him that we were all dedicated to returning to the Moon and going on to explore Mars. I don't know if my silver bullet turned the tables, but George did accept the assignment.

Just before he arrived, on December 2, 1993, NASA launched STS-61 with a crew of seven astronauts. After capturing the Hubble telescope two pairs of astronauts made a total of five EVAs, restoring the crippled instrument. It was one of NASA's brightest moments, and I couldn't have been prouder if I'd commanded the flight myself. Assisted by Mike Mott, I had testified before the House Space Science Subcommittee and its chairman, Rep. Ralph M. Hall (D-Texas), shortly before the launch. At the time I predicted that the flight would achieve 95 percent of its primary objectives and probably 80 to 85 percent of the secondary ones. The team actually accomplished over 100 percent of both.

Randy Brinkley, who did an outstanding job as mission director for STS-61, was selected as head of the new ISS program in Houston. Astronaut Bill Shepherd became his deputy. Later I was awarded the NASA Public Service Medal for chairing the independent review committee that recommended many of the key operational steps.

In May 1994, partly as a result of my recommendations on STS-61, Dan Goldin asked me to serve as chairman of an independent oversight task force that would review technical, safety, and operational readiness issues between the United States and Russia involving the Shuttle-Mir flights. Before each launch I would sign a letter certifying that any open issues had been resolved and that it was safe to proceed with the launch.

For my team I turned to several former astronauts, such as Joe Engle, Jim Adamson, and John Fabian. I also drew in people who had experience in a wide variety of space- or technology-related issues, many of them—such as

Ralph Jacobson and Brad Parkinson—from the Hubble panel. And others, such as Dr. Ronald Merrell, head of the surgery department at Yale University Medical School; Dr. Craig Fischer, a former Army and NASA flight surgeon who did great support work on the Gemini and Apollo flights; and Joe Cuzzuopoli, an Apollo and Shuttle manager from Rockwell.

Other NASA officials who served on the panel included Dr. Arnauld Nicogossian, former crew physician for Apollo-Soyuz, now deputy associate administrator for life sciences; Dr. Michael Greenfield, deputy associate administrator for safety and mission assurance; Milt Heflin (flight director), Chet Vaughn (propulsion and power), William Readdy (astronaut office) and John Young (office of the director) from the Johnson Space Center; and Dave Mobley and Chuck Daniels from the Marshall Spaceflight Center.

Our first subject was the pair of Shuttle-Mir rendezvous missions immediately upcoming, STS-63 and STS-71. STS-63 would only rendezvous with Mir, closing to within a hundred meters, while STS-71, some months later, would dock and transfer Norm Thagard and his Russian crew mates back to earth. After reviewing the schedules for those flights and the five then scheduled to follow, we quickly made three recommendations to NASA: Select a mission commander and payload commander for each Shuttle-Mir flight at launch minus eighteen months (about six months earlier than usual). And we wanted STS-63 to approach to within thirty meters of Mir to fully test a Shuttle in proximity to the station. Finally, we asked that the launch of STS-63, then scheduled for February 1995, be moved forward by several weeks, to allow for "lessons learned" to be incorporated into operations for the more challenging docking.

Leestma and Gibson accommodated our wish for early announcement of Shuttle-Mir commanders by naming Kevin Chilton to STS-76 and Bill Readdy to STS-79, but payload commanders remained unassigned. It was hard to have Readdy leave our committee—he had contributed a great deal to our effort.

We similarly split the difference on our other recommendations: The Russians agreed to allow STS-63 to approach to thirty meters, but the Shuttle program office was unable to move the mission forward in the schedule.

A further meeting between Vice President Gore and Prime Minister Chernomyrdin in December 1994 called for the creation of a "joint expert commission" to resolve expected problems in the ISS relationship, specifically between the United States and Russia. My task force was given the job of representing the U.S. side. A Russian team was organized under the leadership of Academician Vladimir Fyodorovich Utkin, director of TsNIIMash and former director of the Yuzhnoe organization, where he was "father" of the SS-18 Satan ICBM.

Utkin was a tall, kindly-looking gentleman of seventy-one, very smart and articulate. His team, which included engineers from his institute as well as from the Institute of Medical-Biological Problems, Energia, and the Russian Space Agency, was smaller than ours, but much more powerful. Utkin's institute played a major role in the development and execution of Russian space missions. It was as if a former head of Boeing had taken over the leadership of the Aerospace Corporation, and was now "reviewing" the work of Air Force space programs. And Utkin himself was a major figure in Russian science and technology.

Nevertheless, the early going was rocky. For one thing, Russian space officials were completely unused to the idea of an "outside, independent" review team. What could be worse than a review team, which included representatives of their former Main Enemy—the United States? The first meeting in Russia was led by my deputy, Joe Engle, with the help of Joe Cuzzupoli, David Mobley, and Bill Vantine. As I was recovering from surgery at home, the team cabled me to report that our Russian counterparts were uncooperative. I told Joe and the others to make it clear: Either both sides started working together on the outstanding problems, or the American team would pack up and come home. Joe delivered the message with great skill and was soon working well with Utkin's people.

When I met Academician Utkin on his first trip to the United States, we became good friends in spite of the fact that we had differing views of the purpose of our commission: Utkin wanted my team to make decisions that properly belonged to the NASA administrator or to the U.S. Congress. That had to be worked out. Nevertheless, numerous issues fell to us that neither NASA nor the Russian Space Agency could resolve easily.

While our committee was wrestling with matters of policy and procedures, Norm Thagard and his backup, Bonnie Dunbar, were on the Russian Front. Thagard had been one of the first to volunteer for the Shuttle-Mir flight, back when it was just the one. He had had to work hard, even paying for his first language lessons out of his own pocket. Once he got to Russia, he suffered the usual trials of any pioneer—inconsistent support, poor planning, and just bad luck. His wife, Kirby, slipped on the ice and hurt herself.

My group and I traveled to Russia in late February 1995 to meet with Norm. Joe Engle and I had a private dinner with Norm and Kirby at their apartment in Star City, where Norm explained all of the obstacles and frustrations he had encountered. For example, his support equipment was arriving late. I went back to the States and raised hell, saying that everything—training materials, hardware, mockups, procedures—needed to be ready a minimum of three months in advance. We had gone through this late delivery of resources in the preparations for both Gemini and Apollo. I sure didn't want it to jeopardize the Shuttle-Mir missions.

This trip was the first time I had visited Star City since the 1970s, except for the brief visit in 1985, and I was amazed at the deterioration. It wasn't just that there was ice on the sidewalks. The hallways were dirty; many of the lights were inoperative. Facades of buildings were deteriorating.

Norm was launched on Soyuz TM-21 on March 14. He and his Russian crew mates, Vladimir Dezhurov and Gennady Strekalov, linked up with Mir two days later to start their three month–plus mission. Norm would work well with Dezhurov and Strekalov but would still find himself feeling isolated by language difficulties and by lack of equipment and a clear work program. The whole crew returned to earth on July 7 aboard STS-71, which made the first Shuttle-Mir docking.

Norm did an outstanding job under the circumstances. Not just flying the mission—but surviving the training. I admit to being pleased when STS-71 commander, Robert "Hoot" Gibson, reported the successful docking of the orbiter Atlantis to Mir using my words from 1975: "Houston, we have capture."

By fall 1995 Russian cooperation on ISS fell to a minimum, and NASA didn't know why. On December 7, 1995, I was at an Allied-Signal board of directors meeting in New Jersey when Mott called. NASA had a visa and they wanted me to go see Koptev; the meeting had been arranged. I sent Linda back to Washington on a commercial flight then flew to JFK in the Allied-Signal helicopter. There I boarded a flight to Moscow.

I arrived at 11 A.M. Moscow time and was met by astronaut Greg Harbaugh, the JSC Moscow representative, who guided me through customs and drove me to the Penta Hotel. I took a hot bath, a quick one-hour nap, and then walked with Greg the two blocks west to the headquarters of the Russian Space Agency, a big, gold, glass-windowed building that used to house the Ministry of General Machine Building. Nuclear submarines, aircraft, ballistic missiles and space vehicles—all of those programs were managed here.

Koptev met me promptly in his office at 2 P.M., along with Ostroumov, Utkin, and several others. I had an interpreter with me.

The first thing I said was, "Yury Nikolayevich, I'm coming here as a private citizen, and I need to talk to you alone." I hated to leave Utkin out of the conversation and told him we would talk later. But this meeting had to be one-to-one.

We went into his private office, just Koptev, the interpreter, and me. "Look," I said, "I've always supported cooperation with the Russians. Now, from what I understand, funding is not forthcoming for the station work, particularly the service module. Things aren't coming together. What is the problem?"

He was very direct. "General, we have congressional 'Duma' elections coming up in a few weeks. Candidates are calling Mir a national symbol of Russia and saying we can't abandon it." Not only were the political candidates, including former cosmonauts such as Svetlana Savitskaya and Vitaly Sevastyanov, making a fuss, the Russian Academy of Sciences was agitating, too, on the grounds that no Russian experiments would be flown on the ISS for years. "We only have so much money: We can't support Mir and ISS." He added that he was speaking as Yury Koptev, not as head of the Russian Space Agency.

He said that, frankly, he expected the Communists to take over the Duma. He had a potential solution: He took out a tablet and started to sketch a means of shifting the relatively new Spektr and Priroda modules from Mir to the FGB, the first element of the new ISS, once it reached orbit. Looking at Koptev's hasty sketch, my first response was that it would be difficult for attitude and maneuver control for such a configuration. I certainly didn't want to encourage him to think he had a workable solution. All I could do was promise to relay the information to Goldin.

By now it was 4 P.M. We rejoined Utkin, Ostroumov, and the other members of Koptev's staff in his small reception room for the usual toasts and a late lunch. I reaffirmed my belief that we could work together for the common good. "But," I said, "if you start trying to rearrange ISS at the same time we're funding the FGB and Shuttle-Mir, the whole program may collapse. It's like walking in a mine field." They seemed to appreciate my honesty.

I went from there to Dom Spasso, to meet with Thomas Pickering, the American ambassador, and his senior adviser to update them on my conversation. Pickering confirmed that his staff had no knowledge of the Mir-ISS issue in the Duma elections.

Time was of the essence: The Russians were scheduled to arrive in the United States in a couple of weeks to lay out their new scheme. Back in New York, at JFK Airport, I briefed Wil Trafton, head of the ISS program at NASA HQ, and Obie O'Brien, who worked international matters, and then continued to Washington while they headed for Houston. The next morning, I went to Dan Goldin's office and briefed him on the meetings. Later that day he took me to meet with Leon Furth, the vice president's national security adviser.

Ultimately, though, the whole issue died. It was technically impractical. Nevertheless, I felt I had made a major contribution to the survival of the program and the U.S.-Russia relationship by getting that information from Koptev.

Shannon Lucid, a fellow Oklahoman, was the second Shuttle-Mir astronaut, launched aboard STS-76 on March 22, 1996. She moved aboard Mir, joining cosmonauts Yury Onufriyenko and Yury Usachov for a planned 140-day mission, but technical problems extended her stay. Analysis of recovered solid rocket boosters (SRBs) from the STS-78 launch of June 20, 1996, showed signs of charring and discoloration in a field joint, anomalies that required study and replacement of the SRBs for the next scheduled launch. This problem grounded the fleet for almost six weeks.

My task force was asked to review the SRB matter, which was traced, tentatively, to a new insulation cleaning agent used inside the booster. We also examined the effects of an extension on Lucid and her mission, and found that, in most cases, they were positive, allowing her more time to work on her scientific program and delaying the complicated crew transfer until after a visit to Mir by a French astronaut planned for August.

No sooner was NASA ready to launch STS-79 than Hurricane Fran threatened the Cape. The Atlantis stack had to be rolled back to the assembly building—shades of Gemini 2.

In July 1996 I was in San Jose for a Seagate Technology board of directors meeting when I got a call from Andy Turnage, the director of the Association of Space Explorers, who told me that Aleksei Leonov's daughter had died a couple of days earlier. I had met both girls, Viktoria and Oksana, for the first time in 1973 and had seen them on many occasions—more recently as grown-up women with careers and families of their own. Both were married. Vikki had worked for the Russian Navy. Oksana worked at the Military Language Institute.

I immediately got on the phone and was able to get through to Aleksei; he was still crying. "Tom, Vikki is dead. Russian medicine is very bad." Vikki had been misdiagnosed with an ailment, had been given the wrong medication, and it had shut down her liver and resulted in her death. It was very tragic. Aleksei loved his daughters as I loved mine. It was another bond we shared.

The next trip to Russia, I went with Aleksei and Svetlana to visit Vikki's grave. It's in a little cemetery located near Star City, at a place called Leonikha. Cosmonaut Georgy Shonin's grave is nearby. When I was there, Valery Bykovsky came in to visit the grave of his son, who was killed in a MiG-21 crash and is buried in the same cemetery.

Linda was with me on that summer 1996 trip, which actually began in Beijing, where we were among sixty riders on the Orient Express on a trip sponsored jointly by National Geographic and the Naval Academy Alumni Association. I had gone around the world many times by now, via airplane and spacecraft, but this trip took us fifty-five hundred miles—a quarter of the circumference of the earth at that latitude—by train. The cars of the Express dated back to 1920 or earlier, and were still heated by coal-burning stoves. They had been refurbished in other ways, of course. We not only had a dining car, but also a special shower car and one for lectures, too. I was asked to give an impromptu speech on space flight. My most vivid memory of the trip is riding through the Mongolian steps and seeing herds of yaks.

We rode through China and Mongolia into Russia, then turned west, skirting Lake Baikal and making our way across Siberia. After twelve days we reached Moscow. The tour was supposed to terminate in St. Petersburg, but Linda had come down with a bronchial infection that also affected several of the other passengers. The infection resisted the herbal treatment offered on the train by the traveling Russian woman doctor. I asked a NASA doctor in Moscow to give Linda antibiotics, which cleared up the problem in a few days.

As we traveled by rail across Asia, the Shuttle returned to flight with the launch of STS-79 on September 16, 1996. Bill Readdy's crew delivered John Blaha to Mir, returning Shannon Lucid on September 26. With her original 140-day mission extended to 188 days, she was now the American space endurance champion. She seemed to have suffered no ill effects.

Our evaluation of the STS-81 mission, which would deliver astronaut Jerry Linenger to Mir in January 1997, was the smoothest yet. We began to deal with greater numbers of International Space Station matters and looked forward to 1997 as the year we would make a smooth transition from Shuttle-Mir to ISS.

twenty-two
Crises

On February 19, 1997, the Russian space station Mir celebrated its eleventh birthday in space. Originally just a single core module the size of a mobile home, over the years Mir had been expanded with the addition of four other modules the same size (Kvant-2, Priroda, Spektr, and Kristall) as well as the half-sized Kvant-1, plus a special docking module for the Shuttle. At any given time, a Soyuz manned spacecraft and an unmanned Progress supply vehicle docked with the station, giving it a maximum of seven modules totaling 140 tons of mass and about 370 cubic meters of habitable volume—the same as a good-sized four-bedroom home.

Over its eleven-year history, Mir had been host to thirty-four Russians (counting a pair of Kazakh-Russian citizens), fourteen international "guests," and NASA's Norm Thagard. Another twenty-seven astronauts had visited on Shuttle-Mir, with three of those staying aboard for extended missions. One Russian doctor-cosmonaut, Valery Polyakov, had logged 438 days straight aboard Mir from January 1994 to March 1995.

So the station had seen some traffic. And, given that it was originally designed to operate for only five or six years, it had been subject to a lot of wear and tear. Hundreds of pounds of scientific and other equipment had been brought to Mir over the years, and only a small fraction of that had been returned to earth or dumped overboard. The modules were clogged with junk in addition to power cables and ventilation ducts. A lot of netting was attached to the walls, with everything from old clothing to food wrappers stashed behind them. There had been leaks of various fluids over the years, not to mention condensation, causing floating pools that had to be sopped up with towels. According to crew members, some corners of the station smelled of mildew. Crews had to spend a couple of hours a day, at minimum, doing housekeeping and maintenance, which cut into the time available for astronomy, manufacturing, medical study, and scientific experiments. It was as far from pristine as you could get yet was very robust and gave us lots of insight for the future.

On the anniversary itself, the twenty-second Mir main crew consisted of commander Valery Korzun and flight engineer Aleksandr Kaleri. Joining them was NASA astronaut, Jerry Linenger, a forty-one-year-old captain in the U.S. Navy, a medical doctor, and flight surgeon. He had been delivered to Mir just two weeks earlier by STS-81, replacing astronaut John Blaha. Linenger was scheduled to spend the next four months on Mir. The next day, February 20, 1997, Soyuz TM-24 arrived at Mir carrying the next main crew, Vasily Tsibliyev and Aleksandr Lazutkin, as well as German researcher Reinhold Ewald. The Russian main crews got busy handing over their operations while Ewald went to work on his experiments. Linenger was well into his program by now, too.

On the evening of February 23, Armed Forces Day in Russia, five of the six crew members were gathered in the Mir core module around ten thirty in the evening, having a cup of tea, when Lazutkin fired up an oxygen candle in the Kvant module, a few feet away. Mir's main life-support system could really only handle a crew of three for long periods, especially since at this time only one of its two oxygen-producing Elektron units was functioning. With twice the usual number of people aboard, the station's oxygen supply had to be supplemented by cartridges made of lithium perchlorate—cylinders which, when ignited, burned like candles and released oxygen. The same candles had been used for years on Soviet submarines as well as on the Salyuts and Mir. The Mir 22/23 crews needed to burn six candles every day, one per crew member. This particular candle, however, happened to be defective. Instead of burning properly, it exploded inside its holder, setting fire to a nearby filter, spewing flame and molten metal out to a distance of five feet. Kvant quickly filled with green smoke.

You don't want fire of any kind in a spacecraft. Aside from the other dangers, fire eats up oxygen, the one element you need for survival. This fire also threatened to melt a hole in the wall of Kvant, which would vent the station's air in seconds, killing the crew. Fueled by the perchlorate in the candle itself and drawing from the atmosphere of the station, the fire burned on as the crew, realizing they couldn't fight it without using emergency equipment, backed off, donned gas masks, and considered escape options. There were two Soyuz vehicles docked to Mir at the same time, enough to carry the six men safely back to Earth. Both vehicles had their hatches open and were ready to be powered up.

Before anything more serious occurred, though, the fire burned itself out. It had probably taken three minutes. But the crew wasn't out of danger yet. The fire strained Mir's life support and emergency systems to the breaking point. And through it all, the crew had been on its own: The accident took place in what the Russians call a "zone of radio darkness," over the Pacific between Australia and the United States, outside the range of the tracking network. Mir had no contact with Russian mission control in Korolyov, and it wouldn't for another hour.

Linenger used his ham radio to try to send a message about the emergency, hoping it would be relayed to Korolyov, but that effort failed.[7] When Mir finally came in range of Korolyov's antennas, the link was so bad that the only substantive data the crew received from the ground was an acknowledgment of the fire. That was all anybody in Korolyov mission control knew about what had happened. And far more than anybody at NASA knew. The next opportunity for comm was about 4 A.M. Moscow time—over six hours after the accident.

As Shuttle-Mir was dodging a bullet in the form of a potentially-fatal fire, the International Space Station was staring down the barrel of its own loaded gun: The failure of the Russian government to fund construction of the Zvezda service module.

All of the elements of ISS were crucial in some way, but some were more important than others. The first piece planned for launch, for example, the control module (FGB was the Russian acronym, and they later named it Zarya), would provide basic habitation quarters, some power, and propulsion during the first months of ISS assembly. Node One (later named Unity), the first big U.S. element, was to hook up to Zarya and provide a link to later elements, such as the habitation and laboratory modules.

The third big piece of the puzzle, the Zvezda service module, was designed to provide life support and long- term propulsion for the entire station. Zvezda, in fact, was Mir-2, and its aluminum shell had been shaped in Khrunichev's big factory back in 1985, though its electronics and other systems would be upgraded and integrated with other elements of the ISS.

It was clear as early as the end of 1995, during my previous emergency visit to Russia, that the service module was going to be late. I saw the aluminum shell on the floor at the Khrunichev factory, and that's all it was: a shell with no wiring or electronics, just a few brackets on the inside and holders for insulation blankets attached to its exterior. All through 1996, work on the Zarya control module progressed nicely at Khrunichev as the U.S. dollars flowed. The workmanship was excellent, and the factory team impressed both NASA and Boeing with its can-do attitude under director Anatoly Kiselyov. But when it came to the Zvyozda service module, Khrunichev was still a subcontractor to Energia, which was funded by the Russian government.

In August 1996 I met up with Valery Kubasov in Warsaw at that year's Association of Space Explorers meeting. Kubasov was still a senior engineer at Energia, and we discussed the status of the service module in detail. What Valery said both relieved and alarmed me. The good news was that "approximately 85 percent" of the individual system components were already manufactured. (Some had been ordered years ago, as part of an ongoing Mir spares effort.) The bad news was that Energia had received *none* of the components, and they wouldn't be shipped until the government paid the subcontractors—COD. No matter how good the folks at Khrunichev were, they couldn't assemble the service module without parts.

More time passed, and there was no evidence that any significant money was flowing to the subcontractors or that work was being done on the service module. We weren't even sure exactly who these subcontractors were; until recently, all information like that had been classified.

At the Gore-Chernomyrdin meeting in December 1996, Vice President Gore brought up the issue of the service module funding. The prime minister assured him that the Russians would meet their commitments to the program: The service module would go forward, and he would personally look at the situation. Gore didn't want to call him a liar; perhaps Chernomyrdin didn't know the details.

In January 1997 and through February, Dan Goldin let Yury Koptev know that late delivery of the service module could have a major impact on the program. Congress was asking tough questions, and some members were saying we should cancel the program if the Russians didn't meet their commitments. Koptev reassured Goldin that the commitments would be met. Dan didn't want to call the Russians liars, either, but he needed firm answers. So in February 1997 he asked me to go to Russia to get to the bottom of this.

The first thing I did was send Joe Engle of my committee, Gib Kirkham (the executive secretary), and Tom Crimmins (the chief financial officer on ISS) to Russia as my advance team, the good cops warning of the arrival of the bad one: "Stafford's on his way for a come-to-Jesus meeting." Boris Ostroumov welcomed them at Russian Space Agency HQ. Instead of finding a computer flowchart of subcontractors, parts delivery, and integration schedules, what Engle found was a wall covered with four big sheets of paper. The Russian Space Agency people said there that was their management plan, and there were no other copies. So Joe, Gib, and Tom sat down and started making their own notes from the wall data, a tricky business, since none of them read or spoke Russian. Ostroumov's people were stunned to see this. One of them asked Joe, "Don't American generals have better things to do than this?"

Joe told him, "American generals do whatever the job requires."

When the Russians realized that the team was serious, they were able to produce some copies of the material, though not all the data posted on the wall. By the time I arrived, bringing with me Mel Peterson (NASA chief financial officer) and John Schumacher (international relations) from NASA HQ, we had *some* idea of what was supposed to happen, and when. But the question remained: When was the Russian Space Agency going to get the money to start outfitting the service module?

I had a private meeting with Koptev and outlined the problem. I told him I would be in Moscow with my team for the week, but before I left, I needed to have accurate information on funding, delivery, and assembly. I also met with Utkin and laid out the facts. He said he would help in any way he could.

We had been gathering information for three days when Koptev called and sent word that we should meet the following morning in a the reception area of a building near the Kremlin. The building turned out to be the former headquarters of the Central Committee of the Communist Party. I had been there once before in 1986, to meet with then-party president Anatoly Dobrynin on behalf of NL Industries. It was now the Ministry of Finance for the Russian Federation.

When Koptev showed up, I could see he was nervous and probably embarrassed, too. The two of us were met by Andrei Vavilov, deputy minister of finance, who was to take Koptev directly to his boss, Anatoly Chubais. My team and I waited in the outer office, noting the dozen or more phones on a single desk, all but one of them old-fashioned rotaries.

After fifteen minutes, Koptev and Vavilov came out. They sat down opposite me and heard me out: "Mr. Minister, we've had great relationships for many years together in space. We want that to continue. However, the ISS program is really down the road. We've given you hundreds of millions of dollars to build the Zarya. We've provided hundreds of millions for the Shuttle-Mir program, and we're going forward on ISS.

"The problem is, the service module is not coming along. Now, if we don't have action within six weeks—firm evidence that the SM is funded, that there are people working on it, that there is a valid schedule—then the United States is going forward alone. We will leave a docking port open for you, and hope you will be there at some time in the future. We would like for you to be our partners, but we have to face reality." There it was—the line in the sand.

The Russians already knew of our plans to proceed with an interim control module. And I hated to beat up on Koptev, who was being squeezed between the economic realities of Russia in 1997 and political opponents in the Communist-controlled Duma. But Koptev smiled from ear-to-ear. "General Stafford, I have this document just signed by Mr. Chubais down the hall. We have committed 1.8 trillion rubles [four hundred million dollars], which will take care of building the service module, upgrading the flight control center and the Gagarin training center. This money comes in the form of loans from Russian and foreign banks with Russian government guarantees."

It was a creative solution, considering that they just didn't have the cash. All I could say was, "This is wonderful, Mr. Minister. When do you think the service module will actually be funded?"

"In April or May," he said.

I then spoke in Russian to the minister and told him that our long cooperation started with Apollo-Soyuz and presented him with a patch flown on the mission and a coin minted from metal alloys flown on both spacecraft. My business finished, I stood up, shook hands, and headed back to Washington to deliver this news to Dan Goldin and other NASA leaders, knowing we had forged at least a temporary solution to the problem.

The Stafford-Utkin Commission had been forced to take a hard look at continued Shuttle-Mir missions in the wake of the February fire, as well as control system failures which caused Mir to go into free drift from time to time, leaks of toxic ethylene glycol coolant, and worst of all, the failure of the station's Elektron oxygen generator. By late February and early March, I and several members of my panel were beginning to believe that the U.S. presence aboard Mir should probably come to an end.

The Shuttle-Mir program was coming under increased scrutiny from Congress, too. Representative James Sensenbrenner, Republican from Wisconsin, and chairman of the House Science Authorization Committee, even went so far as to propose a bill requiring Dan Goldin to personally vouch for the safety of Americans aboard Mir, but it failed to get out of committee; Dan didn't need a bill to remind him of his responsibilities. None of us did.

By late March, however, the Elektron was back online, producing sufficient oxygen for 2.4 crew members per day. Burning the perchlorate candles made up the balance. STS-84 was also scheduled to deliver a new Elektron to Mir.

Yes, the Russians were using the candles, even though the cause of the February fire had not yet been determined. Data given to our committee claimed that such candles had been used on manned spacecraft over thirty-five hundred times, and on Soviet submarines over ten thousand times, without a failure. Frankly, though, I was still uncomfortable with the situation. There was no way NASA would have flown a spacecraft in that condition. We would have insisted, for example, that both Elektron oxygen units be operational. The Russians were willing to continue the mission with only a single Elektron, as long as they had a repair kit aboard and other systems (candles and oxygen tanks) for backup. But this was what living in space was like. We had not gone into Shuttle-Mir hoping for problems like this, but here we had the opportunity to deal with them—not just as supercautious NASA engineers and managers, but as partners with the Russians.

It was also a question for Mike Foale, who was scheduled to take Linenger's place on Mir in May. Was he willing to fly the mission? He was. So on May 7, 1987, I gave Dan Goldin our recommendation to proceed. STS-84 launched on May 18, with a crew commanded by Charles Precourt, whose job was not only to fly the mission but also to take a good look at conditions aboard Mir before allowing Mike Foale to move aboard. Also in the crew— Russian cosmonaut Yelena Kondakova, veteran of an earlier mission on Mir. She also happened to be Valery Ryumin's wife.

Precourt and his team reached Mir on May 20, and though they spotted some corrosion and other wear, saw no reason to stop the exchange. Mike Foale moved in, and Jerry Linenger returned to earth aboard STS-84 on May 24, 1997, happy to be off Mir.

On June 24, 1997, the Mir-23 crew of Tsibliyev, Lazutkin, and Foale observed as Progress M-34 was backed away from the station. Progress M-35 was to be launched on June 27, and in the normal course of events would be docking with Mir two days after that. The plan was to allow M-34 to fly a trajectory commanded from TsUP to intercept Mir, then to repeat a manual Progress docking. This final approach, using a system known as TORU (a Russian acronym for "teleoperated control mode") would be controlled by Tsibliyev using a hand unit much like a video-game joystick. (This same procedure had failed a test back in early March.)

By his fifth week aboard Mir, Mike Foale was having a better time than Jerry Linenger. Part of this was no doubt due to their different personalities: Jerry had struck the Russians as a bit rigid and inflexible and after the fire had seemed to withdraw. He had also been acutely aware of the fact that back on earth, his wife, Kathryn, was expecting their second child. Foale, much more outgoing, easygoing, more fluent in Russian, seemed to integrate better with Tsibliyev and Lazutkin. He had also been spared the crisis of an onboard fire and its aftermath. The week of June 13–20, 1997, was described by NASA public affairs as the "quietest" in a long time.

The June 25 redocking was attempted in a radio dead zone, since the Russians had yet to get a new Altair comsat on line or complete repairs to a faulty antenna on Mir. All three crew members were in the Mir core module, with Tsibliyev running the TORU joysticks and Lazutkin trying to watch the approaching Progress from the window. Mir was below the Progress, against an Earth background filled with clouds, so the station was hard to see in a fuzzy, black-and-white television picture being transmitted from Progress to Mir. Nevertheless, Tsibliyev fired the thrusters on Progress, which was on a ballistic course initiated by TsUP, sending it toward Mir. Foale used a stop-watch to click off times and rates. It was a very crude way to approach the problem: The rendezvous was being done with Progress approaching from above and Tsibliyev controlling the maneuvers, watching the grids on the black-and-white TV picture transmitted from Progress.

When Progress M-34 was about thirty-five hundred feet away, Foale realized that it seemed to be approaching very fast. Tsibliyev, working the joy-stick, asked him to go over to the Kvant module and look out that window, but Foale couldn't see M-34 out there. He rejoined Tsibliyev and Lazutkin in the core module just in time to see Mir filling the television screen (as seen from M-34), barely 150 feet away, and moving way too fast.

"Michael, get to the spacecraft!" Tsibliyev ordered Foale. He meant the Soyuz.

Foale immediately pushed himself toward the Soyuz as, behind him, Tsibliyev frantically tried to get Progress to respond.

As Foale reached the spherical docking module, he felt the entire station shudder. Progress had hit it—how hard and where, he didn't know. An alarm sounded. All Foale and the others could do was wait to see if the station's air would start whistling out, killing them the way a leak had killed the Soyuz 11 cosmonauts back in 1971.

They started to feel the decreased pressure. The Spektr module had a slow leak. The Progress had slammed into one of its solar arrays, bending the arm that held the array at the root and breaking the structural pressure integrity. Lazutkin immediately began disconnecting all the cables that ran from the base block through the open Spektr hatchway. Foale helped him. (Tsibliyev was telling TsUP about the emergency.) They got the hatchway cleared, then closed it, sealing off the module, and the alarms stopped. Russian engineers later calculated that Mir's whole atmosphere could have leaked out in twenty-four minutes.

I heard about the collision in a call from Joe Engle. Unlike the February fire, this news got around very quickly. Even though Mir had some power, the station was crippled. There was no electrical power from Spektr. With limited power, the Elektron oxygen generator had to be shut down because it drew too much electricity. This forced the crew to rely on the perchlorate candles. They also had to manually orient Mir, to keep its working solar panels pointed toward the sun.

The crew was worn out by now. Mike was in a particularly tough situation, since Spektr had been his living quarters. His computer and all his gear were now sealed off. He didn't even have a toothbrush. But he and Tsibliyev and Lazutkin soldiered on. Three days after the collision, Mir regained automatic control, and the Elektron and Vozdukh systems were back on line.

Officials at the Russian Space Agency and Energia adjusted their own plans. Progress M-35 had been scheduled for launch to Mir on June 27. They had to roll it off the pad and back to the assembly building, so it could be reloaded with repair tools and different supplies. Say what you like about the Russian system, they were able to accomplish this in days, showing their flexibility. It would have taken NASA weeks to roll a Shuttle stack back to the assembly building and change out a payload.

A new launch date was set for July 5, carrying a specially designed replacement hatch for Spektr, along with new EVA tools and fifty pounds of new personal supplies for Mike Foale. Mike had a radio conversation with Dan Goldin on July 10, after the safe arrival and docking of the new Progress, and said he felt comfortable with the level of safety aboard Mir. He was even getting back to some of his scientific work.

But Mir was far from stable. On July 16 one of the crew accidentally disconnected a cable running to the guidance computer. Unknown to the cosmonauts, the whole station began to drift. The problem wasn't discovered until the middle of the night, when they woke up to find they were in the dark. (Mission control didn't know because at the time Mir was in a radio dead zone.) Power had run so low that the crew had to use the radios in their Soyuz to communicate with TsUP. They reconnected the cable and re-oriented Mir manually, bringing systems back on line as the batteries charged up.

But it was a serious lapse. A few more hours, and Tsbiliyev, Lazutkin, and Foale could have had major problems. The initial repair plan was to have Tsibliyev and Lazutkin do an "intravehicular activity" and swap out the hatches, but this episode finally convinced flight directors Vladimir Solovyov and Viktor Blagov that this crew was too worn down to make tricky repairs in an IVA. Leave it to the next Mir crew.

Anatoly Solovyov and Pavel Vinogradov were scheduled for launch in three weeks. This would be Solovyov's sixth visit to Mir; his last had been in June 1995 as a member of the STS-71 crew on the first Shuttle-Mir docking. He was the most experienced EVA cosmonaut in the world, very confident in his own abilities, the perfect choice to take over from Tsibliyev.[8] He and Vinogradov would also be able to simulate the repairs ahead of time in the water tank at Star City.

All during this month I was on the phone daily with Joe Engle, Mike Mott, or Dennis McSweeney (the panel's new executive secretary). There was a tremendous amount of press coverage, some of it overheated, treating the "crisis" aboard Mir as another Apollo 13. It was serious, absolutely, but not that bad.

On July 18 Dan Goldin asked my panel to conduct a special "independent assessment of the safety and operational readiness of the Shuttle-Mir program" and to make recommendations to the NASA Advisory Council. He wanted program assesses before the next Shuttle launch to Mir, STS-86, scheduled for September 26. I decided it would be best to have the Shuttle-Mir assessment performed by a "red team" within my task force, and I asked Gen. Ralph Jacobson to head it up, giving me data I could pass on to Goldin no later than September 19, ten days after the upcoming STS-86 flight readiness review.

The change in Mir IVA plans affected NASA's Shuttle-Mir crewing. Foale was still scheduled to be replaced in September by astronaut Wendy Lawrence, a Navy helicopter pilot and veteran of the STS-67 mission who had been training at Star City since early 1996. She was fully qualified for a mission to Mir except for one thing: She stood five feet, four inches, within the permitted height range for a Shuttle astronaut but too short for a Russian EVA.

Foale was expected to participate in the Solovyov IVA, which, if all went as planned, would take place prior to STS-86. But given the events on Mir throughout 1997, no one wanted to bet that there wouldn't be a delay. The Russians wanted all three Mir crew members to be EVA qualified. Lawrence's backup, Dave Wolf, was qualified—and tall enough. Frank Culbertson, NASA's Shuttle-Mir program manager, and George Abbey made a difficult decision. It fell to Frank to tell Wendy that we couldn't send her to Mir as Mike Foale's replacement. Lawrence took the news like a professional, saying, "I'd have done the same thing, under the circumstances." She remained assigned to STS-86.

Solovyov and Vinogradov launched on August 5, docking with Mir two days later. The handover went smoothly, although with five crew members aboard and the Elektron still not functioning properly, the crew had to ignite several candles each day. Fortunately, there were no problems.

On Thursday, August 14, 1997, Tsibliyev and Lazutkin said good-bye to Mir as they climbed into their Soyuz. "I hope that everything that went wrong here is leaving with us," Tsibliyev said.

Two hours and thirty minutes after undocking, they fired their deorbit engines for four minutes over Africa. Re-entry went as planned, with separation of the orbit module followed by the instrument module and the final dive through the atmosphere. Over the main recovery zone in Kazakhstan, the parachutes on the Soyuz descent module opened normally—and then came the final indignity. The Soyuz soft-landing retro-rocket, designed to cushion the final impact by firing at altitude of six feet, fired early, when the descent module was still five kilometers up, way too high to do the crew any good.

A short time later, they hit, and hit hard. Tsibliyev and Lazutkin were shaken up but fortunately not seriously injured. They were extracted from the descent module and put on a helicopter back to Baikonur. Two days later, in Moscow, still wobbly from their flight, they faced the press. "We should have abandoned the station several times," Tsibliyev said, "if we were following the rules. But we didn't do that." He went on to say that the source of the problems was primarily here on the ground.

He was right to be concerned. There had been a lot of public speculation in Russia that Tsibliyev and Lazutkin had caused the collision by overloading M-34, degrading its preprogrammed parameters. It was a tradition in Russia to "blame the switchman" for a train derailment, and it sure looked as though Tsibliyev, in particular, had been nominated for the role. Aside from damage to his career, Tsibliyev and his partner also stood to lose a good deal of money.

Unlike American astronauts, who fly into space as a routine part of their jobs, Russians cosmonauts are paid bonuses for their missions. Back in Aleksei Leonov's day, this amounted to three thousand rubles, the equivalent of a year's salary. By May 1997 the bonus for a six-month flight aboard Mir could amount to one hundred thousand dollars, a huge amount by any standard. But if a Russian review board faulted the cosmonauts, they would lose most or even all of it. Both Semyonov and Ryumin had told the press that the collision was due to crew error.

The next meeting of the Stafford-Utkin Commission was scheduled to begin on September 15, 1997, in the city of Ryazan, Russia, deep in the heart of the Red Belt. Ryazan was Academician Utkin's home town, and they were honoring him. (There was a giant bust of Utkin, one of the architects of the Soviet "missile shield," in the town square.)

In addition to eleven members of the panel on the U.S. side, including most of Ralph Jacobson's Red Team, we were asked by Roberta Gross, the NASA inspector general, to include two observers. Gross had received a complaint that my task force wasn't far enough outside NASA to conduct a true independent safety review of Shuttle-Mir. But the Russians were adamantly opposed to allowing any "observers" into the meeting, even when we repeated our request. Finally NASA HQ went over our heads, and Utkin's, directly to Yury Koptev. He agreed to let the two inspectors attend the fifth day of our meetings, once we were back in Korolyov.

For four days, the committee met in relative privacy at the Volna Holiday Hotel, about thirty minutes outside Ryazan. It was so isolated that when Dennis McSweeney, our executive secretary, wanted to send a fax, he had to get one of the hotel staff to drive him all the way into Ryazan.

Linda and I returned to Moscow in a van with Academician Utkin and Joe Engle, as well as Paul Kremez, our interpreter from TTI (the company that provided support for the International Space Station program). The subject of Tsibliyev's "fault" in the June collision came up. I asked the academician how much experience he had with orbital rendezvous. "I know how to hit a satellite with an ASAT," he joked.

"I've done more rendezvous in space than anyone to date," I told him, "and the first thing to keep in mind is that Tsibliyev wasn't just being asked to redock the Progress. He had to re-rendezvous, which is a whole lot more complicated." I had no specific reason to go to bat for Vasily Tsibliyev. I had barely met him. But I wanted the Russians to see how inadequate some of their procedures were.

"I'm telling you, this man was set up for failure. There is no way, given his training, given the equipment, that he could have successfully made this rendezvous and redocked."

Because of this conversation, Utkin arranged to bring some of the affected parties together at our final day of meetings, which took place at TsNIIMash itself. In addition to representatives from Energia, the panel, at the request of Russian Air Force chief of staff Gen. Pyotr Deneikin, included former cosmonaut, Col. Gen. Vladimir Kovalenok, now commandant of the Zhukovsky Air Force Engineering Academy. Deneikin and the Russian Air Force were very perturbed at the Energia management for blaming the collision on one of their military cosmonauts.

It sure was interesting to see Kovalenok and Ryumin on different sides of this issue. Both former cosmonauts had once been members of the same crew, Soyuz 25, which had failed to dock with Salyut 6 back in October 1977. Their careers hadn't suffered much damage, though they were the first Soviet cosmonauts to return from a flight without receiving Hero of the Soviet Union medals.

I literally went to the blackboard and sketched out the scenario Tsibliyev had faced, directing my questions to the Energia officials in the room. Had Tsibliyev simulated this procedure? Yes. When? Back on Earth—132 days earlier. Did the simulation of a small image of Mir place the station against a bright background of moving white clouds, ocean, land, and reflected sunlight? No, against a black one. Did he have range and range-rate data? No. (That was the minimum data NASA needed to do a rendezvous back in the 1960s. We called it "R" and "R-dot.") Did he have the roll, pitch, and yaw attitude of the Progress to determine attitude from which he was applying thrust? *No!*

The problem was further compounded by the fact that the thruster specifications for the Progress was plus or minus 15 percent. It turns out from the reconstruction of the data that the thruster was near the top limit. Tsibliyev was to follow instructions to fire thrusters for so many seconds at a given time, not knowing the exact velocity that would result. Looking at the graph that plotted the reconstructed trajectory of Progress, from the start of the

TORU-controlled maneuver right up to the impact with Mir and Spektr, I could fault Tsibliyev for one questionable input immediately prior to the impact—nothing more. No astronaut, including me, would have been able to successfully perform that re-rendezvous and redocking under those conditions. There was an uncomfortable silence in the room. The Russians understood completely, and we moved on to other subjects.

Tsibliyev and Lazutkin received their bonuses. Tsibliyev is now a major general and deputy director of Star City.

We still had to decide whether Mir was safe for further visits by NASA astronauts. Two more were scheduled: Dave Wolf from September 1997 to January 1998, then Andy Thomas from January to May 1998. There was a torrent of criticism in the press, and from Congress, and from a community of self-appointed NASA watchers who were using the Internet and op-ed pages to express themselves. Their objections were these:

NASA had already learned all it needed from Shuttle-Mir. Why risk astronaut lives in a station that was old and crumbling?

Shuttle-Mir was a bad idea in the first place.

Even if Mir was safe and the Russians were honest, the ISS hardware was already designed and largely built. Nothing we could learn on Mir would be directly applicable.

A USA Today poll showed that 82 percent of the American public thought it was too risky to send another astronaut to the aging Mir.

My personal feeling had always been that nine Shuttle-Mir dockings and seven long duration missions by NASA astronauts was a proper amount to set the stage for ISS, just as Gemini did for Apollo. We had gone into Gemini figuring it would take us ten missions to prove the required rendezvous and docking procedures, long-duration flights, and EVA, and that's exactly what it did, though nothing occurred exactly as or when we planned it. There were close calls on Gemini 6 (launch pad shutdown), Gemini 8 (stuck thruster), Gemini 9 (EVA). And we were still learning lessons right through Gemini 12. I was convinced that had the United States tried to go from Mercury to Apollo, we'd never have accomplished a lunar landing on the fifth mission. Or even the fifteenth. In fact, the Apollo program would probably have been cancelled. Shuttle-Mir certainly hadn't gone exactly as planned. But even after the events of spring and summer 1997, I thought there were still benefits to be gained.

General Jake's Red Team delivered its report on September 19. They had looked at Mir's life support systems and the associated risks, and at Mir's electrical power supply—would it be sufficient for life support and scientific experiments? They had also examined the corrective measures taken by the Russians. Jake's conclusion was that Dave Wolf should be cleared for his mission to Mir, to commence with the launch of STS-86. And so he was, just two days before it took place.

Goldin asked me to announce my committee's decision to CNN. The next day, I joined Dan and Tom Young, who did a quick review of the situation, at a press conference where Dan announced the go-ahead.

Shuttle-Mir ended on a high note in June 1998, with the flight of STS-91, commanded by Charlie Precourt, and a crew that included none other than Valery Ryumin of Energia—the same Ryumin who had complained just six years in the past that the Shuttle was "unsafe." STS-91 returned Andy Thomas to Earth. and the Mir crews and their activities dwindled from the minds of most Americans. Meanwhile, Stafford-Utkin Committee turned its full attention to the International Space Station.

In July 1998 government and industrial teams in sixteen countries were hard at work building and integrating modules, solar arrays, trusses, scientific equipment, cargo modules, and other pieces of the giant puzzle that was ISS. George Abbey, adopting the methods of his mentor, George Low, ran regular station development and operations meetings—SDOMs—in which all partners in the program spent a whole day (sometimes a Saturday) evaluating their particular pieces of hardware, explaining delays and making corrections.

The first elements—the Boeing/Khrunichev FGB, and the Boeing Node One—were on track and scheduled for launch in November/December 1998. Four months later, Energia's service module was to follow. Shuttle crews would make two servicing and supply visits, then a Soyuz would launch the first Expedition crew of Bill Shepherd, Yury Gidzenko, and Sergei Krikalyov in July. Four more Shuttle assembly missions would take ISS to the end of Phase I in June.

This schedule became wastepaper within weeks. The first cause was the Russian government's continuing "starvation" of the Russian Space Agency. There simply was insufficient money to complete the work on the service module. Dan Goldin and our panel were getting worried because Mir was still in orbit, requiring a pair of manned launches every year, as well as four or five Progress resupply missions. The Russian commitment to ISS called for a similar number of launches. The total was twice as high as the Russians could deliver, even with regular funding. The second cause was the general collapse of the ruble in late summer. If the Russian Space Agency had funding problems before, it now faced an absolute crisis.

NASA made plans to take over as much ISS work as it could—asking the White House and Congress for additional money for resupply and propulsion modules, but it was told no, make it work with what you have.

So we waited. The Russians took a shellacking in the press. But there were delays on our side, too. Boeing was struggling with software for the laboratory module. The truss hardware was not ready.

Zarya and Unity were on target, however, and Dan Goldin and George Abbey insisted on launching them on schedule, in November/December 1998, even though the vital service module could not fly for at least a year. I wasn't sure this was a good idea: Once those modules reached orbit, they would be exposed to the harsh environment of space. Their electronics would start to degrade, especially in the Russian-built module. And if the service module ran into further delays or failed to reach orbit, we ran the risk of throwing those two elements away.

Nevertheless, Dan and George wanted to stick to the schedule. They felt the whole system needed the pressure of knowing those modules were up there waiting, forcing everyone to meet the launch schedule. And I eventually came around. It was very like the old Irish story cited by President John Kennedy in a speech at Rice University back in 1962, about a boy who motivated himself to climb a wall by throwing his hat over it. He had to make the climb in order to retrieve it. By launching the Zarya and Unity, we threw our hat over the wall.

epilogue
Odyssey Year

In the last week of October 2000, with the new millennium and the "space odyssey" year of 2001 approaching, I flew to Moscow with Dan Goldin and his team for the launch of Soyuz TM-31. This flight would carry a crew of three, Russian cosmonauts Yury Gidzenko and Sergei Krikalyov, as well as NASA astronaut Bill Shepherd. They would be the first "expedition" crew to occupy the International Space Station. STS-92, the vital assembly mission 3A, had just returned to Earth, its two teams of EVA astronauts having successfully installed the Z1 truss on the station. Much work remained to complete the first phase of assembly, but from this point on, ISS would always have a crew aboard.

It had been a long, torturous two years since a Russian Proton thundered into space carrying the Zarya FGB module. Following its checkout by flight control teams at TsUP in Korolyov, STS-88, with a crew commanded by Bob Cabana, was launched with the Unity module. Two days later, Cabana's crew carefully linked the two modules together 140 miles above the earth.

And there they sat.

The year 1999 was an exercise in patience and sometimes frustration. Four ISS Expedition crews were training, sometimes with great difficulty. For one thing, they simply faced endless, demoralizing delays. Then there were problems with training materials and simulators. I was impressed with the way both astronauts and cosmonauts stayed with the program, especially Bill Shepherd. A Naval Academy graduate (Annapolis '71) and a Navy SEAL by training, he had a tremendous commitment to the mission and wasn't going to let delays or equipment problems distract him. He got along great with his Russian colleagues, too.

Russia itself—at least, the Russia I dealt with—seemed to stabilize. There were persistent and continuing problems with money, of course, but we had fewer disputes over unfulfilled agreements. Promises were kept or not made at all. The tiny Russian Space Agency, for example, had grown into Rosaviakosmos, a genuine power in that country, charged with overseeing not only the international space program, but also civilian and some military space activities, and most aeronautical research matters. The lack of a central authority over space had helped kill the Soviet man on the Moon program. Now they had it. I believed that the Russians had learned from us—one of the original goals of ASTP.

Even though I had increasing commitments outside the space program, my committee was very busy reviewing plans for Shuttle missions added to the schedule to deliver supplies and materials to the Zarya-Unity modules: A mission 2A.1 was created, followed by 2A.2, which fissioned into a pair of visits, 2A.2a and 2A.2b. It meant added expense, but also brought added discoveries. The 2A.1 mission, launched as STS-96 in May 1999, turned up some environmental anomalies in the combined modules that we were later able to correct.

One benefit of the delay was that George Abbey was able to get the ISS program office to do an integrated end- to-end test of the U.S. Laboratory (later known as Destiny). Hooked to a mockup of the Unity module then on orbit, Destiny turned out to have an number of software bugs better fixed on the ground. The original ISS contracts had made no provision for this kind of testing nor for such a basic item as hardware schematics for the ground or flight crews to work with. The delays allowed NASA to correct these and other problems.

The Russians finally shipped the Zvyozda service module from Krunichev to Baikonur by train in mid-May 1999. Academician Utkin told me they could have put it on the tracks by April 30, but chose to delay past the May Day celebrations, since they were worried about the increased chances of accidents caused by their locomotive engineers' overcelebration.

Another problem arose when two different Proton launch vehicles failed to reach orbit, one in July 1999, the other in October, both doomed by second-stage engine problems. The failures required me to again dispatch Gen. Ralph Jacobson and a team to the factory in Voronezh, which made the second and third stage engines for Proton. Jake discovered another hard fact of life in post-Communist Russia: the lack of quality control in manufacturing. Both stages, and thus both launches, failed because of contamination when the engines were manufactured in the turbulent era of 1992–93. That sort of laxity was intolerable for the Zvyozda launch, now, finally scheduled for July 2000. We only had that one module. If it failed to reach orbit, the ISS program was in dire trouble.

Vladimir Utkin, in his role as head of TsNIIMash, was put in charge of the accident investigation by Rosaviakosmos. He reported to us the minute details of the accident committee findings and the recommended corrective actions. Fortunately, the teams at Voronezh were able to improve their quality control. And Rosaviakosmos proved it by successfully launching a pair of Protons in June 2000, to pave the way for Zvyozda.

To our great relief, Zvyozda launched smoothly on July 12, 2000. Dan Goldin, Joe Engle, and I were among the VIP guests watching at Baikonur. Two weeks later I was at JSC watching the successful docking of Zvyozda to the Zarya-Unity modules.

There was sad news in 2000, too. Academician Vladimir Utkin died on February 15 at the age of seventy-six. His place as chairman was taken by Nikolai Apollonovich Anfimov, a very capable engineer. But I had lost a dear friend.

Health issues were increasingly on my mind—not necessarily my own. I always had a long-standing interest in medicine: My father was a dentist, and had I not gone into aviation, I might very well have become a doctor myself. So it was natural that I paid attention, back in 1991, when a neighbor of ours in the Keys introduced me to a radiologist who described a new approach to medical diagnostics involving high-tech computer tomography imaging. The idea was to replace invasive procedures for optical colonoscopy with noninvasive scans that would provide a doctor with more data while not subjecting the patient to sedation or discomfort and at a much lower cost. Colon cancer was and remains the number two cancer killer in America, after lung cancer. Such deaths could be nearly eliminated if the population over fifty (or younger, if there was a family history) were screened.

A friend and I helped pay for the initial patent work on the process, and then I played a major role in helping to raise the funding for what became Viatronix, a virtual-imaging software company. Our first offices opened in early 2000.

Joe Engle and I were scheduled to fly from Moscow to Baikonur on a Russian TU-154 along with Dan Goldin, Bill Readdy, and several Russian space officials. Our takeoff was delayed by bad weather in Moscow, and when we finally arrived at Baikonur on the morning of October 31, the whole area was socked in so we landed in conditions that were nearly zero- zero. We checked into a new hotel in Leninsk, a great improvement over my accommodations there during ASTP, then drove north to Area 1, the site of the original Korolyov team assembly building and ICBM launch pads—still in use forty-five years later.

Dressed in their Sokol ascent suits, Shepherd, Gidzenko, and Krikalyov made the ritual appearance at the base of their Soyuz launcher, with Gidzenko reporting the crew's readiness to Col. Gen. Valery Grin, head of the state commission in charge of the launch. Then they clambered up the ladder to the elevator that would take them to their Soyuz. Right on schedule, the old R-7 first stage lit up, the arms of the support structure fell away, and Soyuz TM-31 took off with a roar, disappearing into the low clouds in just a few seconds. Eight minutes later, the first ISS Expedition crew was safely in orbit.

There was a party afterward at one of the hotels in Leninsk, where I met Dennis Tito, an American businessman who had bought a flight to Mir from the Russians for a reported twenty million dollars. At that moment, it appeared that Mir (largely unoccupied for over a year) was headed for destruction, taking Mr. Tito's hopes of a flight to orbit with it.

I was back in the United States by the time Shepherd, Gidzenko, and Krikalyov arrived at the ISS. I was amused to hear, shortly after docking, Shepherd asking Dan Goldin for permission to use the call sign "Alpha" for the station. Dan gave his approval, and ISS finally got a name. (The search for a suitable one had eluded all of the sixteen partners over the years.)

So Alpha was not only crewed, but named. And with mission control centers in Houston and Korolyov, Huntsville, and soon, Germany, making day-to-day operational decisions, fewer matters require intense work by an outside expert commission, though our work continues, with the Russian side headed by Utkin's successor, Nikolai Anfimov. I plan to continue the volunteer work as long as a NASA administrator tells me the commission (task force) is still needed.

But, by and large, the pioneering work is done. NASA and Russia, and the fourteen other international partners, now have a working space station. The first phase of the mission has been accomplished.

My wife, Linda, has been my supportive companion for many of my recent voyages. Our travel schedule is often hectic, but we still find new challenges, such as the round-the-world flight on the supersonic Concorde in August 1995. The route took us from New York to Toulouse, France, then stops in Dubai, Bankok, Guam, Honolulu, Acapulco, and back to New York— 25,000-plus statute miles in thirty-one hours, twenty-seven minutes, and forty-nine seconds, a new world record, both east- and westbound.

We took another Concorde trip around the world in November 1999, with more leisurely stops along the way. It took twenty-two hours of flying time spread over twenty-three days. This was my *slowest* round-the-world trip!

Aleksei Leonov and I still see each other when we can; Valery Kubasov, too, and their families. Aleksei's daughter, Oksana, now lives in the United States six months each year, with her husband and children, including her daughter, Karin (named after my own Karin), and new son, Daniel. My daughter, Dionne, named her second child, born July 1995, Andrew Alexei Harrison, after Aleksei Leonov. So Aleksei is a frequent visitor to the United States. Today if I want to get in touch with him, all I have to do is dial his cell phone number, or send him e-mail.

He has become a successful investment banker, working for Baring Vostok Capital, a British/Dutch/Russian firm headed by—of all people—a young man named Michael Calvey, who attended high school not far from my house in Oklahoma City, and who later earned his BA and MBA from the University of Oklahoma.

When Aleksei and I met on that hot June day in 1971, at the funeral of the Soyuz 11 cosmonauts, neither of us would have predicted our Apollo-Soyuz flight, much less the twists and turns of our space programs over the decades. We were not trained to be ambassadors or emissaries: We were military officers and pilots who found common ground and adapted to changing circumstances. I believe that, together, we helped make that new world a somewhat better place to live.

I am not in the habit of looking back. When I do, I am somewhat amazed that the only child of a dentist and a schoolteacher from a small town in Oklahoma was able to attend the Naval Academy, serve in the Air Force, and fly in space four times. These are accomplishments I couldn't even imagine as a child. Yet now I look back on them from a perspective of decades.

Why me? I am probably not in a position to say. Basic intelligence obviously helped, along with the love and attention of my parents and the support I received from the community of Weatherford. I had the ability to learn from my own mistakes and from the good examples of teachers and leaders. I have tried to be both teacher and leader myself.

Through it all, through my time as a fighter pilot, my tours at Edwards, at NASA, and the Pentagon, whether I was flying a T-38 across the Western United States or piloting an Apollo around the Moon, whether I was visiting the USSR during the Cold War or Russia in the 1990s, I kept my eyes on the sky.

I still do. And hope I always will.

notes

1. Two prior unmanned flights of the Apollo command module were known as AS-201 (CSM 009) and 203 (CSM 011). 202 didn't carry a command module. Gus Grissom, Ed White, and Roger Chaffee were to have flown Apollo CSM 012 on AS-204, and they called it Apollo 1. After the fire, NASA decided, essentially, to retire that name and number and pick up the sequence with Apollo 4.

2. Shatalov was as careful in his contacts as any member of the Soviet delegations, perhaps with reason: Anatole Forostenko heard a rumor that during one of his visits to the United States, Shatalov had received a phone call from an American woman claiming to be a long-lost sister. If that had become known to the KGB, it would have been bad for his career.

3. I was taken into the secure vault at NASA HQ by Associate Administrator Bob Aller, and the tapes of the intercepted conversation were played for me.

4. Republican Jake Garn, Nelson's counterpart in the Senate space subcommittee, had already flown aboard the orbiter Discovery on STS 51-D in April 1985.

5. The entire report is still available at the NASA History Office web site: history.nasa.gov/ Staffordrep/main_toc.PDF.

6. George Abbey and I both said at the time that we really needed ten Shuttle-Mir flights. Ultimately we got a total of nine.

7. The Moscow-area suburb of Kaliningrad, home of Energia, TsNIIMash, and TsUP, was renamed Korolyov in early 1997.

8. In the summer of 1996, Anatoly Solovyov had been assigned to the first planned ISS crew, along with Bill Shepherd and Sergei Krikalyov, but he had pulled out when he realized that Shepherd would be the mission commander.

index